THE CHURCH
Its Changing Image Through Twenty Centuries

VOLUME TWO

1700 to the Present Day

ERIC G. JAY

LONDON

SPCK

First published 1978
SPCK
Holy Trinity Church
Marylebone Road
London NW1 4DU

Text set in 11/12 pt Photon Times, printed and bound in Great Britain at The Pitman Press, Bath

ISBN 0 281 02991 1

Contents

Acknowledgements

Thanks are due to the following for permission to quote from copyright sources:

The Revd Walter M. Abbott, S.J. and the America Press: *The Documents of Vatican II*, edited by Walter M. Abbott, S.J.

George Allen & Unwin Ltd: *The Churches Survey Their Task*, An Oxford Conference Report; and *The Social Teaching of the Christian Churches* by Ernst Troeltsch, translated by Olive Wyon (by permission also of Barnes and Noble)

A. & C. Black Ltd: *A History of the Church in England* by J. R. H. Moorman

T. & T. Clark Ltd: *The Christian Faith* by Friedrich Schleiermacher, translated by H. R. Mackintosh and J. S. Stewart; and *Church Dogmatics* by Karl Barth, edited by G. W. Bromiley and T. F. Torrance

William Collins Sons & Co. Ltd and John Knox Press: *The Humanity of God* by Karl Barth, © 1960 by C. D. Deans

Doubleday & Company, Inc.: *The Suburban Captivity of Churches* by Gibson Winter. Copyright © 1961 by Gibson Winter

Harper & Row, Publishers, Inc.: *On Religion: Speeches to its Cultured Despisers* by Friedrich Schleiermacher

SCM Press Ltd: *Letters and Papers from Prison* (revised enlarged edition) by Dietrich Bonhoeffer, copyright © 1953, 1967, 1971 by SCM Press Ltd; *The Secular City* by Harvey Cox, copyright © Harvey Cox 1965 (both by permission also of Macmillan Publishing Company); *The Kingdom of Christ* by F. D. Maurice, edited by Alec Vidler; *Dogmatics in Outline* by Karl Barth (by permission also of Harper & Row, Inc.)

Search Press Ltd: *The Church* by Hans Küng; and *Structures of the Church* by Hans Küng, copyright © 1974 by Thomas Nelson & Sons (by permission also of Thomas Nelson, Inc.)

Sheed & Ward Ltd: *The Church Against Itself* by Rosemary Radford Ruether; and *God the Future of Man* by Edward Schillebeeckx (USA publisher: Sheed, Andrews & McMeel)

The Society for Promoting Christian Knowledge: *The Ecumenical Advance: A History of the Ecumenical Movement, 1948–1968,* edited by Harold E. Fey; *Thomas Arnold: Principles of Church Reform,* edited by M. J. Jackson and J. Rogan; and *A History of the Ecumenical Movement, 1517–1948,* edited by R. Rouse and S. C. Neill

The University of Chicago Press: *Systematic Theology* by Paul Tillich, copyright © The University of Chicago 1951

The World Council of Churches: *The New Delhi Report: The Third Assembly of the World Council of Churches, 1961,* edited by W. A. Visser't Hooft.

Abbreviations

CD   Karl Barth, *Church Dogmatics*

Church   Hans Küng, *The Church*

E.T.   English translation

F. and O.   Faith and Order

L'Eglise   Yves Congar, *L'Eglise de saint Augustin à l'époque moderne*

N.T.   New Testament

O.T.   Old Testament

R.S.V.   Revised Standard Version of the Bible

Speeches   Friedrich Schleiermacher, *On Religion: Speeches to its Cultured Despisers*

ST   Paul Tillich, *Systematic Theology*

Structures   Hans Küng, *Structures of the Church*

W.C.C.   World Council of Churches

Part 5

THE EIGHTEENTH AND
NINETEENTH CENTURIES

15

The Age of Reason and the Church

The middle of the seventeenth century was 'the beginning of a new era in western thought'.[1] It ushered in a period during which 'many of the important movements in modern Christianity have their rise, and many of the problems which distinguish the modern era first assume their familiar form'.[2] Many factors contributed to the new situation: the challenge of the Reformation to long-accepted authority; the establishment of more unified and powerful states in western Europe, and the rise of national spirit; the widening of world horizons by the discovery of the New World, its colonization, and the consequent development of trade and enrichment of the seafaring European powers; the enlargement of man's knowledge by striking advances in the physical sciences; weariness and disgust after decades of bitter, bloody, and often fratricidal fighting (the 'Religious Wars') which ended with the Peace of Westphalia in 1648, leaving central Europe exhausted economically, and engendering in many minds a scepticism concerning the truth and value of a religion which had plunged so many into such suffering. For all these reasons the Church found itself in a world which was loudly challenging the assumptions of seventeen hundred years.

THE AGE OF REASON

The eighteenth century is often called 'the age of Reason' or the 'Enlightenment' (German, *Aufklärung*; French, *l'illumination*). It is a true description, although it draws attention to but one, albeit very important, element in the thinking and culture of the time, namely, the emphasis on rationality. There were other strong elements: pietism in religion and, well before the end of the century, romanticism in reaction both to philosophical rationalism and to classicism in art and literature, each stressed the importance of the emotional side of man's nature.

The scientific successes of the late sixteenth and the seventeenth century were taken as tokens of what human reason could achieve. Isaac Newton (1643–1727) had unravelled the workings of the universe. John Locke (1632–1704) had discovered the workings of the mind. It began to be assumed that illimitable possibilities lay before man, provided that he took reason for his guide. The philosophical trends known as rationalism and empiricism received great impetus. Some thinkers noted that the success of science was closely related to mathematics, a discipline which demands a rigorous use of reason, and pursued their studies on the assumption that pure reason is capable of attaining truth. These were the rationalists (Descartes, 1596–1650; Spinoza, 1632–77; Leibniz, 1646–1716). Others, impressed by the scientific results of close attention to sense experience, adopted the view that knowledge is ultimately derived from sense experience. These were the empiricists (Locke; Bishop George Berkeley, 1685–1753; David Hume, 1711–76). The rationalism of this period was not usually atheistic. Those to whom the scientific advances of the time were due, like Robert Boyle, the chemist, Isaac Newton, the physicist, and John Ray, the naturalist, were convinced that they were making plain not only the existence of God but the workings of his laws. The philosophers also for the most part (Hume is an exception) found that reason led them to the conclusion that God exists. Locke in *An Essay Concerning Human Understanding* spoke of the existence of God as 'the most obvious truth that reason discovers' and one 'equal to mathematical certainty'. But the rationalists were sceptical about divine revelation: the competence of man's reason rendered it unnecessary. For them, God exists as the creator who has given to the universe the laws by which it runs, laws which human reason is fully capable of discovering, and he exists aloof in transcendent majesty. Man's responsibility is to discover and live by the laws which God has laid down for his human creation, and in proportion to his achievement rewards or punishments await him after death. This concept of God is known as Deism.

Close to the English Deists in some ways were the Latitudinarians, of whom Dr Samuel Clarke (1675–1729) is the best known representative. 'While continuing to conform with the Church of England they attached relatively little importance to matters of dogmatic truth, ecclesiastical organization, and liturgical practice.'[3] Like the Deists they held that the essence of religion could be expressed in rational yet simple terms. God is the wise and beneficent creator, and he requires of his children a like wisdom and kindliness. But whereas the Deists rejected the idea of revelation, the Latitudinarians defended it, contending that the Scriptures contained nothing contrary to reason.

The period is an important and fascinating one in many respects. Our concern, however, is with the doctrine of the nature of the Church. How was this affected by the movements of thought in the late seventeenth century and the eighteenth? The period produced no treatises on the Church of comparable influence with some which we have already studied and others which were to appear later. The ecclesiologies set forth in the catechisms, articles, and confessions which were discussed at the end of volume one, remained normative for Anglicans, Catholics, Congregationalists, Lutherans, and Presbyterians. But the spirit of the time did engender certain new ideas about the Church which, although not accepted into official formulae, have been very influential. These are the idea of the Church as an ethical society, and the concepts of toleration and the 'denomination'.

THE CHURCH AS AN ETHICAL SOCIETY

The philosopher John Locke, as we have seen, believed that the existence of God could be proved by reason. But unlike many other thinkers of the period, he also held that God had revealed his will to man through the Scriptures, and pre-eminently through the teachings of Jesus Christ. He sees Christ as primarily the teacher of an ethical code:

> Next to the knowledge of one God; maker of all things; a clear knowledge of their duty was wanting to mankind ... he that shall collect all the moral rules of the philosophers, and compare them with those contained in the new testament, will find them to come short of the morality delivered by Our Saviour. ... Such a body of Ethics, proved to be the law of nature, from principles of reason, and reaching all the duties of life, I think nobody will say the world had before Our Saviour's time (*The Reasonableness of Christianity* 241–2).[4]

The Reasonableness of Christianity abounds in phrases which describe the Christian life as 'sincere obedience to his law' (178), 'sincere obedience to the law and will of Christ' (179), 'a sincere endeavour after righteousness, in obeying his law' (181). What Christ expects from his followers, we are told, 'he has sufficiently declared as a Legislator' (220).[5]

> Our Saviour not only confirmed the moral law, and ... shewed the strictness, as well as obligations of its injunctions; but moreover ...

requires the obedience of his disciples to several of the commands he afresh lays upon them; with the enforcement of unspeakable rewards and punishments in another world, according to their obedience or disobedience (212).[6]

What is being proposed here is the idea of the followers of Christ as an ethical society of those who have voluntarily accepted a set of moral principles which is both advantageous to society and to themselves as individuals, and who endeavour to live in accordance with it. Such an idea was not unacceptable to the Latitudinarians. Benjamin Hoadly (1676–1761), successively Bishop of Bangor, Hereford, Salisbury, and Winchester, preached a sermon before George I in 1717 in which he made it clear that he had a negative view of the value of creeds, sacraments, and the ministry, and saw no need for the Church as a visible institution. The prevailing view among Latitudinarians was that Christianity is essentially a reasonable ethical code, that the *raison d'être* of the Church is to promote that code, and that therefore the Church is a useful institution deserving the support of the government in power. There were not lacking churchmen to oppose these ideas with considerable theological power, among whom William Law (1686–1761) and Joseph Butler (1692–1752), Bishop of Durham, are outstanding. But the interpretation of Christianity in moralistic terms, and the idea of the Church as primarily an institution for the improvement of moral standards has persisted to the present day, not least because churchmen have not infrequently used the idea as a valuable apologetic when the Church has come under attack and ridicule from the intelligentsia.

TOLERATION

In the wake of the Reformation came persecution of Protestants in Catholic lands and of Catholics in Protestant territory. There followed also the religious wars which devastated and impoverished large tracts of central Europe until the middle of the seventeenth century. By that time not only was Europe weary and sickened by bloodshed in the cause of religion, but the voice of reason was beginning to be heard. As early as 1554 Sebastian Castellio, who was converted to Protestantism by John Calvin and proved to be a somewhat unorthodox Calvinist, had argued in his *De Haereticis* that persecution could not be the will of Christ: 'If thou, O Christ, hast commanded these executions and tortures, what hast thou left for the devil to do?'[7] But such words fell on deaf ears for many decades.

At the Peace of Augsburg in 1555 the disputes between Catholics and Lutherans within the German empire had been settled by acceptance of the principle that the religion of the ruler determines the religion of the territory (*cuius regio, eius religio*). At the Peace of Westphalia, which in 1648 concluded the Thirty Years' War, the same principle was accepted, and extended to all the territories of the Holy Roman Empire and to include the Calvinists. But, despite provisions for the protection of minorities, toleration was as yet far from being achieved.

In England the question was vigorously debated, and Locke's *A Letter Concerning Toleration*[8] (1689) was widely read and most influential. Castellio's plea is again voiced, but in the more measured tones of the rationalist:

> If, like the Captain of our salvation, they [zealots] sincerely desired the good of souls, they would tread in the steps and follow the perfect example of the Prince of Peace, who sent out His soldiers to the subduing of nations, and gathering them into His Church, not armed with the sword or other instruments of force, but prepared with the Gospel of peace and with the exemplary holiness of their conversation. . . .

> The toleration of those that differ from others in matters of religion is so agreeable to the Gospel of Jesus Christ, and to the genuine reason of mankind, that it seems monstrous for men to be so blind as not to perceive the necessity and advantage of it in so clear a light.[9]

> It will be very difficult to persuade men of sense that he who with dry eyes and satisfaction of mind can deliver his brother to the executioner to be burned alive does sincerely and heartily concern himself to save that brother from the flames of hell in the world to come.[10]

Locke argues for 'the mutual toleration of private persons differing from one another in religion'; against the right of any person, church, or commonwealth 'to invade the civil rights and worldly goods of each other upon pretence of religion'; for the Christian duty of preaching peace, goodwill, and toleration; against religious compulsion by rulers or magistrates: 'Men cannot be forced to be saved whether they will or no'; and against the intervention of the magistrate *qua* magistrate in Church affairs unless there is any question of danger to the public good. And in respect of this proviso, 'the magistrate ought always to be very careful that he do not misuse his authority to the oppression of any church, under pretence of public good'.[11]

Locke would extend religious liberty widely, even to include idolaters,[12] but would withhold it from four groups. First, any whose opinions are contrary to the law and order of civil society;[13] second, such groups as are themselves intolerant;[14] third, the Roman Catholic Church:

> That church can have no right to be tolerated by the magistrate which is constituted upon such a bottom that all who enter into it do thereby *ipso facto* deliver themselves up to the protection and service of another prince.[15]

He gives as an instance one who professes to be 'a Mahometan only in his religion, but in everything else a faithful subject to a Christian magistrate, whilst at the same time he acknowledges himself bound to yield blind obedience to the Mufti of Constantinople'. There were few Muslims in England in the late seventeenth century. Locke was thinking of Roman Catholics. The fourth group is that of the atheists:

> Those are not at all to be tolerated who deny the being of a God. Promises, covenants, and oaths, which are the bonds of human society, can have no hold upon an atheist.[16]

In the same year that Locke published this letter the Toleration Act gave freedom of worship to dissenters, except Roman Catholics and Unitarians. They remained, however, under many civil disabilities most of which were removed in 1828. In 1829 the Roman Catholic Emancipation Act removed most of the disabilities from Roman Catholics.

DENOMINATIONALISM

The climate of opinion which promoted toleration also fostered the idea that the separated Christian bodies are all more or less acceptable categories of Christianity. The word 'denomination'[17] came to be used to describe them.

In *A Letter Concerning Toleration*, John Locke wrote:

> A church ... I take to be a voluntary society of men, joining themselves together of their own accord in order to the public worshipping of God in such manner as they judge acceptable to Him, and effectual to the salvation of their souls.[18]

This is reminiscent of the definitions of the Church which we found given by exponents of the congregational type of Church order. Locke, however, is speaking of all Christian groups, whether congregational, national, or transcending national boundaries. They are all voluntary, or in his opinion should be so regarded, in the sense that every man has liberty to join them or to dissociate himself from them.

They may differ from each other in respect of the doctrines which they consider essential, in forms of ministry, modes of worship, and rules of discipline, and therefore may be looked on as so many options open to a Christian person. As the spirit of toleration gained ground, they were increasingly looked on as tolerable options. That Christendom was divided into denominations came to be regarded as a natural, even desirable state of affairs. 'Denominationalism' denotes this position.[19] Concern for the unity of the body of Christ drops into the background.

The word 'denomination', which was not used by Locke, has passed into common currency. Those churches, however, which hold themselves to be representative of the one Church of Christ, or even to be *the* Church of Christ, tend not to use it of themselves, though they may do so of other Christian bodies. Nor is it much used by those Christians who, looking beyond a mere tolerance which leaves churches separated from, and even in competition with, one another, hope for a union of all Christian people on the basis of a common faith and order.

REACTION

During the period of the Enlightenment the talents of theologians were, for the most part, directed to the defence of the Christian faith against the most powerful and bitter attacks it had received since the *True Word* of Celsus in the second century, which drew forth Origen's apology, *Contra Celsum*, several decades later. At the official level, the intellectual resources of the churches were stretched to the utmost in the negative task of maintaining and justifying the status which the churches enjoyed in the various regions where they were recognized. This endeavour met with indifferent success. The papacy still asserted its full claims in those countries where its writ still ran. But, despite the zealous activity of the Jesuits, in almost every Catholic country those claims were ignored, and papal privileges were whittled away by 'enlightened' monarchs and their advisers. In France, for instance, the independent 'Gallican' spirit of French Catholics, which had frequently been expressed in previous centuries, renewed itself. Kings, the *parlements*, and the bishops each for their own reasons resisted the papal claims. In 1682 an assembly of the French clergy accepted four principles, known as the Four Gallican Articles, which had been drawn up by Jacques Bénigne Bousset, Bishop of Meaux. They asserted (1) the independence of kings from the pope in all things temporal; (2) the authority of general councils as superior to that of the pope, in accordance with the Council of Constance;[20] (3) that so far as France was concerned the pope must conform to the laws and customs of the French Church; (4) that, while in matters of faith the pope had the principal part, his decrees are not irreformable, unless the Church has given its consent. The ambitious and autocratic Louis XIV at once promulgated these articles, demanding their acceptance by all the clergy. They were revoked before the end of the century, and a compromise was worked out with the papacy. Gallicanism, however, has continued to be a potent force up to modern times.[21]

The Church of England, protected by its establishment, pursued a somewhat somnolent way, suspicious of all that savoured of enthusiasm, resisting change, and reluctant to see the lifting of the legal disabilities on dissenters. For several generations after the end of the Thirty Years' War, theologians of the Lutheran and Reformed Churches expended their energies in producing volumes of dogmatic theology. G. R. Cragg writes:[22] 'The intellect was in the ascendant, and in a particularly arid form, while vast and intricate dogmatic systems fortified the rival positions of Lutheran and Calvinist theologians. . . . Strict orthodoxy became an obsession.'

Reaction against formalism and sterile scholastic theology, whether Catholic or Protestant, prompted the most significant religious movements of the period. These were Pietism, Methodism, and Jansenism. Pietism flourished in Germany under the leadership of Phillip Spener (1635–1705) and August Francke (1663–1727), and in Bohemia under that of Count Nikolaus von Zinzendorf (1700–60) who in 1722 gave refuge to a group of exiled Moravian Brethren at Herrnhut on one of his estates. In England the revival of evangelism and spiritual life known as Methodism was pioneered by John Wesley (1703–91), his brother Charles (1707–88), and George Whitefield (1714–70). The movement was influential in America, and the preaching of Whitefield and Jonathan Edwards in New England in 1740–43 led to the widespread revival known as the Great Awakening. Within the Roman Catholic Church Jansenism, which takes its name from Cornelius Jansen (1585–1638), Bishop of Ypres, was a movement of a different kind. It began as a revival of St Augustine's doctrines of election and of grace as irresistible, giving rise to bitter theological controversies which do not directly concern us here. The Jansenists taught that man can only be saved by the predestinating love of God which creates faith. They stressed, therefore, man's need of personal conversion. They demanded a rigorous discipline, and opposed the principle of *probabilism*[23] taught by the Jesuits. Jansenism quickly spread from the Low Countries to France, and the Convent of Port-Royal became a centre of propaganda for the movement. In spite of official condemnation and persecution it remained a powerful influence on the French Church throughout the eighteenth century.

These movements in their different ways laid stress on the importance of an individual conversion experience, on a warm devotional life, and a strict, even puritanical discipline. Each sought to strengthen the Church by rekindling the fervour of the gospel where formalism in matters of doctrine and in worship was prevalent. In their early phases there was no thought of separation and the formation of a new 'denomination'. But in the event each movement led to the creation of a new church. After the condemnation of Jansenism in the papal Bull *Unigenitus* (1713), the Jansenists of the Netherlands rejected the papacy and in 1724 elected their own bishop of Utrecht. This was the first of the small national bodies now known as Old Catholic Churches, which have originated from groups that have seceded at different times from the Church of Rome. They exist also in Germany, Austria, and Switzerland. Their numbers were to be greatly increased by defections from the Roman Catholic Church after the promulgation of the dogma of the infallibility of the pope, at the First Vatican Council, in 1870.

A Methodist Church was organized in America in 1784. In England separation from the Church of England was a gradual process. It was effected after the death of the Wesley brothers, when in 1795 the 'Yearly Conference of the People Called Methodists' decided that preachers admitted by the Conference had authority to administer the sacraments without ordination.[24]

The Moravian Brethren of Herrnhut, under the inspiration and example of Count von Zinzendorf, showed from the beginning a remarkable missionary zeal in many countries both in Europe and the Americas. Separate communities have been established. In Europe they are known as the Moravian Brethren or the Moravian Church, and in North America, where they are far more numerous, as the Church of the Brethren.

These new churches developed no unique ecclesiologies. The Old Catholic Church represents a western Catholicism which rejects the claim of the pope to plenitude of ecclesiastical power over all dioceses, and the dogma of papal infallibility.[25]

The Methodist Church, in the words of a twentieth-century document,[26] 'claims and cherishes its place in the Holy Catholic Church which is the Body of Christ'. When, in the late eighteenth century, Methodists seceded from the Church of England, they needed an ecclesiology and a Church order. It may fairly be said that the Methodist ecclesiology is expressed by the definition of the Church in the Confession of Augsburg as 'the congregation of saints in which the Gospel is purely taught and the sacraments are rightly administered'.[27] The word 'saints' indicates not the morally perfect, but has the Pauline sense of those who have a living faith in God through Christ. While Methodism emphasizes the necessity for believers to persevere towards holiness and the perfection of love for God and man, it is not a Holiness Church of the Novatianist or Donatist type. It recognizes that the Church is a mixed society of good and bad. Much emphasis is placed on the priesthood of all believers, and abundant opportunities are provided at all levels, from the local 'society' to the Annual Conference, for lay participation in the Church's decisions and work. Ministers are trained, tested, and appointed to their pastorates by the authority of the Conference after ordination by prayer and the laying on of hands by ministers. In England the Methodist Church polity is most closely akin to the Presbyterian, though with a centralization of more authority in the Annual Conference than the Presbyterian Churches invest in their General Assemblies.

In the United States the size of the country has necessitated a different structure for the Methodist Church. The General Conference meets only every four years. Annual conferences are held on a regional basis, and these bodies elect representatives to six Jurisdictional Conferences. All these conferences consist of equal numbers of ministers and lay people. The Jurisdictional Conferences elect bishops. The bishops, who confer together in an annual Conference of Bishops, are charged with general oversight of the Church, the supervision of the Annual Conferences and the smaller District Conferences, and with the direction of evangelism at home and missions abroad. The Methodist Church makes no claim that its bishops are within the historic succession of bishops from apostolic times. Methodism sees its continuity with the Church of the past rather in the succession of believers from the days of the earliest disciples to the present:

> The true continuity with the Church of past ages which we cherish is to be found in the continuity of the Christian experience, the fellowship in the

gift of the one Spirit; in the continuity of the allegiance to one Lord, the continued proclamation of the message, the continued acceptance of the mission. ... The influence of one human personality on others is the chief means used by God for propagating the truth by which the Church lives. ... Behind each believer there stretches a long chain, each link a Christian man or woman, till we find ourselves, with the first disciples, in the company of the Lord Himself. ...

This is our doctrine of apostolic succession. It is our conviction, therefore, that the continuity of the Church does not depend on, and is not necessarily secured by, an official succession of ministers, whether bishops or presbyters, from apostolic times, but rather by fidelity to apostolic truth.[28]

The ecclesiology of the Church of the Brethren approaches more closely to the Holiness and Separatist type. The Church is seen as the fellowship of the saints, membership in which is based on faith in Christ as Saviour, repentance of sin, and baptism which is administered by immersion after a confession of faith. Church polity is of the congregationalist type. Elders, ministers, and deacons are elected by each congregation, and inducted into their office by the laying on of hands. Only in the case of elders is this called ordination. Traditionally the Church of the Brethren has stood aloof from the State and from other Christian bodies. It has insisted on the complete separation of the Church from the State, believing that the latter has its own autonomous function in the material sphere, and has refused to participate in political affairs even to the extent of advising its members against voting. At the same time it has tended to isolate itself in a close community life from the rest of the Christian world. In recent decades there are many signs that the Brethren are emerging from this isolationism by a more positive attitude to civic responsibility and to co-operation with other Christian groups.[29]

ROMANTICISM

As the eighteenth century progressed, the reign of reason was increasingly challenged, aside from the pietistic reaction within the churches, by what is known as the Romantic Movement. It marked an awareness that there was another ingredient in human nature besides rationality and common sense which could introduce man to reality and meaning. This was man's emotional side, his *sensibilité*, his feeling. The claim that scientific rationalism alone could provide a full and satisfying life and set mankind on the way to a golden age was rejected. 'Mystery and wonder, beauty and spontaneity asserted their right to a place in any adequate conception of a satisfying life.'[30] Romanticism touched almost every field of human activity, philosophy, ethics, politics, art and literature, the crafts. Jean-Jacques Rousseau (1712–78) is usually spoken of as 'the father of the Romantic Movement'. Influential in Germany were the poets J. W. Goethe (1749–1832), J. C. F. Schiller (1759–1805), and F. W. J. von Schelling (1775–1854), whose idealistic philosophy was in strong contrast with the systems of the rationalists.

The challenge to the omnicompetence of human reason, and the rehabilitation of a sense of wonder and of emotion as having a vital place in human affairs encouraged a religious attitude, but this did not necessarily lead men to Christian faith. It is true that reaction from the arid rationalism of the age engendered in some Romantics a wistful longing for things medieval, and a number of them espoused Catholicism. Usually they did not remain long within it: their individualism was neither comfortable nor congenial there. The Romantics for the most part found God in the emotions of the human heart; and since strong emotions could be called forth by the beauty, wonder, and might of nature, God was there too, conceived as immanent within the universe. With some this was close to a primitive nature-worship. Even in theologians influenced by the Romantic Movement there is a discernible tendency towards pantheism. This is true of Friedrich Schleiermacher (1768–1834) and of Samuel Taylor Coleridge (1772–1834).

'In the closing years of the eighteenth century,' writes G. R. Cragg,[31] 'the German people were awaiting a prophet who could relate with authority a living message to their sense of need. Frederick Schleiermacher proved to be that prophet. In a unique degree he possessed the gifts necessary for reinterpreting the Christian faith to a generation weary of rationalism and disillusioned by the course which the French Revolution had taken.' In chapter 16 we shall consider the doctrine of the Church of this German theologian who is frequently spoken of as the father of modern Protestantism.

THE CHURCH OF ROME AND THE AGE OF REASON

The Roman Catholic Church was not untouched by the movements of thought which ushered in the modern era. The rationalism of the eighteenth century, the Romantic reaction, and growing nationalism all had their effect.

French nationalism gave rise to a certain independent attitude towards papal claims. This was the Gallicanism which I have already mentioned.[32] A similar movement, known as Febronianism, occurred in Germany. Febronius was the pseudonym of Johann von Hontheim (1701–90), Bishop of Trier. Encouraged by the German archbishops, he conducted a lengthy historical research into the status of the papacy, and in 1763 published his findings in his book, *On the Present State of the Church and the Legitimate Power of the Roman Pontiff.* The Gallican principles appear again, but in a German setting. The Cyprianic concept of the corporate episcopate is asserted. The pope has only an honorific primacy, and, moreover, it is the responsibility of the civil ruler to hear appeals and check abuse. The book was immediately placed on the Index of Prohibited Books, but the views it expressed were widely disseminated, and accepted by many of the German bishops and clergy.

In Austria, Joseph II, Holy Roman Emperor from 1765 to 1790, introduced an attempt at ecclesiastical reform, known as Josephinism, which sprang directly from the 'enlightened' principle that, in so far as it has any place at all, religion must be rational, useful, and beneficial to the State. Religious toleration was granted, but the ruler's right to regulate ecclesiastical affairs was strongly asserted. So far as the Roman Catholic Church was concerned, the pope's authority was strictly spiritual, and his decisions must have the consent of the ruler. The bishops in each state were considered to have equal authority, but within limits imposed by the ruler. On the Emperor's death, Josephinism also died in those parts where it had been introduced: Austria, Hungary, the Netherlands, and Tuscany. As with Gallicanism and Febronianism, the ideas behind it, however, remained influential.

ROMANTICISM AND THE ROMAN CATHOLIC CHURCH

The Romantic reaction to the Enlightenment also influenced Roman Catholic ecclesiology, especially in Germany. While Romanticism emphasized the importance of the individual, it also fostered a sense of the community of man in and with nature. Yves Congar considers that 'the most common characteristic of the complex phenomenon of German Romanticism is the idea of life as a total movement uniting diversity in unity'.[33] Moreover, the renewed interest of the Romantics in the Middle Ages led churchmen back to the conception of the Church as the mystical body of Christ rather than as primarily a structured institution. These themes can be discerned in the ecclesiology of a group of German theologians, several of whom were members of the

Catholic Faculty of Theology which was opened at Tübingen in 1817. J. M. Sailer (1751–1832) saw the Church as 'the living mediation of an interior and living Christianity'.[34] J. S. Drey (d. 1853) conceived of the Church as, within the context of God's plan, 'the manifestation of the Kingdom of God, the instrument of his revelation, an organism vitalized from within by the Spirit'.[35]

More influential has been Johann Adam Möhler (1796–1838) of Tübingen. Möhler, a patristic and medieval scholar, cherished the hope of the reunion of the churches, and acquainted himself thoroughly with the Protestant thought of his day. He was particularly attracted by the idealism of Schelling and the mystical immanentism of Schleiermacher, whom he knew. Their influence is especially apparent in his early work, *Die Einheit in der Kirche*, 'Unity in the Church' (1825), in which he asserts that the Church as hierarchy and institution is 'an effect of Christian faith, the result of the living love of the faithful who have been united by the Holy Spirit', the answer to a human need first stirred up by God. But even so, Möhler does not deny the necessity of the hierarchy and external forms of the Church. They too are of the Holy Spirit, and the faithful can only draw their life from the visible community which the Spirit creates.

In his later works it is clear that he had come to realize that a predominantly pneumatological ecclesiology carried the danger of excessive subjectivism, and might be construed as the acceptance of the idea that the Church is essentially invisible. His study of the life and work of St Athanasius in preparation for his *Athanasius der Grosse* (1827) enabled him to see the importance of Christology and the doctrine of redemption, and to appreciate the role of the papacy.[36] Consequently, in his *Symbolik* ('Symbolism')[37] of 1832 he provides a more christological and objective view of the Church:

> By the Church on earth, Catholics understand the visible community of all believers, founded by Christ, in which the activity he exercised during his earthly life for the reconciliation and sanctification of mankind is continued to the end of the world, by means of an apostolate of uninterrupted continuity which was instituted by him; and into it in the course of time all peoples are to be led back to God. ... The Church ... is not a purely human institution. ... As in Christ divinity and humanity, although distinct, are closely united, so in his undivided wholeness he abides in his Church. The Church, his continuing manifestation, is at once both divine and human. ... It is he who, hidden in human forms, continues to act in it; and it necessarily has both a divine and human side.[38]

The ecclesiology of Möhler is still highly regarded by Roman

Catholic theologians. 'His equanimity and genius have proved an inspiration for modern scholars who find him a guide to the problems raised by the ecumenical movement of today.'[39]

ULTRAMONTANISM

Even in the countries most affected by the Gallican and similar movements, many remained loyal to the papacy and supported its universal claims. These were the Ultramontanes, so called from the Latin *ultra montes*, 'beyond the mountains'. The mountains were the Alps, beyond which lay Rome. Ultramontanism is the position which supports the centralization of ecclesiastical authority and administration in the bishop of Rome and the papal curia, and regards the pope as the sole judge of the orthodoxy of doctrine. The excesses of the French Revolution were seen as the inevitable product of the rationalism tinged with emotionalism of the preceding decades, and when the 'Terror' had subsided, the forces of conservatism reasserted themselves. Within the Roman Catholic Church, Ultramontanism now gained ascendancy. The Jesuit Order, always a strong support of the papacy but which had been suppressed in 1773 under pressure from European monarchs, was restored by Pope Pius VII in 1814. Pope Gregory XVI (1831–46), who in 1799 had published a treatise, *The Triumph of the Holy See*, in support of papal infallibility, condemned the liberalism of the French priest, Hugues Lamennais, although the latter had fondly supposed that the pope would endorse his crusade for freedom and his concept of the Church as authoritative in matters of faith but not of politics.

PIUS IX AND THE FIRST VATICAN COUNCIL

Gregory XVI was succeeded by Pope Pius IX (1846–78). His pontificate, in which the temporal power of the papacy was at its weakest, was marked by a considerable increase of authority in spiritual matters. The Roman Catholic hierarchy was established in England in 1850; he defined the doctrine of the Immaculate Conception of the Blessed Virgin Mary in the papal Bull, *Ineffabilis Deus*, in 1854; in 1864 he issued an encyclical, *Quanta Cura*, together with the *Syllabus Errorum*, a series of theses which condemned rationalism, socialism, and various contemporary philosophical trends; and in 1867 he convoked a General Council which was to meet at the Vatican in 1869.

The First Vatican Council was preceded by vigorous debate on the question of infallibility. Henri Maret, Dean of the Sorbonne, in *On the*

Ecumenical Council and Religious Peace (1869) advocated a moderate Gallican view: 'Neither the papacy nor the episcopate, but the papacy *and* the episcopate are the depositaries of infallibility.' In England, Henry Manning, the former Anglican, and now Archbishop of Westminster, and the layman W. G. Ward pressed for the definition of papal infallibility. Professor J. J. I. Döllinger (1799–1890) of Munich strongly opposed the doctrine, and found an equally doughty opponent in Professor Matthias Scheeben (1835–88) of Cologne. There were also those who held that a definition of infallibility was inopportune, in view of possible political repercussions and further alienation of the Orthodox and Protestants.

When the Council, which comprised some 700 bishops, met on 8 December 1869, the infallibility question was not on the agenda. A schema 'On Faith' first occupied the Council, and this, in revised form, was promulgated on 24 April 1870, as the constitution *Dei Filius*. It reaffirmed many of the theses of the *Syllabus*. The Council then proceeded to what was to be its most important business, the doctrine of the Church. A preparatory commission had proposed two schemata. One was in two parts, dealing with the Church itself, and Church and State relations. The subject of the second was *De Romano Pontifici*, 'On the Roman Pontiff', but no discussion of infallibility was proposed. But a majority of the bishops had petitioned for the inclusion of the infallibility question. This was successful, and, moreover, it was agreed to deal with the schema *De Romano Pontifici* first. Procedural matters occupied some weeks but the constitution *Pastor Aeternus*, which defined the infallibility of the pope, was passed on 18 July with 533 votes in favour, two against, and about sixty abstentions.[40] The Constitution states:

> We, with the approval of the sacred council, teach and define that it is a divinely revealed dogma: that the Roman Pontiff when he speaks *ex cathedra*, that is, when, acting in the offices of shepherd and teacher of all Christians, he defines, by virtue of his supreme apostolic authority, doctrine concerning faith or morals to be held by the universal Church, possesses through the divine assistance promised to him in blessed Peter the infallibility with which the divine Redeemer willed his Church to be endowed in defining faith or morals; and that such definitions of the Roman Pontiff are therefore irreformable of themselves, but not because of the agreement of the Church.[41]

On the next day the Franco-Prussian War broke out, and because of the political turmoil the Council was suspended without having completed its agenda. Thus, the Council had defined the magisterium of the pope without relating it to the authority of the bishops or of general councils. The Council was never formally closed, however, and it is possible, therefore, to regard the Second Vatican Council of 1963–5 as a continuation of the First to deal with its unfinished business. But at the time Vatican I seemed to mark the final failure of what Conciliarists and Gallicans had striven for, and the triumph of Ultramontanism. There were secessions from the Roman Church, notably that of Döllinger, resulting in the formation of a new section of the Old Catholic Church which received episcopal succession from the Jansenist Bishop of Deventer.

THE MODERNIST CRISIS

The denunciations in *Quanta Cura* and in Vatican I's constitution *Dei Filius* of a great deal of contemporary intellectual endeavour, posed problems of conscience for Roman Catholic scholars who took seriously the critical study of the Scriptures, or were aware that the new concept of historical process, closely associated with evolutionary theory, demanded a rethinking of scholastic theology, or believed that the philosophers of the day might have something to say to the Church. Liberal thinking gained momentum towards the end of the nineteenth century, and provoked the so-called Modernist crisis in the first decade of the twentieth. Here we trespass a little beyond the proper bounds of our Part 5.

Among, the leaders of the movement were Alfred Loisy (1857–1940), Maurice Blondel (1861–1949), Lucien Laberthonnière (1860 –1932), George Tyrrell (1861–1909), and Friedrich von Hügel (1852–1925). Their major interests ranged from biblical criticism and the study of Christian origins to contemporary trends in philosophy such as the pragmatism of William James and the intuitionism of Henri Bergson. But as Yves Congar says, their views cannot be reduced to a single uniform position.[42] The more radical were sceptical about the foundation of the Church by Jesus, but nevertheless held it to be a legitimate development from his teaching, and valued it as the setting in which the spiritual and moral life may best be fostered. Even if they were not convinced that the sacraments were instituted by Christ, they valued them, and in particular the Mass, as nourishing this spirituality.

The well-known phrase of Loisy in his *The Gospel and the Church* (1902): 'Jesus announced the Kingdom, and it is the Church which came', may suggest the Modernists' scepticism about the Church's origin. His argument, against Harnack, that the essence of the Church is to be discerned in the form which it developed under the guidance of the Holy Spirit illustrates their interest in evolutionism. He later became more radical, and was prepared to accord little historical worth to the Gospels. Tyrrell, a Jesuit, had a strong interest in the devotional life of the Church, and wrote much on the subject. But he came to interpret the devotional life as an immanental *élan vital* in the human conscience, and to see the sole task of the Church and its hierarchy as the protection of the open-endedness of this interior drive which must not be restricted by the imposition of unalterable dogma. In his posthumous book, *Christianity at the Crossroads* (1909), Tyrrell suggested that Christianity was not final, but was to develop into a more perfect and universal religion.

Seeing in the movement a threat to the Church as an historical institution, and to the objective truth of its affirmations of the faith, Pope Pius X (1903–14) condemned Modernism in 1907 in the decree *Lamentabili* and the encyclical *Pascendi* which asserted strongly that the Church was not merely the expression of religious experience, nor a phase in the evolution of another and truer institution. Loisy, Tyrrell, and others were excommunicated. Others again were prohibited from teaching and publishing.

The Baron Friedrich von Hügel, son of an Austrian father and a Scottish mother, and whose home was in London, exercised a moderating influence among the Modernists, with many of whom, both in England and on the Continent, he was on close terms of friendship. Well abreast of the state of biblical and historical criticism, he was convinced that these were valuable scholarly tools which only cast doubt on Christian origins if those who used them brought to their work purely rationalistic presuppositions which excluded the transcendent. And he argues cogently against the position of Modernists who taught that 'Christianity and Catholicism are essentially a system of principles and laws ... [which] would remain true, even if every one of the alleged happenings and historical facts [viz., those recorded in the N.T.] turned out to be pure creations of the imagination'.[43]

He shared Tyrrell's emphasis on the mystical, but for him the life of devotion was not the subjective experience of a principle immanent in human nature, but the converse of the soul with the transcendent God. For von Hügel there was a 'fundamental and decisive difference ...

between religion conceived as a purely intra-human phenomenon, for which no evidence is to be found beyond the aspirations of humanity, and a religion conceived as having a basis in evidence and metaphysics; as the effect on us of something greater than ourselves—of something greater than any purely human facts and ideas'.[44]

Von Hügel was greatly distressed by the excommunications of Loisy and Tyrrell. He had exercised his considerable influence to prevent them. But he believed religious individualism to be a deviation. The religious life demands a social framework, an institution, and for him this was the Roman Catholic Church, to which, despite his acknowledgement of its weaknesses,[45] he remained completely loyal.

He believed the Church to have its origin in the explicitly declared will of Jesus Christ who gave it a hierarchy with Peter at its head. So he interprets Matthew 16.13–20.[46] The Church is not a static institution, but an organic reality manifesting a living energy which has developed from the original revelation. It works towards the universal goal of the transformation of society and the conversion of souls. Its unity is incarnated in a visible authority which must have a hierarchy and a supreme head. The Church, however, does not exist for itself, but to bring the world to the God who became incarnate in Christ. The Church itself incarnates spiritual realities within the temporal. The sacraments, which von Hügel associates intimately with the incarnation, are essential to its life, for in them Christ is present and active. But Christ died upon the cross. The element of tragedy is therefore to be expected in the Church. 'Von Hügel clung to the Church of Rome partly because he knew it was a Church in which he would have to suffer.'[47] And this, he believed, called for patience, courage, humility, and, moreover, a toleration and sympathy for the consciences of others.[48]

16

Schleiermacher and Ritschl

FRIEDRICH SCHLEIERMACHER, 1768–1834

Friedrich Schleiermacher was born in Breslau, the son of an army chaplain of the German Reformed Church. His parents were converted to the Moravian Brethren, and he received his early education at a Moravian school and seminary. He found Moravian teaching too restrictive for his independent mind, and his speculations led to his expulsion from the seminary. He always retained, however, much of what he had learned there, in particular a warm devotion and love of Christ. In 1787 he went to the University of Halle, was ordained in the Reformed Church in 1794 and appointed as preacher at the Charity Hospital in Berlin. In Berlin he came under the influence of the Romantic Movement, and in 1799 published the first edition of his *On Religion: Speeches to its Cultured Despisers*, which Rudolf Otto describes[1] as 'a veritable manifesto of the Romantics in its view of nature and history; its struggle against rationalist culture and the Philistinism of rationalism in the state, church, school, and society', Schleiermacher was appointed professor of theology at Halle in 1804, but returned to Berlin three years later to become preacher at Trinity Church, and in 1810 dean of the Faculty of Theology of the new Berlin University.

J. M. Creed says[2] that Schleiermacher was 'the first great Protestant theologian since the classical age of the Reformation to lay a primary doctrinal emphasis upon the idea of the Church'. This may seem surprising since he was brought up in a pietistic home, is known as the theologian of Romanticism, held the proper sphere of religion to be feeling, and defined theology as the expounding of one's self-consciousness of relationship with God. All these things suggest an individualism in which a doctrine of the Church would seem to have little place. Yet Creed is right. In both Schleiermacher's major works, the *Speeches* and *The Christian Faith* (1821–2), the Church receives much attention.

1 ON RELIGION: SPEECHES TO ITS CULTURED DESPISERS

The *Speeches*, as the full title makes plain, are addressed by Schleier-macher to his educated contemporaries for whom religion did not merit the consideration of a cultured person:

> In your ornamented dwellings, the only sacred things to be met with are the sage maxims of our wise men, and the splendid compositions of our poets. Suavity and sociability, art and science have so fully taken possession of your minds, that no room remains for the eternal and holy Being that lies beyond the world. I know how well you have succeeded in making your earthly life so rich and varied, that you no longer stand in need of an eternity. Having made a universe for yourselves, you are above the need of thinking of the Universe that made you (*On Religion*, pp. 3–4).

It is in the fourth speech, 'Association in Religion, or Church and Priesthood', that he deals directly with the Church. He notes that 'op-position to every institution meant for the communication of religion is always more violent than . . . opposition to religion itself'.[3] He asks his readers to consider that 'if there is religion at all, it must be social, for that is the nature of man, and it is quite peculiarly the nature of religion'. Man has an impulse to communicate all that is in him. It would be unnatural and morbid to fail to do so. Therefore, 'if a religious view become clear to him, or a pious feeling stir his soul, it is rather his first endeavour to direct others to the same subject and if possible transmit the impulse'.[4] Moreover, realizing his own limitations, man needs association with others in order that his own understanding of religion may be filled out by theirs.[5] Conversational groups are neither adequate nor suitable to fulfil these impulses and needs: 'There must be a higher style and another kind of society en-tirely consecrated to religion.'[6] There follows a rhetorical description of a congregation assembled for worship. Here the preacher 'presents to the sympathetic contemplation of others his own heart as stirred by God'; here 'are sacred mysteries discovered and solemnized that are not mere insignificant emblems'; here 'in sacred hymns and choruses . . . are breathed out things that definite speech cannot grasp. The melodies of thought and feeling interchange and give mutual support, till all is satiated and full of the sacred and the infinite.'[7]

THE PRIESTHOOD OF THE PEOPLE

Schleiermacher now turns to the distinction between priests and laity which the despisers, he says, believe to be the source of many evils. He asserts that they are mistaken:

You have been deluded; this is no distinction of persons, but only of office and function. Every man is a priest, in so far as he draws others to himself in the field he has made his own and can show himself master in; every man is a layman, in so far as he follows the skill and direction of another in the religious matters with which he is less familiar. That tyrannical aristocracy which you describe as so hateful does not exist, but this society is a priestly nation, a complete republic, where each in turn is leader and people, following in others the same power that he feels in himself and uses for governing others (ibid., p. 153).

In his explanation of this passage,[8] Schleiermacher says that if Christianity had attained its goal of being a royal priesthood (1 Pet. 2.9) 'so that there was no more need to awake religion in others', there would have been no need for a distinct priesthood. With the spread of Christianity the need arose 'to organize the more advanced for more effective operation on the rest'. But the distinction between priest and laity, teacher and taught, is not an original and essential difference. The more the function of the special priesthood succeeds, 'the more superfluous this organization will become'. The disappearance of the distinction is not to be expected quickly, but meanwhile its validity 'must ever more and more be limited to the sphere in which finally alone it can have a reason', that is, the training of the community to be a royal priesthood.

NO SALVATION OUTSIDE THE CHURCH

Schleiermacher condemns, as much as do the cultured despisers, 'the wild mania for converting to single definite forms of religion ... and the awful watchword, "No salvation save with us".'[9] Such a watchword is not to be used by one religious association against another. Nevertheless:

> The maxim *nulla salus* ... has for the great communion of the pious an absolute verity, for without any piety it can acknowledge no salvation. Only in so far as one religious party utters it against another, does it work destructively, which is to say, in so far as a universal communion is denied (ibid., p. 188).

Schleiermacher here asserts the existence of a universal religious communion, 'the great communion of the pious'. It is a graduated communion made up of 'different pious communions', Christian and non-Christian, of different historical origin, arising in different cultures, or representing different stages of development. Between these there should be no 'wild mania for proselytizing'. Yet he draws a distinction between 'that wild irreligious mania which easily degenerates into persecution' and 'a praiseworthy zeal for conversion' which, following the example of St Paul at Athens, finds a connecting link with the piety of others and seeks to build it up.[10] Moreover, 'the spread of our own form of religion is a natural and permissible private business of the individual';[11] and Schleiermacher is prepared to allow that 'individual' here need not be interpreted 'with too painful accuracy', and that such 'mild proselytizing' may rightly be the work of associations of individuals.[12]

THE INVISIBLE CHURCH

Schleiermacher proceeds to discuss the distinction between the visible Church and the invisible Church which he calls the true Church.[13] He departs from traditional usage in speaking of the true Church also as the Church triumphant. The Church militant is 'the Church that fights against what the age and the state of man place in its way', and the Church triumphant is 'the Church that has vanquished all opposition, whose training is completed'.[14] The visible Church comprises the great mass of people who 'wish to receive . . . but of reaction on others they do not so much as think. . . . They exercise no reaction because they are capable of none; and they can only be incapable because they have no religion.' Using 'a figure from science', Schleiermacher says that

> they are negatively religious, and press in great crowds to the few points [i.e. the religious associations or denominations] where they suspect the positive principle of religion. Having been charged, however, they again fail in capacity to retain. . . . They then go about in a certain feeling of emptiness, till longing awakens once more, and they gradually become again electrified. . . . Being without knowledge or guess of true religion . . . they repeat a thousand times the same endeavour, and yet remain where and what they were.[15]

It is a contemptuous description which in his later 'explanation'[16] he modifies considerably.

On the other hand, the true Church consists of those who 'have reached consciousness with their piety, and in whom the religious view of life is dominant'. They are 'men of some culture and much power', few in number and never to be found all together where 'many hundreds . . . are assembled in great temples'. They form a true religious society in which all communication is mutual, and they know 'how to estimate the Church, commonly so called, at about its true value, which is to say, not particularly high'.[17]

Yet Schleiermacher does not wish for the dissolution of the visible Church, nor that those who are of the true Church should stand aloof from it:

> In comparison with the more glorious association which, in my view, is the only true Church, I have spoken of this larger and widely extended association very disparagingly, as of something common and mean. This follows from the nature of the case, and I could not conceal my mind on the subject. I guard myself, however, most solemnly against any assumption you may cherish, that I agree with the growing wish that this institution should be utterly destroyed. Though the true Church is always to stand open only to those who have already ripened to a piety of their own, there must be some bond of union with those who are still seeking. As that is what this institution should be, it ought, from the nature of the case, to take its leaders and priests from the true Church (ibid., p. 161).

There needs to be a relationship between the true Church and the visible institution: 'Were persons of more individual emotion now to withdraw from those common forms of presentation, both parties would suffer loss.'[18] The visible Church, 'this institution for pupils in religion, must take its priests only from the members of the true Church'.[19] These latter must compassionately go to the help of those who are as yet beginners.[20] They themselves, too, need this sphere of activity, for 'if the true Church nowhere shows itself in actuality, nothing remains for (them) but an isolated, separatist existence, always decaying for want of a larger circulation'.[21]

Because of the unfavourable circumstances of the time, Schleiermacher sees this relationship between members of the true Church and the actually existing religious associations as yielding only 'scanty fruit'.[22] No more can be expected, he intimates, than 'the peaceful cosmopolitan union of all existing communions, each being as perfect as possible after its own manner'.[23]

CHURCH AND STATE

In the last part of this fourth speech on 'Association in Religion', Schleiermacher eloquently expresses his opposition to the domination of the Church by the State. A few extracts will illustrate his point of view: .

> Listen to what may possibly seem an unholy wish that I can hardly suppress. Would that the most distant presentiment of religion had for ever

remained unknown to all heads of states, to all successful and skilful politicians! (ibid., pp. 166–7).

As soon as a prince declared a church to be a community with special privileges, a distinguished member of the civil world, the corruption of that church was begun and almost irrevocably decided (ibid., p. 167).

The members of the true church the visible church may contain . . . are not in a position to do for it even the little that might still be done. . . . There are worldly things now to order and manage, and privileges to maintain and make good (ibid., p. 168).

If it is the interest of the proud, the ambitious, the covetous, the intriguing to press into the church, where otherwise they would have felt only the bitterest *ennui*, and if they begin to pretend interest and intelligence in holy things to gain the earthly reward, how can the truly religious escape subjection? (ibid.).

[The State] treats the church as an institution of its own appointment and invention . . . and it alone presumes to decide who is fit to come forward in this society as exemplar and priest (ibid., p. 169).

It is very apparent that a society to which such a thing can happen which with false humility accepts favours that can profit it nothing and with cringing readiness takes on burdens that send it headlong to destruction; which allows itself to be abused by an alien power, and parts with the liberty and independence which are its birthright, for a delusion; which abandons its own high and noble aim to follow things which lie quite outside of its path, cannot be a society of men who have a definite aim and know exactly what they wish. This glance at the history of ecclesiastical society is, I think, the best proof that it is not strictly a society of religious men. At most it appears that some particles of such a society are mixed in it and are overlaid with foreign ingredients (ibid., pp. 170–71).

The state may be satisfied, if it so pleases, with a religious morality, but religion rejects consciously and individually every prophet and priest that moralizes from this point of view. Whosoever would proclaim religion must do it unadulterated (ibid., p. 173).

Away then with every such union between church and state! That remains my Cato's utterance to the end, or till I see the union actually destroyed (ibid., p. 174).

In his later 'explanations' Schleiermacher puts forward his views about the relation between Church and State in such matters as marriage, law and education. He stands firm on the principle of separation, but adds, in words which echo John Locke:

Yet it is impossible that the church should be without any union with the state. That appears even where the church is freest. The least is that the state treat the religious societies like any other private society. As a general principle of association it takes knowledge of them and puts itself in a position to interfere in case they should cherish anything prejudicial to the common freedom and safety. With this least, however, it is seldom possible to escape, as appears even in North America where the church is freest. The freer the churches are, the easier it happens that some dissolve and some combine ... [in which case] there are difficulties of settlement in which the state is the natural arranger and umpire (*ibid.*, p. 205).

2 THE CHRISTIAN FAITH

Schleiermacher's *The Christian Faith* is a systematic presentation of Christian theology. 'In the opinion of competent thinkers (it) is, with the exception of Calvin's *Institutes*, the most important work covering the whole field of doctrine to which Protestant theology can point.'[24] It is a work of dogmatic theology, and since dogmatics is the systematization of the teachings of the Christian Church, Schleiermacher holds that he 'must begin with a conception of the Christian Church, in order to define in accordance therewith what Dogmatics should be and should do within that Church'.[25] In his Introduction, therefore, he puts forward certain propositions about the Church, derived not from biblical or dogmatic sources, but from other disciplines, ethics primarily, but also philosophy of religion and apologetics: 'The general concept of "Church", if there really is to be such a concept, must be derived principally from Ethics, since in every case the "Church" is a society which originates only through free human action and which can only through such continue to exist.'[26] The first proposition derived from ethics is:

> The piety which forms the basis of all ecclesiastical communions is, considered purely in itself, neither a Knowing nor a Doing, but a modification of Feeling, or of immediate self-consciousness (*The Christian Faith*, p. 5).

The words immediately following show that for Schleiermacher a church is essentially an association of those who share substantially the same kind of religious feeling:

> That a Church is nothing but a communion of association relating to religion or piety, is beyond all doubt for us Evangelical (Protestant) Christians, since we regard it as equivalent to degeneration in a Church when it begins to occupy itself with other matters as well, whether the affairs of science or of outward organization; just as we also always op-

pose any attempt on the part of the leaders of State or of science, as such, to order the affairs of religion.[27]

The second and third propositions derived from ethics are:

The common element in all howsoever diverse expressions of piety, by which these are conjointly distinguished from all other feelings, or, in other words, the self-identical essence of piety, is this: the consciousness of being absolutely dependent, or, which is the same thing, of being in relation with God (ibid., p. 12).

The religious self-consciousness, like every essential element in human nature, leads necessarily in its development to fellowship or communion; a communion which, on the one hand, is variable and fluid, and, on the other hand, has definite limits, i.e. is a Church (ibid., p. 26).

Up to this point Schleiermacher is giving the word 'Church' a wide sense which includes all religious groups. The propositions which he now borrows from the philosophy of religion lead him to develop ideas which he had touched on in the *Speeches*: that the various religious communions are related to each other as different stages of development and as different kinds;[28] that monotheistic forms of piety are on the highest level;[29] and that those which 'subordinate the natural in human conditions to the moral' are superior to those which 'subordinate the moral to the natural'.[30]

From apologetics he derives a proposition which defines the peculiar essence of Christianity:

Christianity is a monotheistic faith ... and is essentially distinguished from other such faiths by the fact that in it everything is related to the redemption accomplished by Jesus of Nazareth (ibid., p. 52).

Christianity, however, 'takes a greater variety of forms than other faiths and is split up into a multiplicity of smaller communions or churches'.[31] Schleiermacher concludes that 'Dogmatic Theology is the science which systematizes the doctrine prevalent in a Christian Church at a given time'.[32] However,

Limitation to the doctrine of one particular Church is not a characteristic universally valid, for Christendom has not always been divided into a number of communions definitely separated by diversity of doctrine. But for the present this characteristic is indispensable; for, to speak only of the Western Church, a presentation suitable for Protestantism cannot possibly be suitable for Catholics, there being no systematic connection between the doctrines of the one and those of the other. A dogmatic presentation which aimed at avoiding contradiction from either of these two parties would lack ecclesiastical value for both in almost every proposition (ibid., p. 89).[33]

Schleiermacher, therefore, undertakes to present the doctrine of one communion only, that of the Evangelical (Protestant) Church. Of this, he says, there are two principal branches, the Reformed and the Lutheran, whose 'original relation was such that, notwithstanding their different starting points, they might just as well have grown together into an outward unity as they have come to separate from each other'.[34] A union of the Lutheran and Reformed Churches had been effected in Prussia in 1817, and Schleiermacher was a member of this united Church. He feels able to proceed to his systematic presentation of doctrine with 'the assumption that the separation of the two has lacked sufficient grounds, inasmuch as the differences in doctrine are in no sense traceable to a difference in the religious affections themselves'.[35]

Schleiermacher's major treatment of the Church is found in the second part of his system, which is the 'Explication of the Facts of the Religious Self-Consciousness, as they are determined by the Antithesis of Sin and Grace'.

THE CHURCH AS A DIVINELY EFFECTED CORPORATE LIFE

In the Introduction to the 'Second Aspect of the Antithesis: Explication of the Consciousness of Grace'[36] he presents a doctrine which is close to the idea of the Church as the mystical body of Christ.[37] The religious consciousness which is specifically Christian is consciousness of the need of redemption and that redemption is made available by Jesus Christ. It is not a consciousness which is achieved by Christians as individuals, but is given in the experience of the Christian corporate life.

> We are conscious of all approximations to the state of blessedness which occur in the Christian life as being grounded in a new, divinely effected corporate life, which works in opposition to the corporate life of sin and the misery which develops in it (ibid., p. 358).

Schleiermacher is insistent that the blessedness (i.e. essentially the consciousness of redemption) which develops in the Christian fellowship proceeds directly from Christ himself:

> To regard our corporate life as divinely created, and to derive it from Christ as a divinely given One, are the same thing; just so, at that time [i.e. the lifetime of Christ], to believe that the Kingdom of God (that is, the new corporate life which was to be created by God) had come, were the

same thing. Consequently, all developing blessedness had its ground in this corporate life (ibid., p. 360).

While these propositions may apply to very different conceptions of Christianity, he maintains that they exclude two things:

> First, the idea that one can share in the redemption and be made blessed through Christ outside the corporate life which He instituted, as if a Christian could dispense with the latter and be with Christ, as it were, alone (ibid.).

And, second:

> the supposition that, without the introduction of any new factor, and within the corporate life of sin itself, the better individuals could attain to such an approximation to blessedness as would remove the misery (ibid., pp. 360–61).

Thus, the principle that Christianity is essentially corporate is strongly affirmed, and the idea of self-salvation by works is firmly rejected. These things are summed up in a further proposition:

> In this corporate life which goes back to the influence of Jesus, redemption is effected by Him through the communication of His sinless perfection (ibid., p. 361).

The sinless perfection which Jesus possessed is communicated in the fellowship which he founded. It was not, and is not faith that makes Jesus the Redeemer. He is Redeemer by his own work, 'constraining us to the new corporate life'.[38] In summary Schleiermacher says:

> We posit, on the one side, an initial divine activity which is supernatural but at the same time a vital human receptivity in virtue of which alone that supernatural can become a natural fact of history (ibid., p. 365).

Jesus Christ is the Second Adam, 'the beginner and originator of the more perfect human life, or the completion of the creation'.[39] The community which has its origin in him is the 'new creation' of 2 Corinthians 5.17.

Schleiermacher's more detailed exposition of the doctrine of the Church is contained in the second section[40] of his 'Explication of the Consciousness of Grace'. He includes here his discussion of holy Scripture, the ministry of the Word of God, baptism, the Lord's Supper, the power of the keys, and prayer in the name of Christ, all of which are 'essential and invariable features of the Church'.[41] We shall limit ourselves to his treatment of the origin of the Church, with which he closely associates the doctrines of election and the Holy Spirit,[42] of the Church visible and invisible,[43] and of the consummation of the Church.[44]

THE ORIGIN OF THE CHURCH

Schleiermacher begins by noting that fellowship may be understood in a narrower or wider sense. Within the one fellowship of believers or the Church an outer and an inner fellowship may be distinguished, each belonging to the Church 'though obviously in a different sense'.

> The new life of each individual springs from that of the community, while the life of the community springs from no other individual life than that of the Redeemer. We must therefore hold that the totality of those who live in the state of sanctification is the inner fellowship; the totality of those on whom preparatory grace is at work is the outer fellowship, from which by regeneration members pass to the inner, and then keep helping to extend the wider circle (ibid., p. 525).

At first, 'the power of the inner circle was entirely confined to Christ'.[45] Then, from among those who awaited the fulfilment of the messianic hope, some (the first disciples) recognized Jesus as the Christ, came under his redemptive influence, and at the same time began to exercise an influence upon others who had not yet attained to the recognition of Christ. 'These latter thus formed the outer circle, receiving from the first the preparatory operations of grace, in contrast to the inner circle from which the operations proceeded.'[46] Thus 'the Christian fellowship gradually expands as individuals and masses are incorporated into association with Christ'.[47]

The origin of the Church, then, is no different from what happens daily: redeeming activity reaches out from the community to lead the unconverted to conversion. It is a movement outward towards the world from the fellowship of believers, and a movement from the world to the Church. The corporate Christian consciousness, Schleiermacher says, is that the Church 'confronts us as something growing out of the world and gradually, of itself, expelling the world'.[48]

ELECTION

Schleiermacher sees the doctrine of election as intimately connected with the doctrine of the Church in that those who are to form the Church must be separated out from the world,[49] and this is a matter of divine government, a divine ordinance, or election, which rests in the divine good-pleasure.[50]

He does not hold a doctrine of election to damnation. This would be incompatible with the Christian self-consciousness of God.[51] There is a 'single divine fore-ordination to blessedness, by which the origin of the Church is ordered'.[52] 'Each man, when his time is fully come, is regenerated.'[53] The difficult theological question, then, is why some are regenerated later than others. This is similar to the question why the incarnation of Christ occurred when it did and not earlier. The answer can only be that it is 'when the fullness of time was come', which rests on the divine good-pleasure and knowledge of what is truly the best for every individual and group. In his postscript to this doctrine Schleiermacher says that 'it is an essential of our faith that every nation will sooner or later become Christian'.[54]

THE COMMUNICATION OF THE HOLY SPIRIT

All who are living in the state of sanctification feel an inward impulse to become more and more one in their common co-operative activity and reciprocal influence, and are conscious of this as the common Spirit of the new corporate life founded by Christ (ibid., p. 560).

This common Spirit is the Holy Spirit of whom Scripture speaks:

He is promised to the whole community, and where an original communication of the Spirit is spoken of, it comes by a single act to a multitude of people (John 20.22–3; Acts 2.4), who *eo ipso* become an organic whole (ibid., p. 562).

This common Spirit is the Spirit of Christ. This affirmation is based on the Christian self-consciousness:

For everyone is conscious of the communication of the Spirit as being connected in the closest fashion with the rise of faith in him, and everyone recognizes that the same is true for all the others. For faith only comes by preaching and always goes back to Christ's commission and is therefore derived from Him. And as in Christ Himself everything proceeds from the Divine within Him, so also does this communication, which becomes in everyone the power of the new life, a power not different in each, but the same in all (ibid., pp. 563–4).

After his departure from earth Christ fully communicated his Spirit to his followers,[55] and among them prolongs his 'fellowship-forming activity'.[56]

Every regenerate person partakes of the Holy Spirit, so that there is no living fellowship with Christ without an indwelling of the Holy Spirit, and *vice versa* (ibid., p. 574).

> Regeneration is not a sudden transformation; even though delight in God's will has become man's proper self, there remains in him everywhere an activity of the flesh striving against the Spirit; and thus even in those who taken together compose the Church, there is always something that belongs to the world (ibid., p. 676).

Only if it were possible to 'isolate and collect the effects of the divine Spirit' in the members of the Church, should we be able to see the Church in its purity.[58] A distinction between the Church visible and invisible is therefore necessary, but Schleiermacher prefers to use the antithesis he has already employed[59] between the Church's outer and inner circles:

> By the Invisible Church is commonly understood the whole body of those who are regenerate and really have a place within the state of sanctification; by the Visible Church, all those besides who have heard the gospel and therefore are called, and who confess themselves outwardly members of the Church, or who (as we should prefer to express it) form the outer circle of the Church, inasmuch as they receive preparatory gracious influences through the medium of an externally constituted relationship (ibid., p. 677).

The visible Church is divided and subject to error; the invisible is an undivided unity and infallible in the sense of possessing the whole truth of redemption.[60] The separations of the visible Church are not to be condoned. There must be 'endeavour to unite the separates',[61] and 'the complete suspension of fellowship between different parts of the Visible Church is un-Christian'.[62]

THE CONSUMMATION OF THE CHURCH

> We ... cherish the hope that the expansion of Christianity will be accelerated in proportion as the glory of the Redeemer is ever more clearly reflected in the Church itself. It is an undeniable possibility that this might take place in the course of human history; yet we cannot forget that during all that time the propagation of the species goes on, and that sin develops anew in each generation. ... The Church is thus ever anew admitting worldly elements ... and hence is never perfected. In this state it is usually designated the 'Church militant' because it has not only to stand on the defensive against the world but must seek to conquer the world. Just for that reason, as conceived in the state of consummation it is called the 'Church triumphant', because all that in this sense was worldly has

now been wholly absorbed in it, and no longer exists as its opposite (ibid., pp. 696–7).

But this takes us into the doctrine of 'the Last Things', and the 'Christian consciousness has absolutely nothing to say regarding a condition so entirely outside our ken'.[63] In Schleiermacher's view, therefore, this is a very uncertain part of Dogmatics. Nevertheless the Church's doctrines about personal immortality and the consummation have their source in the prophetic teaching of Christ. Consequently,

> this idea of the consummation of the Church is rooted in our Christian consciousness as representing the unbroken fellowship of human nature with Christ under conditions wholly unknown and only faintly imaginable, but the only fellowship which can be conceived as wholly free from all that springs from the conflict of flesh and spirit (ibid., pp. 697–8).

It is the Christian consciousness as hope and 'as a pattern to which we have to approximate'.[64]

ALBRECHT RITSCHL, 1822–89

The most influential theologian in Germany in the latter part of the nineteenth century was Albrecht Ritschl, the son of a Lutheran pastor. He became Professor of Theology at the University of Bonn in 1859, after more than a dozen years there as a lecturer. In 1864 he was appointed Professor of Theology at Göttingen where he remained until his death. His main publication was *The Christian Doctrine of Justification and Reconciliation* in three volumes (1870–74), the first presenting the history of the doctrine, the second its biblical basis, and the third Ritschl's own systematic theology.[65] His theology reacts sharply from the position of Schleiermacher, for whom theology was the explication of the Christian self-consciousness. It reacts equally sharply from the philosophical idealism of Hegel and his disciples. For Ritschl neither man's feelings nor intellectual speculation provided a firm foundation for theology. His starting-point is the revelation of God in Christ.[66] He regards all attempts to establish, for example, the divinity of Christ by philosophical methods as mistakes:

> Luther's warning against teachers who would determine the things of God *a priori*, from above downwards, previous to all definite Divine revelation, holds good (*Justification and Reconciliation*, p. 399).

Since Christ is received by the Christian as 'the Bearer of the final revelation of God'[67] the task of theology is to provide 'an orderly reproduction of the thought of Christ and the apostles'.[68] Ritschl believed he was rescuing Protestant theology from both the subjectivism of Schleiermacher[69] and the intellectualizing of the Hegelian school, and returning to the theological principles of Luther and to the firm basis of God's revelation in Christ.

A paragraph from his Introduction to volume 3 in which he defines 'Christianity', reveals the special characteristics of Ritschl's theology:

> Christianity, then, is the monotheistic, completely spiritual, and ethical religion, which, based on the life of its Author as Redeemer and as Founder of the Kingdom of God, consists in the freedom of the children of God, involves the impulse to conduct from the motive of love, aims at the moral organization of mankind, and grounds blessedness on the relation of sonship to God, as well as on the Kingdom of God (ibid., p. 13).

He bases his theology on the historical facts of Christ's life. It is practical, not speculative, concerned with man's will rather than with his feelings, and therefore has a strong ethical emphasis with both personal and social implications.

THE NECESSITY OF THE CHURCH

On the first page of the Introduction Ritschl speaks of Jesus as the Founder of the Christian Church and of the apostles as its earliest representatives. At once he goes on to assert the essential place which the Christian community (he prefers this term to 'Church') has in the purposes of God. The significance of Jesus' teachings about Redemption

> becomes completely intelligible only when we see how they are reflected in the consciousness of those who believe in Him, and how the members of the Christian community trace back their consciousness of pardon to the Person and the action and passion of Jesus (ibid., p. 1).

Only those who imagine themselves competent to discover 'the religion of Jesus' by themselves, or who conceive of him only as the originator of a new moral code, or as one who has contributed to the picture of an ideal humanity, can ignore the necessity of the Church and of membership of it.[70]

> Authentic and complete knowledge of Jesus' religious significance—His significance, that is, as a Founder of religion—depends, then, on one's reckoning oneself part of the community which He founded, and this precisely in so far as it believes itself to have received the forgiveness of sins as His peculiar gift.... We can discover the full compass of His

historical actuality solely from the faith of the Christian community. Not even His purpose to found the community can be quite understood historically save by one who, as a member of it, subordinates himself to His Person (ibid., pp. 2–3).

The idea of the Church as the essential *locus* where man in history comes to know and can appropriate the redemption offered in Christ occurs in several places. Thus:

Even the Evangelical Christian's right relation to Christ is both historically and logically conditioned by the fellowship of believers; historically, because a man always finds the community already existing when he arrives at faith, nor does he attain this end without the action of the community upon him; logically, because no action of Christ upon men can be conceived except in accordance with the standard of Christ's antecedent purpose to found a community (ibid., p. 549).[71]

There is much in common with Schleiermacher here,[72] but whereas for the latter the sharing of the God-consciousness of Jesus is primarily distinctive of the community, Ritschl places the emphasis on the acceptance of the moral standards and teaching of Christ.

THE CHURCH DISTINGUISHED FROM THE KINGDOM OF GOD

Ritschl affirms that the Christian religion has two focal points: redemption through Christ and the Kingdom of God. Protestant theology generally has taken the concept of redemption through Christ as the single centre from which all Christian faith and practice flow. 'But', says Ritschl, 'Christianity, so to speak, resembles not a circle described from a single centre, but an ellipse which is determined by two *foci*.'[73] In Christianity everything is related to redemption through Christ, but everything is related also to 'the moral organization of humanity through love-prompted action'. The former is 'the private end of each individual Christian'; the latter is the setting-up of the Kingdom of God—'the final end of all'.

The Church has a close relationship to the Kingdom of God, but is not to be identified with it. Ritschl rejects such an identification, which he believes to be characteristic of western Catholicism. He rejects also the view, which he attributes to Luther, Melanchthon, and Calvin, that the Kingdom is 'the inward union between Christ and believers through grace and its operations'.[74] Both views assume that the Kingdom is already fully in being. For Ritschl the Kingdom of God is a teleological concept, and its characteristics have a greater ethical content than either western Catholicism or the early Reformers allowed:

> In Christianity, the Kingdom of God is represented as the common end of God and the elect community, in such a way that it rises above the natural limits of nationality and becomes the moral society of nations . . . . Christ made the universal moral Kingdom of God His end, and thus He came to know and decide for that kind of redemption which He achieved through the maintenance of fidelity in His calling and of His blessed fellowship with God through suffering unto death . . . a correct spiritual interpretation of redemption and justification through Christ tends to keep more decisively to the front the truth that the Kingdom of God is the final end (ibid., p. 10).[75]

Ritschl is prepared to describe the Church as 'the fellowship of believers',[76] and to affirm that its unity is 'essentially bound up with the pure preaching of the Gospel and the proper administration of the two sacraments'.[77] The distinction between the Church, so understood, and the Kingdom of God is the distinction between acts of devotion or worship and moral activity:

> Those who believe in Christ . . . constitute a Church in so far as they express in prayer their faith in God the Father, or present themselves to God as men who through Christ are well-pleasing to Him. The same believers in Christ constitute the Kingdom of God in so far as, forgetting distinctions of sex, rank, or nationality, they act reciprocally from love, and thus call into existence that fellowship of moral disposition and moral blessings which extends through all possible gradations, to the limits of the human race (ibid., p. 285).

Ritschl justified this distinction on the ground that worship and devotional acts are ends in themselves in that a devotional act 'never can be at the same time a means to an act of the same kind', whereas a moral act is both an end and a means to other possible moral acts. Christians engaged in the first are the Church, while Christians engaged in moral action are the Kingdom of God.[78]

He goes on to say:

> The fellowship of Christians for the purpose of religious worship manifests itself in the sphere of sense, and therefore betrays its peculiar nature to every observer. On the other hand the moral Kingdom of God, even while it manifests itself sensibly in action, as a whole reveals its peculiar nature to Christian faith alone. Moreover, the fellowship of Christians for worship gives rise to legal ordinances which it requires for its own sake; but the Kingdom of God, while not injuriously affected by the fact that

moral action under certain circumstances assumes the garb of legal forms, does not in the least depend on them for its continued existence (ibid., p. 285).

Ritschl's distinction between Church and Kingdom appears, therefore, to bear a resemblance to that of the Reformers between the Church visible and invisible. The resemblance, however, is only superficial. The latter distinction does not fit into his theological framework, and he nowhere discusses it. Although Luther and Calvin broke with the idea that the Kingdom of God is the historical Catholic Church (which Ritschl takes to be Augustine's teaching),[79] he argues that they erred in identifying the Kingdom of God with the 'inward union between believers and the Mediator',[80] conceived of as purely spiritual. 'This conception of the Kingdom of Christ is very far indeed from expressing the fellowship of moral action prompted by love.'[81] Moreover, the Reformers involved themselves in contradictions by according to the State the function of preserving true religion by means of laws and government,[82] and by including preaching ('a legal institution') in their conception of the Kingdom of Christ.[83]

The distinction which Ritschl wishes to make is of a different kind. It is that between the Christian community constituted and organized for the conduct of worship (the Church), and the Christian community as engaged in common action inspired by love (the Kingdom of God):

A legally constituted Church, be it Catholic or Lutheran, is not the Kingdom of God or the Kingdom of Christ, for the simple reason that the Church is not the Kingdom of God. Activity of the most important kind for the service of the Church may be of no value whatever for the Kingdom of God. Nor is devotion to the Church a virtue which could in any way compensate for the absence of conscientiousness, justice, truthfulness, uprightness, tolerance. While we must at present put up with a great deal which contradicts this principle, I have always counted what Christ says in Matthew 7.21–3[84] as part of the consolations of the Gospel.

According to the canons of the New Testament, then, we find that the self-same subject, namely, the community drawn together by Christ, constitutes the Church in so far as its members unite in the same religious worship, and, further, create for this purpose a legal constitution; while on the other hand it constitutes the Kingdom of God in so far as the members of the community give themselves to the interchange of action prompted by love. These two modes of activity, however, are not unrelated to one another. They rather condition one another reciprocally. For Christians must get to know one another as such in the exercise of Divine worship, if they are to make sure of occasions to combine together in mutual action from love. On the other hand, the whole range of this loving activity serves to support the maintenance and extension of fellowship in Divine worship. For there is nothing from which the latter suffers more than from slackness in discharging the tasks of the Kingdom of God (ibid., pp. 289–90).

Ritschl's teaching on the distinction and relation between Church and Kingdom has been criticized on several scores. His conception of the Church as an external organization for the purpose of worship and as a preliminary school for moral action bears little relation to the fullness of the N.T. idea of Church. Nor in the N.T. does the Kingdom of God connote the moral endeavour of man, but rather the act of God in judgement and the inauguration of his reign on earth.

THE HOLY SPIRIT AND THE CHURCH

Ritschl regrets the neglect of the doctrine of the Holy Spirit by theology, and that his own book allows him no space to make good this lack.[85] He does, however, engage in several brief discussions in each of which the Holy Spirit is related to the community.[86] He is reluctant to enter into the question of the eternal relations within the Godhead: 'Our time-conditioned view of things'[87] makes this hazardous. Scripture, he asserts, uses the name of God always as 'a compendious description of his revelation', which is imparted through his Son, Jesus Christ, a process which is only completed when the revelation is accepted by the community under the influence of the Spirit:

> The name God has the same sense when used of Father, Son, and Holy Spirit (Matt. 28.19). For the name denotes God in so far as he reveals Himself, while the Holy Spirit is the power of God which enables the community to appropriate His self-revelation as the Father through His Son (1 Cor. 2.12). That the revelation of God through His Son, however, embraces the community which acknowledges His Son as her Lord, and how it does so, is explained by saying that God manifests Himself to the Son and to the community as *loving will* (ibid., p. 273).

Although 'for us, as pre-existent, Christ is hidden',[88] our estimate of him, based on the revelation of God in Christ, is that he is 'the eternally beloved Son of God', the 'object of the Divine mind and will'.[89] So also we may hold that

> the spirit of God is the knowledge God has of Himself, as of His own self-end. The Holy Spirit denotes in the New Testament the Spirit of God, in so far as the latter is the ground of that knowledge of God and that specific moral and religious life which exist in the Christian community. Since the community has for its conscious purpose the realization of the

Kingdom of God as the Divine self-end, it is correct to say that the practical knowledge of God in this community which is dependent upon God, is identical with the knowledge which God has of Himself even as the love of God is perfected in the fact that within the community love is practised towards the brethren. But if in His Son God loves eternally the community that is like His Son, in other words, if the community is *eo ipso* the eternal object of God's will of love, then also it is God's eternal will that His Spirit should be the Holy Spirit in the community of the Kingdom of God. In the form of this eternal purpose, the Spirit of God proceeds from God, inasmuch, namely, as He is destined to enter into the community which enjoys the perfect knowledge of God (ibid., pp. 471–2).

Ritschl presents the same doctrine of the Holy Spirit in the community in a later passage, more briefly:

The Spirit of God or the Holy Spirit, Who in relation to God Himself is the knowledge which God has of Himself, is at the same time an attribute of the Christian community, because the latter, in accordance with the completed revelation of God through Christ, has that knowledge of God and of His counsel for men in the world which harmonizes with God's self-knowledge (ibid., p. 605).

The Christian community, because it shares in God's knowledge of himself through his self-revelation in Christ, shares in God's Spirit. Ritschl goes on to assert that the Holy Spirit is at the same time the motive-power of the life of all Christians, directing that life to the common end of the Kingdom of God. Consequently, he argues, 'it is not permissible for any man to determine his relation to the Holy Spirit by observation of himself in which he isolates himself from all others'.[90]

Regarding the justification and regeneration of the individual, then, nothing further can be objectively taught than that it takes place within the community of believers as a result of the propagation of the Gospel and the specific continuous action of Christ's personal character in His community, through the awakening in the individual of faith in Christ as trust in God as Father and of the sense of union rooted in the Holy Spirit (ibid., p. 607).

'Rules for the objective operation of Divine Grace upon individuals are not to be found, the less so as the relations between men and God always manifest themselves in experience solely in the form of subjective self-consciousness.'[91] Claims about individual experiences of the Spirit, therefore, while open to psychological inquiry, are not subject-matter for dogmatic theology. Ritschl is suspicious of such claims in that 'sectarian or half-sectarian practice customarily appeals to the

Holy Spirit just in so far as thereby justification is supposed to be found for passionate zeal, or pathological experiences or forced, vague, aimless efforts to reach passive assurance of salvation'.[92] Here his antipathy towards subjectivism, enthusiasm, and pietism generally is apparent. At the same time his limiting of the activity of the Holy Spirit to the Christian community fails to do full justice to the biblical doctrine of the Spirit who is likened in John 3.8 to the wind which blows where it wills.

Ritschl's theology was very influential in Germany in the last quarter of the nineteenth century and the first quarter of the twentieth. Its chief exponents were W. Herrmann (1846–1922), J. Kaftan (1848–1926), A. Harnack (1851–1930), F. Loofs (1858–1928), and E. Troeltsch (1865–1923). In Harnack's widely read *Das Wesen des Christentums* (1900)[93] the Ritschlian interpretation of the Kingdom and ethical emphasis are very prominent. A question mark against the assumptions of the Ritschlian theology was, however, placed by two books. These were Johann Weiss's *Die Predigt Jesu vom Reiche Gottes*[94] (1893) and Albert Schweitzer's *Von Reimarus zu Wrede* ('From Reimarus to Wrede')[95] (1906), which made clear that, although the conception of the Kingdom of God as the gradual ethical development of mankind under Christian influence was thoroughly in accord with the prevalent optimism about historical progress, it bore little relation to the Kingdom of God which Jesus preached. Between the two world wars the Ritschlian school was greatly weakened under the impact of the 'Crisis theology' of Karl Barth and Emil Brunner.

Ritschlian influence was strong also in America. The Social Gospel Movement, of which Walter Rauschenbusch (1861–1916) was the most able theological exponent, owed much to Ritschl's doctrine of the Kingdom of God.

17

The Church of England
Its Parties

The nineteenth century brought great changes to the churches in Britain. The repeal of the Test and Corporation Acts in 1828 meant that the non-conformist churches, among which were the now rapidly increasing Wesleyans, were free of the most serious civil restrictions which had been laid on them for over 150 years. The Catholic Emancipation Bill of 1829 likewise lifted these disabilities from Roman Catholics. In 1850 a Roman Catholic hierarchy was set up in England with the appointment as Archbishop of Westminster of Cardinal N. P. S. Wiseman. At once the Roman Catholic Church made great strides, increasing in membership, building churches and schools, and reintroducing monastic communities. But as the century proceeded, no church was more markedly transformed than the established Church of England. When the century opened, three parties may be discerned within the Church of England: Evangelicals, Liberals or Broad Churchmen, and High Churchmen.

THE EVANGELICALS

Many who shared the Methodist concern for personal conversion to Christ, and the conviction that the sole work of a Christian minister is to convince hearers that justification is by faith alone in the efficacy of Christ's atoning sacrifice, remained within the Church of England. The formalism and suspicion of 'enthusiasm' of the Church sorely tempted these Evangelicals to secede. Much pressure was brought also upon bishops to discipline clergy who engaged in itinerant preaching or set up meeting places outside their own parishes.

Some leading Evangelical clergymen had done these things. Henry Venn (1725–97) had left Huddersfield in 1771 because of ill-health for the less demanding parish of Yelling in Huntingdonshire. Fearing that his successor at Huddersfield would not continue the 'gospel preaching', he encouraged the building of a chapel within the parish for those who were dissatisfied with their new incumbent. The tragedy of this was that when, two years later, another Evangelical was appointed, few seceders returned to the Church, and another permanent dissenting body was thus created.[1] As Rector of Yelling Venn still practised itinerancy, preaching in houses and barns in neighbouring parishes, and also visiting London regularly to preach at the Surrey Chapel[2] even after it had been registered as a dissenting chapel. John Berridge (1716–93), whose extraordinarily powerful preaching as incumbent of Everton in Cambridgeshire marked the beginning of the Evangelical Movement in that county, also did not hesitate to engage in preaching in the fields as well as in chapels of the Countess of Huntingdon's Connexion.

It is generally agreed that it was principally the influence of Charles Simeon (1759–1836) which held Evangelicals within the established Church. A Fellow of King's College, Cambridge, in 1783 he was appointed Vicar of Holy Trinity Church, Cambridge, where he remained until his death. He held that the object of Evangelical preaching is 'To humble the sinner. To exalt the Saviour. To promote holiness'.[3] This he determined to do in the spheres which had been assigned to him by ecclesiastical authority, his parish, and his College. He encountered not only the derision of Fellows and undergraduates of his College, but also opposition from his churchwardens and parishioners who had hoped for the appointment of their afternoon lecturer as vicar. They made the church as inaccessible to Simeon as possible. They locked their rented pews, leaving only the side aisles for any who attended. They refused his visits. Simeon's friends, Henry Venn among them, counselled patience and humility, and he heeded their advice. His quandary, however, led him to one irregularity which his enemies might have used against him, but oddly did not. When, after a few months, a few parishioners began to attend church, he felt the need to give them further instruction. His church being barred against him for this purpose, he hired a room in his parish and, as their numbers grew, a larger room in an adjoining parish. His dilemma (and that of other Evangelicals) is well expressed in his own Memoir: 'I was sensible that it would be regarded by many as irregular, but what was to be done? I could not instruct them in my church; and I must of necessity have them all drawn away by the dissenters, if I did not meet them myself; I therefore committed the matter to God in earnest prayer.'[4]

Early in his ministry (*c*.1785) Simeon also preached several times in a barn within another parish. Henry Venn, who had frequently preached in the same place, remonstrated with him on this. It is likely that the older man, ready himself to accept the opprobrium and penalties which itinerancy might bring, saw in Simeon a man who could bring the established Church to a recognition of the value of Evangelical principles. In later life, being reminded of his preaching in the barn, Simeon replied: 'O spare me! Spare me! I was a young man then.'

The history of Simeon's overcoming of opposition in his parish and in the University is told by his successor at Holy Trinity, William Carus, in his *Memoirs of the Life of the Rev. Charles Simeon, M.A.*[5] His incumbency, which lasted fifty-four years, was a remarkable instance of devoted pastoral work which sought to humble his people (and himself) and to exalt Christ.

We do not find in the writings of Simeon or other Evangelicals of the early nineteenth century any systematic exposition of the doctrine of the Church. It may safely be said that they held the Augustinian and Calvinistic doctrine of the Church Invisible. But they were also convinced that the Church of England embodied a divinely sanctioned Church order, and that it was there that they were called by God to serve. They were well aware of its faults. They would have subscribed to the view that the Church regarded as institution is a mixed society. Speaking of baptism in his University Sermons of 1811, 'On the Excellency of the Liturgy', Simeon said:

> We must distinguish between a change of state and a change of nature. Baptism is a change of state: for by it we become entitled to all the blessings of the new covenant. ... A change of nature may be communicated at the time that the ordinance is administered; but the ordinance itself does not communicate it. ... Simon Magus was baptized; and yet remained in the gall of bitterness.[6]

The idea of the 'mixed Church' is implicit here.

The common assumption that the Evangelicals saw the Church simply as a gathering of individual believers is not true. As for Simeon, it is belied both by his use of corporate terms in speaking of the Christian community ('fold of Christ', 'one family', even 'mystical body') and by his pastoral policy. He was a pioneer in encouraging the laity of his parish to realize that they were members of a body, and to show this by taking their part in pastoral care of the sick, needy, and troubled.

Simeon had a great regard for liturgical worship. In the series of sermons mentioned above he declared that if an objective comparison of the extemporary prayers offered in dissenting chapels over a period of time could be made with those of the Book of Common Prayer, 'there is scarcely a man in the Kingdom that would not fall down on his knees and bless God for the Liturgy of the Established Church'.[7] Elsewhere he wrote: 'The finest sight short of heaven would be a whole congregation using the prayers of the Liturgy in the true spirit of them.'[8] He was meticulously loyal to his bishop, and Charles Smyth notes[9] also 'his feeling that the Priestly benediction was more than a prayer . . . his recognition of the priestly power of Absolution'.

To many enthusiastic Evangelicals Simeon seemed 'more of a churchman than a gospel man'. As Smyth says,[10] Simeon had learned from his contact with John Berridge that 'although the Kingdom of Heaven is indeed taken by violence, it is not to be held by indiscipline'. This lesson he passed to those who came under his influence at the University, many of whom were to be the Evangelical leaders of the next generation. 'Do not attempt to act in a parish with which you have no connection,' he wrote to a young clergyman in 1817.[11]

However, an urgent problem faced the Evangelicals. How were Evangelicals to be placed in a sufficient number of parishes thus securing the continuity of 'gospel-preaching' in England without the formation of new dissenting groups, which too often was the result of preaching in fields, barns, and private houses? The solution was found in the purchasing of advowsons,[12] initiated by John Thornton, a wealthy layman, and enthusiastically adopted by Simeon, who devoted a great deal of his own money to it, and collected much more. The Simeon Trust, which administered the money and controlled the appointments, was constituted in 1817. This well-meant policy (Simeon was convinced that it was for the advancement of the established Church and the Kingdom of God) had unforeseen and unfortunate results. Other groups which did not share Evangelical principles adopted the practice of buying advowsons, and this did much to exacerbate party strife within the Church of England until well into the twentieth century.

Of much more positive value to the Church of England was the Evangelicals' zeal for overseas missions and social reform. Simeon was a co-founder in 1799 of the Church Missionary Society, which supplied a steady stream of missionaries first to India and other parts of the East, and later to Africa. From the Evangelical ranks came many of the nation's leaders in the campaigns for the abolition of the slave trade in British dominions (finally achieved in 1833), for the introduction of legislation to improve the inhuman conditions in factories and mills, and for educational reform. William Wilberforce, Hannah More, and Anthony Ashley Cooper, the seventh Earl of Shaftesbury, were all Evangelicals.

Later in the nineteenth century many Evangelicals took a course which their predecessors would hardly have approved. In violent reaction to the Oxford Movement (see pp. 51 ff), prompted by an irrational fear of the Church of Rome, they formed a strange alliance with the Liberal successors of the Latitudinarians. Virulent anti-Romanism became their chief preoccupation, and often the theme of their preaching rather than the gospel of Christ's love for souls. Simeon's charitable attitude to dissenters and Roman Catholics ('the clergyman ought to visit them all, visiting even their Ministers ... treating them with gentleness and delicacy, and making himself felt as their friend'),[13] and Wilberforce's defence of the Catholic Emancipation Bill were forgotten. Happily, this phase of their history has passed, and Anglican Evangelicals are to be found among those engaging in the ecumenical dialogues with Roman Catholics which are a feature of the post-Vatican II era.

THE LIBERALS

The Liberals were the successors of the Latitudinarians. They disliked dogmatic definition in theology, saw the maintenance and inculcation of a high moral standard in accordance with the teachings of Christ as the main significance of the Church's existence, and opposed the limitation of Church membership by rigid theories of Church order and ecclesiastical regulations.

Dr Thomas Arnold (1795–1842), the famous headmaster of Rugby School, would doubtless not have agreed that he was 'a party man', but it may certainly be said that his *Principles of Church Reform*[14] (1833) sets out an ecclesiology representative of the Broad Church party, or Liberals. It is often remarked that he took what he had been able to achieve at Rugby as a model for his proposals for a reformed national Church.[15] At Rugby, with great single-mindedness and courage he had brought into being, out of something akin to anarchy, a community for the good order and common purpose of which each member accepted responsibility: headmaster, masters, seniors, and even the newest boys. This was based on acknowledgement of faith in

Christ and the acceptance of Christian moral standards. Arnold envisaged a Christian state in which, just as at Rugby School, the Christian religion was related to all activities, whether in classroom, house, or on the sports field. Christianity would penetrate very aspect of the national life. To this end there should be one national Church in which the great majority of sincere Christians could unite.

In his Preface Arnold declares the following principles:

> that a Church Establishment is essential to the well-being of the nation; that the existence of Dissent impairs the usefulness of an Establishment always, and now, from peculiar circumstances, threatens its destruction: and that to extinguish Dissent by persecution being both wicked and impossible, there remains the true but hitherto untried way, to extinguish it by comprehension (*Principles of Church Reform*, p. 87).

Arnold was convinced that Church reform was impossible unless the problem of sectarianism, 'that worst reproach of the Christian name',[16] were boldly tackled, and he devoted several pages to a consideration of sectarianism in England. It arose, in his opinion, because the Establishment mistakenly identified unity with unanimity of opinion. Divisions among Christians are indeed evil, but 'whoever is acquainted with Christianity, must see that differences of opinion are absolutely unavoidable'.[17] The Establishment also made the mistake of assuming that dissent could be prevented by setting up a statement of doctrine and appointing a form of worship to which men were obliged to conform under the threat of severe legal penalties. 'But [our fathers] forgot that while requiring this agreement, they had themselves disclaimed, what alone could justify them in enforcing it—the possession of infallibility.'[18] The 'vindictive oppression' of the Clarendon Code[19] was replaced by the Toleration Act of 1689—'a strange measure by which the nation sanctioned the non-observance of its own institutions',[20] but there was no determined effort to effect a union with the non-conformists. 'The Church and the Dissenters lived in peace; but their separation became daily more confirmed.'[21] That separation was now widened in that dissenters, to their credit, exercised a great influence among the poorer classes, while the Establishment, confined by its prescribed forms of worship and operating from centres and buildings which were unstrategically placed for effective work in the new industrial areas, had little influence outside the upper and middle classes. The situation, moreover, was exacerbated by rivalry, jealousy, and recrimination, the established Church and dissenters each accusing the other of the sin of schism.[22]

Is it not, then, worth while to try a different system? And since disunion is something so contrary to the spirit of Christianity, and differences of opinion a thing so inevitable to human nature, might it not be possible to escape the former without the folly of attempting to get rid of the latter; to constitute a Church thoroughly national, thoroughly united, thoroughly Christian, which should allow great varieties of opinion, and of ceremonies, and forms of worship, according to the various knowledge, and habits, and tempers of its members, while it truly held one common faith, and trusted in one common Saviour and worshipped one common God? (ibid., pp. 107–8).

As a basis for such a national Church, Arnold proposes the following points, on which all Christians, he holds, are agreed: belief in God as creator and sustainer; belief in Jesus Christ, the Son of God, and in his atoning death and resurrection; belief that the Old and New Testaments uniquely contain the revelation of God's will to men; acceptance of Christian moral standards, 'that pride and sensuality are amongst the worst sins; that self-denial, humility, devotion, and charity, are amongst the highest virtues . . . that our first great duty is to love God; our second, to love our neighbour'.[23] It is not unreasonable that those who are united in these principles should be content to live as members of the same religious society. Leaving aside different opinions on Church government, Arnold argues that no differences on the important points of pure doctrine need prevent Presbyterians, Methodists, Independents, Baptists, and Moravians from entering, with the established Church, into a united national Church. Of the Quakers, Roman Catholics, and Unitarians, however, he says that 'so long as these sects preserve exactly their present character, it would seem impracticable to comprehend them in any national Christian church; the epithet "national" excluding the two former, and the epithet "Christian" rendering alike impossible the admission of the latter'.[24] He proceeds to discuss what changes would be necessary in these bodies, and how a national Church, given these changes, might make it possible for them to unite by framing articles, creeds, and prayers for public use not to serve as tests for latent error, but 'to provoke the least possible disagreement, without sacrificing, in our own practical worship, the expression of such feelings as are essential to our own edification'.[25]

Arnold next considers the kind of 'government and administration' which this national Church will need. Its ministers are to be drawn from all classes of society: 'As all classes of society require the services of ministers of religion, the ministry should contain persons taken from all',[26] even from the poorest. The laity are to have a large share in the government of the Church at all levels. In the parishes a social organization must be built up which will involve the parishioners as a body. The lack of it compels passivity: 'The love of self-government, one of the best instincts in our nature, and one most opposite to the spirit of lawlessness, finds no place for its exercise.'[27]

As for the government of the Church, 'Episcopalians require that this should be *episcopal*; the Dissenters of almost every denomination would insist that it should not be *prelatical*. But it may be the first without being the last.'[28] Dioceses must be smaller. Each diocese is to have a council consisting of clergy and lay members, appointed partly by the bishop and partly by the clergy and laity of the diocese. The bishop must not act without his council. This would 'destroy that most mischievous notion ... that the Church is synonymous with the clergy'.[29]

Arnold advocates a part-time ministry, where need warrants it, of men who, having another profession or trade, would not be wholly dependent on the ministry for support.[30] He requires a radical revision of the patronage and appointments systems of the established Church.[31] He strongly defends the membership of bishops in the House of Lords, and argues that representative clergy should sit in the House of Commons: 'They are wanted in the national assembly of a professedly Christian nation.' He indignantly rejects the suggestion that they should be there only to vote on ecclesiastical matters.[32] He would wish the liturgy of the Church of England to be used once on every Sunday and great festival, but there should also be at other times of the day and week other services of a freer kind, even at the risk of 'some insipidity and some extravagance'.[33]

The commuting of tithes, the equalizing of the incomes of bishops and of clergy, the evils of pluralism and absentee incumbents, the exclusion of dissenters from the universities all come briefly under his review[34] before he turns to the question by what power the national Church should be brought into being. It would be by legislative enactment of the government. This would be prepared for by a commission charged with the revision of the Thirty-nine Articles. Arnold is insistent that any such commission should not consist of clergymen alone. It would also be necessary to draw up in detail the proposed constitution of the national Church. The body charged with this task would necessarily seek 'information on many points ... from persons locally or professionally qualified to furnish it'.[35]

Arnold concludes with an appeal to his fellow-members of the established Church:

> that they would regard those thousands and ten thousands of their countrymen, who are excluded from [the Church of England's] benefit; that they would consider the wrong done to our common country by these unnatural divisions amongst her children. . . . For the sake, then, of our country, and to save her from the greatest possible evils—from evils far worse than any loss of territory, or decline of trade—from the sure moral and intellectual degradation which will accompany the unchristianizing of the nation, that is, the destroying of its national religious establishment, is it too much to ask of good men, that they should consent to unite themselves with other good men, without requiring them to subscribe to their own opinions, or to conform to their own ceremonies? They are not asked to surrender or compromise the smallest portion of their own faith, but simply to forbear imposing it upon their neighbours. They are not called upon to give up their own forms of worship, but to allow the addition of others; not for themselves to join in it, if they do not like to do so, but simply to be celebrated in the same church, and by ministers, whom they shall acknowledge to be their brethren, and members no less than themselves of the National Establishment (ibid., p. 148).

On the last few pages of the book Arnold discusses some of the objections which he foresees to his proposals. The book won little assent. His proposals were not taken up by the Liberals. The Evangelicals saw the conversion of individuals as the nation's greatest need, and, as J. R. H. Moorman remarks, 'the High Church party, now on the eve of its great revival, had other ideas of what the Church should be'.[36]

THE HIGH CHURCH PARTY AND THE OXFORD MOVEMENT

The smallest of the three 'parties', the High Churchmen, were the successors of the seventeenth-century divines like Andrewes, Cosin, Bramhall, and Pearson to whom they looked with great veneration. In their ecclesiology they upheld the view, against both Roman Catholics and Protestant dissenters, that the Church of England was the successor in England of the primitive Church. They placed great emphasis on apostolic succession, and on the authority of the creeds and conciliar decisions of the patristic period. They greatly desired the renewal of the much neglected sacramental life of the established Church and the restoration of a stricter discipline. They were opposed to the authority over the Church which Parliament had come to exercise. It was against State control as much as against dissenters that they stressed the doctrine of apostolic succession, inasmuch as implicit in that doctrine is the concept that authority over the Church resides in the bishops who have received it in succession from the apostles and from Christ.[37]

During the eighteen-thirties the High Church party gained vigour under the leadership of a remarkable group of Oxford dons, chief among whom were John Keble (1792–1866), E. B. Pusey (1800–82), R. H. Froude (1803–36), and John Henry Newman (1801–90). With them began the Oxford Movement, whose supporters were variously named Tractarians, Puseyites, and, at a later stage, Ritualists and Anglo-Catholics.

In July 1833, Keble preached a sermon on 'National Apostasy' before the judges assembled for the Assizes in Oxford. It was directed against parliamentary legislation which proposed the suppression of a number of Irish bishoprics. This proposal was not without justification, in view of the small Anglican population of Ireland and the expense of maintaining an unnecessarily large number of sees. To High Churchmen, however, it was a glaring instance of State interference in ecclesiastical affairs, and Keble called on the nation to recognize that the Church was more than a mere creation of the State.[38] Shortly afterwards the Oxford High Churchmen met to discuss a campaign for the promotion of High Church principles and the defence of the Church against Erastianism. They decided to issue a series of *Tracts for the Times*,[39] twenty of which were issued in the same year. The ecclesiological interests of the Tractarians are prominent throughout the tracts, and often evident from their titles alone.

1 APOSTOLIC SUCCESSION

Several deal with apostolic succession and episcopacy. Tract 1, 'Thoughts on the Ministerial Commission', argues that even if the government should cast off the Church, the real ground of the authority of the Church's ministry would remain—'our apostolical descent'.[40] Tract 4 is entitled 'Adherence to the Apostolical Succession the Safest Course', and Tract 7, 'The Episcopal Church Apostolical'. Tract 12, 'On Bishops, Priests, and Deacons', argues that the threefold order of ministry is implicit in the N.T. and supported by the Apostolic Fathers: Clement of Rome, Polycarp, and Ignatius. Tract 15 is entitled 'On the Apostolical Succession in the English Church', and Tract 19 'On Arguing concerning Apostolical Succession'. Tract 74 cites at length support for the doctrine from post-Reformation English divines.

2 THE IDEAL OF THE PRIMITIVE CHURCH

Several tracts urge a return to the primitive practice of the Church in general (Tract 6, 'The Present Obligation of Primitive Practice') and in particular ways such as fasting (Tracts 18 and 66, two learned tracts by Pusey), and frequent communion (Tract 26). Tract 36 pleads for a greater appreciation of the value of primitive rites and customs in connection with Christian initiation and the celebration of the eucharist.

3 THE BRANCH THEORY

What has been called 'the Branch Theory' of the Church is implicit in several tracts. This is the notion that those Christian communions which have maintained the doctrinal standards of the early creeds and general councils are to be deemed true branches of the Church even though they are not in communion with one another. Tract 5, 'On the Nature and Constitution of the Church of Christ, and of the Branch of it established in England', claims that the Church of England is 'a pure and apostolic branch of Christ's holy Church'.[41] Tract 71, 'On the Controversy with the Romanists', speaks of the Church of England as 'that particular branch of the Church Catholic through which God made us Christians. . . . The only conceivable reasons for leaving its communion are . . . first, that it is involved in some damnable heresy, or second, that it is not in possession of the sacraments.'[42] It is admitted that the Church of Rome is 'a branch of Christ's Church', and that its orders are valid. Nevertheless its errors are such that the English churchman must resist the argument that it is 'safer' to unite with Rome, despite the imperfections of the English Church which the tract readily admits.[43] The Branch Theory was expounded at length in a *Treatise on the Church of Christ* (1838) by William Palmer, an early supporter of the Oxford Movement.

4 ANTI-ROMANISM

The Tractarians were consciously in controversy on several fronts: against State control, liberalism, dissent, but also against 'the Papists'. Several tracts deal with grievances against Rome. Tract 71 specifies the denial of the cup to the laity, insistence that the validity of sacraments depends on the priest's intention, compulsory auricular confession, unwarranted anathemas, the doctrine of Purgatory, the invocation of saints, the worship of images.[44] Tracts 27 and 28 reprint Bishop Cosin's *History of Popish Transubstantiation*. Tract 30, 'Christian Liberty; or Why should we belong to the Church of England?', rejects the pope's claim 'to control all the branches of the Church on earth'. The bishops of the Church of England rightly rejected the claim, and the conclusion is drawn that papists in England and Ireland are to be regarded as schismatic.[45]

5 THE CHURCH OF ENGLAND AS THE VIA MEDIA

Tracts 38 and 41, written by Newman and entitled 'Via Media', present the idea that the Church of England holds the middle path, *via media*, between the errors and exaggerations of Rome on the one hand, and Protestantism on the other.

> The glory of the English Church is, that it has taken the *via media*, as it has been called. It lies *between* the (so-called) Reformers and the Romanists (*Tracts for the Times*, p. 277).

> In the seventeenth century the theology of the divines of the English Church was substantially the same as ours is [i.e. the Tractarians]; and it experienced the full hostility of the Papacy. It was the true Via Media; Rome sought to block up that way as fiercely as the Puritans (ibid., p. 281).

Newman then adds a list of the errors of Rome. To those mentioned in the Anti-Romanism section, above, he adds: that it is unscriptural to say that 'we are justified by inherent righteousness', or that 'the good works of a man justified do truly merit eternal life'; that the sacrifice of masses as practised in the Roman Church is unscriptural and blasphemous; that indulgences are a gross and monstrous invention; that to celebrate divine service in an unknown tongue is a corruption; that there are not seven sacraments; that the Roman doctrine of tradition is unscriptural.[46]

In Tract 41 he discusses the catholic elements in the Book of Common Prayer. He acknowledges that in practice the established Church has neglected many of them, and suggests the need for another reformation:

> I would do what our Reformers in the sixteenth century did: they did not touch the existing documents of doctrine—there was no occasion; they kept the creeds as they were; but they *added* protests against the corruptions of faith, worship, and discipline, which had grown up round them. I would have the Church do the same thing now, if I could: she should not

change the Articles, she should add to them: add protests against the Erastianism and Latitudinarianism which have incrusted them. I would have her append to the Catechism a section on the power of the Church (ibid., p. 299).

J. H. NEWMAN

At this time Newman, it is clear, was convinced that the Church of Rome had in many respects declined from the doctrines and practices of the primitive Church. In the next few years, however, certain influences were to alter his attitude to Rome. J. R. H. Moorman[47] describes these:

In 1839 N. P. S. Wiseman, a half-Irish and half-Spanish fanatical Roman Catholic priest, was sent to England and began publishing articles on the Donatist schism, suggesting that the Church of England was schismatic in just the same way that the Donatists had been pronounced schismatic in the fourth century. Newman was deeply impressed by this line of thought. Then again a small group of radical thinkers among the Tractarians, including W. G. Ward and F. W. Faber were becoming attracted, not, like Froude, to medieval Rome, the Church out of which the Anglican Church had emerged, but to the Rome of the Counter-Reformation and to post-Tridentine theology and practice. Newman was not, at first, impressed by this. The Church of Rome, he was convinced, had wandered far from the customs of the Primitive Church and, in so doing, had erred from catholic simplicity. But at this point he was introduced to the doctrine of 'Development'. Christ had promised that the Holy Spirit should guide the Church into all truth. The Primitive Church did not know the whole truth; this was revealed only slowly in the course of history. It was not the Primitive Church that should be taken as the model, but that Church which showed most signs of holiness, of being the true Body of Christ. From that moment Newman began to look on Rome with new eyes. What if her wandering had led her not away from catholic simplicity but on into wider fields of divine truth?

In February 1841 Newman's famous Tract 90 appeared, entitled 'Remarks on Certain Passages in the Thirty-nine Articles'.[48] It sought to show that the Anglican Articles are capable of being interpreted in harmony with the decrees of the Council of Trent. It occasioned violent opposition. For many it confirmed what they had long suspected, that the Tractarian aim was to Romanize the Church of England and undo the work of the Reformation. It was condemned by the heads of the Oxford Colleges, and Bishop Bagot of Oxford forbade the publication of more tracts. Newman resigned his benefice in

1843, and in 1845 was received into the Roman Catholic Church. Later in the same year his *Essay on the Development of Christian Doctrine* appeared, on which he had been working for some time.[49] The principle of development enabled Newman now to see the Roman Catholic Church of his day as one with the Church of the Nicene era and the Church which was founded by Christ. It was 'a sort of test which the Anglican [teaching] could not exhibit, that modern Rome was in truth ancient Antioch, Alexandria, and Constantinople, just as a mathematical curve has its own law and expression'.[50] He can therefore say of the Church of Rome in the *Essay on Development*:

> When we consider the succession of ages during which the Catholic system has endured, the severity of the trials it has undergone, the sudden and wonderful changes without and within which have befallen it, the incessant mental activity and the intellectual gifts of its maintainers, the enthusiasm which it has kindled, the fury of the controversies which have been carried on among its professors, the impetuosity of the assaults made upon it, the ever increasing responsibilities to which it has been committed by the continuous development of its dogmas, it is quite inconceivable that it should not have been broken up and lost, were it a corruption of Christianity. Yet it is still living, if there be a living religion or philosophy in the world; vigorous, energetic, persuasive, progressive; *vires acquirit eundo*;[51] it grows and is not overgrown; it spreads out, yet is not enfeebled; it is ever germinating, yet ever consistent with itself. . . . That its long series of developments should be corruptions would be an instance of sustained error, so novel, so unaccountable, so preternatural, as to be little short of a miracle, and to rival those manifestations of Divine Power which constitute the evidence of Christianity (*Essay on Development*, pp. 437–8).

Newman's reasons for concluding that the Church of Rome *alone* can be identified with the primitive Church are given in the following typical[52] passage:

> On the whole, then, we have reason to say, that if there be a form of Christianity at this day distinguished for its careful organization, and its consequent power; if it is spread all over the world; if it is conspicuous for zealous maintenance of its own creed; if it is intolerant towards what it considers error; if it is engaged in ceaseless war with all other bodies called Christian; if it, and it alone, is called 'catholic' by the world, nay, by those very bodies, and if it makes much of the title; if it names them heretics, and warns them of coming woe, and calls on them one by one, to come over to itself, overlooking every other tie; and if they, on the other hand, call it seducer, harlot, apostate, Antichrist, devil; if, however much

they differ one with another, they consider it their common enemy; if they strive to unite together against it, and cannot; if they are but local; if they continually subdivide, and it remains one; if they fall one after another, and make way for new sects, and it remains the same; such a religious communion is not unlike historical Christianity, as it comes before us at the Nicene Era (ibid., pp. 272–3).

In the years that followed there were other secessions to Rome. Pusey and Keble stood fast to the Tractarian principles. The Oxford Movement went on, gaining more support even as it aroused opposition both from within and outside the established Church. To the Tractarians and the 'Anglo-Catholics', as their later successors were called, the whole Anglican Communion owes a great debt, whether acknowledged or not. The renewal of the Church's sacramental life, greater appreciation of beauty in worship, the founding of many schools and colleges, a new impetus in missionary work abroad and in the slums of England, the reintroduction of religious communities all spring from the Tractarian conviction of the essential catholicity of the Church of England.

18

F. D. Maurice;
The Lambeth Conferences

FREDERICK DENISON MAURICE (1805–72)

F. D. Maurice was a theologian of original and independent mind. Although he had affinities with Evangelicals, Liberals, and High Churchmen, he abhorred party spirit, and stood aloof from them all. Since his lifetime, hardly a decade has passed without the appearance of a book or major article on his thought, and interest in him has increased by the recognition that certain principles, now commonly taken as guidelines in discussions on Christian unity and often assumed to be the invention of twentieth-century ecumenists, were expounded by Maurice over a century before. In many respects he 'was a hundred years in advance of his time'.[1] This is true of his ecclesiology, although it must be added that in other respects it is dated.

Maurice, who had a Unitarian upbringing, became a member of the Church of England in 1830 and was ordained in 1834. His best known book, which chiefly concerns us here, is *The Kingdom of Christ* (1838). It was first published under the title *Letters to a Member of the Society of Friends* in 1837, and a revised and enlarged edition appeared in 1842. Its themes recur in many of his other writings, especially *The Lord's Prayer* (1848), *The Gospel of the Kingdom of Heaven* (1864), and *The Commandments considered as Instruments of National Reformation* (1866). His ecclesiology is summarized here in the order he himself presents it in *The Kingdom of Christ*, and under four headings.

1 THERE EXISTS IN THE WORLD A UNIVERSAL AND SPIRITUAL KINGDOM FOR MAN

Maurice begins from the Quaker assertion that spiritual principles imply the rejection of outward ordinances. The Society of Friends sought to establish a spiritual kingdom in the world; but, Maurice asks, 'Did not such a Kingdom exist already, and were not these ordinances the expression of it?'[2]

> There rose up before me the idea of a Church Universal, not built upon human inventions or human faith, but upon the very nature of God Himself, and upon the union which He has formed with His creatures: a Church revealed to man as a fixed and eternal reality by means which infinite wisdom had itself devised (*Kingdom of Christ*, Dedication, vol. 2, p. 363).[3]

Maurice is convinced that if such a Church is a reality, 'apprehensions of the different sides and aspects of it' must be found in 'the different schemes which express human thought and feeling', apprehensions which will find their highest meaning in the 'Universal Society' which God has created. His method, therefore, in the early part of the book is to examine the most prominent of these 'different schemes', to distinguish the fundamental principles of each from the systems which have often distorted them, and to inquire whether the fundamental principles of each may be reconciled with those of the others, and so point, by way of agreement, to the reality of a universal society grounded in God. It is his belief that

> all sects and factions, religious, political or philosophical, were bearing testimonies, sometimes mute, sometimes noisy, occasionally hopeful, oftener reluctant, to the presence of that Church Universal, which is at once to justify their truths, explain the causes of their opposition, and destroy their existence (ibid., Introductory Dialogue).[4]

In turn there come under his review Quakerism, Protestantism both in its Lutheran[5] and Calvinist forms, Unitarianism, Methodism, the Irvingites (or Catholic Apostolic Church), the philosophical thought of the eighteenth and early nineteenth centuries, the political movements which inspired the American and French revolutions, the teachings of Jeremy Bentham, and the socialism of Robert Owen. Maurice's comprehensive review suggests that he was attempting to do for the early nineteenth century what Augustine did for the fifth in his *City of God*.

He argues that the positive principles of each of the post-Reformation religious bodies are valid, or at least contain the element of truth: the Quaker principles that there is in all men an inward light or an indwelling word of God, and that Jesus Christ came to establish a spiritual kingdom and to encourage men to lead a spiritual life; the Protestant principles of justification by faith, election, the Bible as the witness to these doctrines addressed to and intended to be heard by every man in his own language, the authority of the national sovereign, the importance of the individual man and at the same time the importance of national distinctness; the Unitarian principle of 'the deep primary truth' of the unity of God, the assertion of his absolute and unqualified love, and 'a benignant view of things' in general.

Maurice presents the objections to these various principles made by other religious bodies and schools of thought. Out of this dialectic, he holds, the truth in the principles stands more clearly revealed. It is the systems to which they have given rise which are at fault. The principles become distorted when they are used as weapons in controversy. The resulting ecclesiastical systems or organizations never exemplify the principles in a credible way. In its systematic working-out, Protestantism, for example, began to advance propositions about justification, illustrated them from the working of the law-courts and from the practices of common life, became involved in scholastic debate, and tended more and more to ethicize and rationalize its Christianity.

> What I wish the reader to observe here, is, how little the body which took justification by faith as its motto and principle, has been able, in any stage of its history, to assert that doctrine; how constantly the system, whether interpreted by earnest believers or stiff dogmatists, by orthodox doctors or mere moralists, has been labouring to strangle the principle to which it owes its existence (ibid., vol. 1, p. 115).

Similarly, he argues, the Quaker and Unitarian systems have introduced ambiguities, even contradictions which conceal the witness of the former to the existence of a universal kingdom, and of the latter to the concept of God as a universal and loving Father.

Maurice sees philosophical movements of thought as each contending for a true principle, but as losing sight of those principles as their systems harden. The principle of the Romantics, that 'the perfection of a man is to be in harmony with nature',[6] and the Kantian principle that there is a region which lies beyond human experience and that man possesses a faculty by which that region is cognizable,[7] each testify to a conviction that there exist bonds between man and the universe which 'do not depend for their reality upon our consciousness of them',[8] but are there antecedent to man's experience of them. Such insights, he believes, are capable of being reconciled, and in a universal and spiritual society which already exists:

> If reason affirm a truth which must have always been; if the communion with nature be something implied in our constitution, and therefore im-

plied in the constitution of those who lived a thousand years ago; if humanity be essentially spiritual, the reconciling method may already exist, and ... the work of our age may not be to create it afresh, but to discover its meaning and realize its necessity (ibid., p. 182).

In political movements and the reactions to them Maurice also discerns the expression of principles which can only find their true embodiment in a universal and spiritual society. Revolutionary movements beginning with the assertion of individual rights moved towards concepts of fellowship and even of a universal society. In Bentham's 'greatest happiness of the greatest number', Saint-Simon's recognition of the importance of the family and his principle of 'each according to his capacity', and Robert Owen's idea of co-operation, there is enshrined the feeling that 'a universal society is needful to man'.[9]

At the beginning of Part 2 Maurice recapitulates. The principles asserted by the religious societies formed since the Reformation are 'solid and imperishable', but 'the systems in which those principles have been embodied were faulty in their origin, have been found less and less to fulfil their purpose as they have grown older, and are now exhibiting the most manifest indications of approaching dissolution'.[10] The philosophers of the eighteenth century first rejected the idea of a spiritual kingdom, assuming that men possessed no faculties by which they could take cognizance of any such thing. In opposition to Christianity the idea of a comprehensive *world*, including all nations, systems, and even religions, knit together by benevolent philanthropy, became prevalent.

Yet a religious awakening occurred, born of a conviction that a spiritual influence is at work among men. Personal religion was emphasized, as was the need to co-operate in promoting spiritual objects. Among philosophers also there was a growing tendency to think of man as essentially a spiritual creature whose highest acts are of a spiritual kind, and to acknowledge the existence of a region for their exercise. Some would go no further than to identify this region with the universe of sight and sound into the understanding of which only a few gifted poets and sages had entry. Yet others were driven to recognize 'the existence of something which man did not create himself, but to which he must in some sort refer all his acts and thoughts, and which must be assumed as the ground of them'.[11] Men were searching for a universal constitution into which all men as men might enter. But each attempt to construct it was defeated by men's determination to assert their own wills. Maurice declares that a true universal society must not ignore these wills, for they are the very principle and explanation of its existence. He also says that 'it is equally impossible for men to be content with a spiritual society which is not universal, and with a universal society which is not spiritual'.[12]

He now asks again whether such a society, which he believes to be implied by the human constitution itself, has not been made known to men in the course of history. Are there traces of it in the early ages? Do the Scriptures, to which many of the religious groups he has examined have appealed, provide any evidence?

He sees the first indication that there is a spiritual constitution for mankind in the fact that men live in families, 'a state which is designed for a voluntary creature; which is his, whether he approve it or no'.[13] That man is inclined to rebel against it shows not that the bonds of the family are unnatural, but that man is meant also for other relationships, not necessarily incompatible with the family. History records the development of the national community. To be able to say 'I am a brother' reveals man's true nature as more than a self-contained unit; but to be able to say 'I am a citizen' is an onward step. Ancient history tells of the awakening of the desire for even a larger and more comprehensive constitution. The empire of Alexander the Great, however, was short-lived. That of Rome eventually perished. Maurice sees the cause of its break-up in its failure to maintain the health of family and national life. If there is to be a universal *Church*, he says, it must not set aside family or national life, but rather justify their existence and reconcile them to itself.[14]

He now turns to the Bible. The O.T. speaks of a covenant of God with a family, that of Abraham. Abraham recognized, and this is the essence of his faith, that there is a God who is related to men, and made known to them through their human relations. He may therefore rightly be called 'the beginner of the Church on earth'.[15] Despite rebellion against God and his laws Abraham's family was to become a nation. The national polity of the Jews, like that of other nations, ancient and modern, was exclusive. But among them were prophets who proclaimed God as the God of all nations and had a vision of a king who should reign in righteousness and whom all nations would own.

The N.T. speaks of the coming of one who is a son of David and of Abraham to establish a kingdom. All the words and acts of Jesus relate to this kingdom and the whole N.T. affirms him to be its king. Although this kingdom is not to be observed with the outward eye and is not of this world (Luke 17.20–21; John 18.36), it extends to all men and over all nature. At the last supper Jesus declared that his followers were united with him, and through him with his Father, and that his spirit would be with them, witnessing to him and cementing this union. He translated these words into acts by his sacrificial death and resurrection. He still communes with them, and they recognize that the union between heaven and earth is 'no longer a word, it is a fact'.[16] He bids his disciples go out, testify to it, and adopt men into a society based on its accomplishment, a society continuous with the past (being 'the child which the Jewish polity had for many ages been carrying in its womb'),[17] but containing a principle of expansion in its freedom from all national exclusions.

Although this universal society historically grew out of the Jewish family and nation, it is theologically prior. Aristotle's dictum, 'that which is first as cause is last in discovery', is caught up in the Epistle to the Ephesians which speaks of members of the Church as created by God before all worlds, and of God's 'transcendent economy as being gradually revealed to the apostles and prophets by the Spirit. . . . The mystery of the true constitution of humanity in Christ is revealed.'[18]

2 THE PRESENT SIGNS OF A SPIRITUAL SOCIETY

There are two possible kinds of universal society, 'one of which is destructive of the family and national principle, the other the expansion of them'.[19] Scripture calls the first 'this world', the latter 'the Church'. If the latter exists it must be a *distinct* body, and to say this does not negate its universality. Are there, Maurice now asks, any signs of the spiritual and universal society, that is to say, of the Catholic Church, upon the earth? He sees six such signs: baptism, the creeds, forms of worship, the eucharist, the episcopal ministry, and the Scriptures. His discussion of these and of the objections to them or views upon them of the Quakers, the Protestant Churches, philosophers, and the Roman Catholics of his day occupies most of Part 2 of the work. Into these dialogues we cannot follow him here, but must summarize.

Baptism is 'the sign of admission into Christ's spiritual and universal kingdom', and consequently every person receiving that sign is '*ipso facto* a member of that kingdom'.[20] Baptism announces to a man what his position is and the conditions by which he is to live. Conflicts lie in front, temptations and hindrances in the way of his entering into the blessing which has been obtained for him. But he is and remains a son of God, a member of Christ. 'We do not ... cease to be children because we are disobedient children.'[21] There will be constant need of repentance for living the lie that denies our baptismal status.

The creeds are documents, closely connected with baptism, which declare the name into which men are adopted by baptism. They are not digests of doctrine, but a man's declaration of belief in a Father and Creator, his Son who became incarnate to be man's redeemer, and his Holy Spirit who has established a holy universal Church. They are acts of allegiance. They affirm 'belief in a name and not in notions'.[22] They are signs of a spiritual and universal society, and a protection of the meaning of the Scriptures against the tendency of the learned to mangle them.[23]

Forms of worship have persisted through all the vicissitudes of Christian history. They vary according to time, locality, and culture, but have an underlying unity not only in the remarkable persistence of certain ancient forms, but in their purpose, which is 'the adoration of the one living and true God'.[24] Forms of worship have sometimes been made badges of distinction and instruments of controversy, but their preservation through so many generations is a sign of the existence of 'a community which the distinction of tongues and the succession of ages cannot break'.[25]

The eucharist is the service of worship which interprets all other acts of worship. In instituting this sacrament Christ meant that his disciples

> should have the fullest participation of that sacrifice with which God had declared himself well pleased, that they should really enter into that Presence, into which the Forerunner had for them entered, that they should really receive in that communion all the spiritual blessings which, through the union of the Godhead with human flesh, the heirs of this flesh might inherit. ... The new life which they had claimed for themselves, as members of Christ's body, was here to be attained through the communication of his life (ibid., vol. 2, p. 62).

The eucharist is misinterpreted if it is conceived of individualistically as a means of communion with a Lord who is somehow made present by a man's faith. A presence which is not a presence until we make it so is a strange conceit. In the eucharist men enter into the presence of Christ *where he is*. It is a continuing witness 'that the Son of man is set down at the right hand of the throne of God, and that those who believe in him, and suffer with him, are meant to live and reign with him there'.[26] It is a sign of the existence of a universal and spiritual kingdom.

The ministry   The foregoing signs imply the agency of men. The universal society is 'not a kingdom ... if it have not certain magistrates or officers',[27] and such there are.

> It has been believed, as a necessary consequence of the importance attached to the Eucharist, that an order of men must exist in the Christian Church corresponding to the priests of the old dispensation, with the difference that the sacrifice in the one case was anticipatory, in the other commemorative (ibid., p. 99).

Priesthood has commonly been held to imply dominion over men's minds. In the Christian Church, however, it is *ministry*. From the Bishop of Rome to the founder of the latest sect the name of 'minister' is acknowledged. The minister's characteristic function is to absolve or set free. There are differences within Christendom about the nature of this power and the method of its exercise, but not about its existence.

The most conspicuous order of ministers, the episcopate, has assumed a universal character. Bishops have felt themselves to be 'the bonds of communication between different parts of the earth'.[28] Episcopacy has been preserved in the Orthodox churches of the East and in western Europe, and has developed in the New World. Christ came to minister, to absolve, and to bind men into a kingdom. He called and commissioned the apostles to the same ministry and to announce the same kingdom. They, not supposing that the kingdom was to die with them, appointed successors 'to bring before men the fact that they are subject to an invisible and universal Ruler'.[29] Consequently, 'those nations which have preserved the episcopal institution have a right to believe that they have preserved one of the appointed and indispensable signs of a spiritual and universal society'.

The view that it is a secret call of God that makes a man a minister runs into the danger of confounding man's spiritual faculty with the Holy Spirit. Moreover, there needs to be a formal, public, and open endowment of authority so that all may understand the extent and derivation of an office which is claimed. This was the practice of the N.T. Church.[30] Maurice opposes also the view that episcopal succession is the transmission of some part of the effect of Christ's ordination of the apostles. Rather, the episcopate receives the functions committed to the apostles (administering the sacraments, absolving, preaching, ministering) and the authority to exercise them directly from Christ; and the bishops' connection with previous ages and the apostles is maintained as a witness to the permanent constitution of the Church and to the continued presence of Christ.[31]

Maurice also opposes a doctrine of vicarial priesthood: that 'ministers are deputed by our Lord to do that work now which he did himself while he was upon earth'—as though Christ were absent. He holds that in baptism and the other signs there is 'a direct, real, and practical union between men and their Lord',[32] and therefore the priest is not Christ's *vicar*, as though the veil between men and God was not yet withdrawn, but his representative, commissioned with authority to absolve, set free, and bid men be what they are—members of Christ and his kingdom.

The Scriptures are also a continuing sign of the existence of a spiritual and universal kingdom. They declare a divine constitution for man, revealed first to a family, then to a nation, and through them to mankind. 'They make us conscious of the existence of two societies, one formed in accordance with the order of God, the other based upon self-will.'[33] Their object 'is to withdraw us from outward sensual impressions of the divine majesty, to make us feel the reality of the relation between him and his creatures, to make us understand that it is a spiritual relation, and that, therefore, it can manifest itself in outward words and acts'.[34] Consequently, it was a grievous mistake to attempt to conceal the Bible from men in order to exalt the Church.

Although Maurice discusses at length different views about these signs, he is chiefly concerned, as A. M. Ramsey remarks,[35] to emphasize the *fact* of each sign as a witness to the existence of a universal Church.

3 THE IDEA OF A CATHOLIC CHURCH DOES NOT EXCLUDE NATIONAL CHURCHES

Maurice is convinced that the universal and spiritual society must express itself in national societies. The O.T. is the story of a family which acknowledges God as Father, and a nation which acknowledges God as King. The principles of this kingdom which the ten commandments lay down are spiritual, but they also concern man as a mundane creature, in a particular place, with a defined circle of human relationships. They deal with such matters as family, sexual, and neighbourhood relations; property, tribunals, and oaths. Jewish history contains the 'divine specimen of a national life'.[36] The N.T. develops the principles of a universal society, but without superseding those of a true national society. The ten commandments are not abrogated, but shown to be basic not for one nation only, but for all nations, and in their deepest meaning for the universal society which is the Church of God.

In a historical survey[37] Maurice traces the relationship of the Church to empires and nations. The alliance, initiated by Constantine, between a 'superannuated despotism' based upon mere power with a body which recognized a King who rules in righteousness and whose strength is in weakness was a dispensation of God, but was not intended to last. The Roman, Carolingian, and Byzantine empires perished. As the Church penetrated barbarian lands, the bishops, had they been able, would have 'reduced Europe into one great society, having a common language, scarcely acknowledging any territorial or political distinctions'. This might have seemed appropriate to the idea of a divine commonwealth. In the event, the bishops were the main instruments in creating distinct national organizations, different from, though acting in concert with the ecclesiastical organization. Distinctions in character and institutions between the original tribes were slight, but in the course of time, by Christian nurture and education, the latent peculiarities and gifts of each were brought out. It would seem that in Europe the form of the national society was brought into existence by that very society which might have been supposed to displace it. Maurice sees here 'a higher will, another power at work, crossing human calculations'.[38] The universal society negates neither the family nor the nation.

In the early stages of European nationhood a spiritual element was found to be necessary to uphold a legal society. Maurice contends also that 'a legal element, a body expressing the sacredness and majesty of law, is shown to be necessary in order to fulfil the objects for which the spiritual and universal society exists'.[39] There is mutual benefit from the relationship of Church and nation. Many answers have been given to questions about the authority and function of each in relation to the other, and many experiments made. Some are now anachronistic, such as any claim of the legal power to use compulsion to enforce ecclesiastical conformity. That relationship took many forms, some of them gravely distorted but Maurice is in no doubt that two powers, one of which wishes to set men free, and the other to have a free intelligent people 'must be meant continually to act and react upon each other, and to learn better, by each new error they commit, their distinct functions, their perfect harmony'.[40] For its part the Church must acknowledge

> that she is not meant to have an independent existence; that she is not meant to be extra-national; that she has no commission or powers which dispense with the necessity of positive, formal law and with outward government; that her highest honour is to be the life-giving energy to every body in the midst of which she dwells (ibid., p. 254).

But can one Catholic Church be recognized under the distinctions and limitations of national bodies? Must it not inevitably lose the features which constitute its identity? Maurice distinguishes between 'certain ordinances in which the character and universality of the Church are expressed' and 'everything which is but accidentally connected with them'.[41] The ordinances are the six signs which he has discussed; the accidents are modes of treating the ordinances, such as particular modes of administering baptism and the eucharist or particular rules about the jurisdiction of bishops. There has been an unfortunate tendency to efface this distinction by identifying particular decrees and ceremonies with the very being of the Church, both by the papacy and by the Church within each nation. A national Church must learn that its substance is the ordinances which it shares with Christians everywhere and the powers it has in common with other parts of the body. Its convocations and synods are to be used with the purpose

> of determining those ceremonies which to a people of a particular climate, character, and constitution best express the great ideas of the Church, of more effectually establishing and directing discipline and education, of promoting fellowship with national Churches which are willing to acknowledge themselves as part of a great Catholic body (ibid., p. 262).

Maurice's diagnosis of the condition of Christendom since the Reformation is that two principles have been struggling for supremacy: one, 'embodied in Protestantism, resisting the claims of the spiritual power to any extra-national domination, and always tending to set at naught spiritual authority altogether'; the other, 'embodied in Romanism, resisting the attempts of the particular states to divide their own subjects from the rest of Christendom, continually striving to uphold the Church as a separate Power, and to set at naught the existence of each particular nation'.[42] He believes that it is

God's purpose to reconcile these principles and eliminate what is contrary to his will in each, so that 'the unity of the Church shall be demonstrated to be that ground upon which all unity in nations and in the heart of man is resting'.[43]

Eschatology Maurice is aware that his conception of the Kingdom of Christ as already established is open to the criticism that it ignores the eschatological element in the N.T. and sets aside the doctrine of the second coming of Christ. He defends himself against this charge. The Church has reason to live in expectation of the appearance and triumph of its Head. Scripture, however, gives no hint that this will be the beginning of a *new* order and constitution of things. Rather it will be 'the appearance of a light which shall show things as they are ... the day of judgement and distinction, the gathering of all together into one, the restoration of all things ... the full evidence and demonstration of that which *is now*',[44] the clearing away of all that hides from view the existence now of a kingdom, constitution, order which men have been trying to deny, but under which nevertheless they have been living, and which will then be shown to be the only one under which they can live.

Christ's second appearance will also make clear that his dominion is 'not merely over the heart and spirit of man ... but over all his human relations, his earthly associations, over the policy of rulers, over nature and over art',[45] all of which is as much the truth now as it ever can be in any future period. The principle of his book, Maurice contends, is not inconsistent with a sound apprehension of the second coming, but only with any system that leads men to think that present responsibilities may be taken lightly, and that God's providence means nothing much now and is leading only to something hereafter.

4 THE CHURCH OF ENGLAND IS AN EMBODIMENT OF THE UNIVERSAL AND SPIRITUAL ORDER

In Part 3 of *The Kingdom of Christ* Maurice applies his criteria to his own church. While he has much to criticize in it, he is convinced that it preserves the signs of a universal and spiritual constitution which again he enumerates, and now discusses in relation to the Church of England.[46] In a brief analysis of the Thirty-nine Articles,[47] he claims that they assert the *positive principles* of all the post-Reformation religious bodies and repudiate the *systems* which they have 'grafted' on them. Likewise the Articles repudiate the Roman Catholic system 'in every point wherein it is opposed to the distinct affirmations of the Reformers'.

In the English Church 'ecclesiastical and civil institutions are united'.[48] History is silent about the origin of this union. From the very beginning the relationship was presupposed. Maurice agrees that the Reformation in England originated with the sovereign, but it was not a purely political movement. For several centuries not only rebellious, but also most orthodox kings had attempted to break the relationship with Rome. 'The difference in the reign of Henry VIII was ... that a large body of the bishops and clergy had been led by their religious feelings to desire that this correspondence should be broken off.'[49]

Since the Reformation a number of sects had grown up in the country. He describes the attempts to coerce them into union with the national Church as stupid. That these various religious bodies still exist in England does not 'destroy a union which has cemented itself by no human contrivances, and which exists in the very nature of things'.[50]

In a most interesting section[51] on the particular characteristics of Englishmen, Maurice asserts that they are politicians at heart, and inclined, whether they would be artists, philosophers, or even mystics, to link thought with action. This political bias has had the beneficial result that it has led Englishmen to think of the Church as a kingdom rather than a system. Yet there was too great a tendency to forget that the Church is 'the type of all kingdoms, and is not moulded after the maxims of any',[52] and too ready an assumption that what is expedient for the ruling class must determine ecclesiastical matters. The English Church in the eighteenth century became identified with the aristocracy who regarded it as the upholder of the *status quo* in matters of property and privilege. It neglected the rising class of industrial workers and showed little sympathy with the Methodists who endeavoured to evangelize them. Maurice admits all this with shame, but believes that this kind of State churchmanship belonged to 'the spirit of an age of our national Church, not of the Church itself'.[53]

In Maurice's own day young and active churchmen were seeking alternatives to 'the dreariness of political Anglicanism'. Within the Church, parties were forming: the Liberals, the Evangelicals, and the High Church party.[54] Under the pressure of controversy there was a tendency to systematize in each of them. What he said in Part 1 about the various post-Reformation religious bodies he now says of these parties: that there is likely to be in each of them something which ought not to be rejected. It may be 'that there is a divine harmony, of which the living principle in each of these systems forms one note, of which the systems themselves are a disturbance and a violation'.[55] The Liberal contention that 'the Church is meant to comprehend and not to exclude', the Evangelical insistence on the power of the gospel, and the Catholic idea of a Church which God himself has established, possessing powers which the State neither gave nor can take away, are important. But when hardened into a *system* in opposition to other systems, each leads to error: Liberalism to the denial that anything is given to man in revelation; Evangelicalism to the denial of the idea of Church fellowship and unity; and the catholicism of the High Church party to the denial of the distinction of national Churches.[56]

Speaking again of the various religious systems, Maurice says: 'These systems, Protestant, Romish, English, seem to me each to bear witness of the existence of a *divine order*; each to be a miserable, partial, human substitute for it. In every country, therefore, I should desire to see men emancipated from the chains which they have made for themselves, and entering into the freedom of God's Church.'[57] He desires the acknowledgement of one Church, the universal and spiritual society, in which Christians of each nation, as a national Church, may claim their rightful place. He believes that in England, more clearly than elsewhere, there is an indication how this may be effected, for, although the English political bent does tend towards the creation of parties, 'system-building is not natural' to the English. Churchmen, and especially the younger ones, must seek for *principles* and grounds of action. The various systems and Church parties have made known certain principles, none of which may be disregarded; there is need of them all.[58] But the way forward is not to identify oneself with a party. That is to become involved in unfairness, libel, name-calling, polemics, and to merit judgement.

Much of the opposition to the national Church by sectarians and dissatisfaction with it by adherents of the parties is because 'it has put itself forth merely as an English church. Its character as a Catholic body, as a kingdom set up in the world for all nations, has been kept out of sight. Secondly ... it has taken a negative, that is a sectarian, form.'[59] It has accused those who have separated from it of wickedness, regarded its episcopacy and sacraments as excluding those who do not possess them, and made little attempt to show that the institutions which it requires others to accept are of a spiritual character and belong intrinsically to the divine kingdom. But those who are convinced that the English Church has the signs of the universal society must 'not despair of seeing all the true hearty dissenters gradually receiving them also'.[60] There must be patience, no forcing of ideas on others, concern that they should preserve the true principles and the faith which they already have, and the wish 'to make them integral members of the body from which they fancy that it is the object of our pride and selfishness to exclude them'.[61] The results of such a method are in God's hands. Other methods have been tried without success. This one has not been tried.

The final pages of *The Kingdom of Christ* show that Maurice finds much to criticize in the national English Church of his day: its identification with the aristocracy; neglect of the industrial districts; the subservience of churchmen in Ireland to English interests; the setting-up of episcopacy in Scotland 'as if it were an English thing', and the continued failure to understand the needs and aspirations of the Scots.[62]

Its experience in Ireland, Scotland, and North America has, he suggests, clear lessons for the English nation in its colonial policy and the English Church in its missionary policy elsewhere:

> See that you do not merely establish an English kingdom in those soils; if you do, that kingdom will not be a blessing to the colonists, to the natives, or to the mother country. See that you do not merely send forth preachers in your ships to tell the people that all they have believed hitherto—if they have believed anything—is false, and that we hold a doctrine which sets it all aside (ibid., p. 341).

The need is rather to raise up a kingdom which the inhabitants know to be 'as real as the one which is presented to them in the persons of governors and judges'; a kingdom which claims both settlers and natives for its citizens, does justice to both alike and extends its privileges to all,

> a kingdom which comes to subvert nothing, but to restore that which is decayed and fallen; to adopt into itself every fragment of existing faith and feeling; to purify it and exalt it; to cut off from it only that which the conscience of the native confesses to be inconsistent with it; to testify that wherever there is a creature having human limbs and features, there is one of that race for which Christ died, one whom he is not ashamed to call a brother (ibid., pp. 341–2).

Nearly a hundred years were to pass before Christian missionary strategists began to speak in similar terms.

As for its relationship with foreign churches, Roman or Protestant, Maurice says that the English Church has no cause to call itself better than they; in many respects it is worse. However, it holds an advantageous position. Its faith, represented in its liturgy and articles, is that of a Church, not a system; nor is it derived eclectically from elements taken from other systems. English churchmen, he claims, are better able than others to understand the difference between a church and a system.[63] It must seek to unite with foreign churches not 'on the ground of any one of their systems', but 'on the grounds of the universal Church'. Maurice, then, sees possession of the signs of the universal and spiritual society which he has described in Part 2 as the basis for the coming together of separated national churches. The nations will still be distinct, for the bonds which unite the churches of the nations themselves imply the peculiar characteristics and independence of national life.

If sects within the nation are to be reconciled, if the Church is rightly to be planted in the mission fields, and if a proper relationship with foreign churches is to be set up, there is need for discipline, study, and a spirit far different from the spirit of party and selfishness. National confession and reformation are needed, and the clergy must be foremost in both.

Maurice's final paragraph reiterates his detestation of systems, parties, and schools which attempt to amalgamate the doctrines of other schools:

> I do pray earnestly that, if any such schools should arise, they may come to naught; and that, if what I have written in this book should tend even in the least degree to favour the establishment of them, it may come to naught (ibid., pp. 346–7).

I have given much space to Maurice's conception of the Church because of its relevance to the Church of the late twentieth century. What many modern ecclesiologists and ecumenists contend for was already expounded eloquently in the pages of *The Kingdom of Christ*.

In the final section of this chapter I note the growth of the Anglican Communion, and the institution of the Lambeth Conferences which were to have an important influence on the ecumenical movement.

LAMBETH CONFERENCES

The nineteenth century saw the growth of the Anglican Communion.

In 1800, apart from the United States which then had several diocesan bishops, there were only two dioceses outside the British Isles: Nova Scotia and Newfoundland. Increasing emigration to the various parts of the British Empire, and the intensification of missionary work led to the expansion of the English Church on all continents and to the creation of dioceses which in some countries were organized into provinces, and eventually into national churches. There were seventy-two bishops overseas in 1882, the year of the death of A. C. Tait, Archbishop of Canterbury, who had done much to encourage this growth.

In these new lands the Church of England found itself faced with many unfamiliar problems. Among these were questions of organization and of relation to the mother church of England, questions not unlike those which in the twentieth century confront the Eastern Orthodox communities which have sprung up in new lands.[64] The bishops of the Church of England in Canada proposed in 1865 that a council should be held in England at which all Anglican bishops might discuss their common problems, and the first of a series of such meetings, known as the Lambeth Conferences, took place in 1867.

These conferences, usually at intervals of ten years, have been held at Lambeth Palace, the London residence of the Archbishop of Canterbury, and under his chairmanship. The Lambeth Conference has no legislative authority; its resolutions may or may not be ratified by the synods of the autonomous Anglican churches. Its influence, however, is strong. From the first, Christian unity was high on its agenda, and in this we may see the concern of bishops from parts of the world where Christian disunity was more clearly recognized as a scandalous hindrance to the gospel than it was in England.

The third Lambeth Conference in 1888 had before it reports from several committees which had been considering Anglican relations with other churches. It adopted in a revised form four basic conditions for the restoration of Christian unity which had been drawn up by the General Convention of the Protestant Episcopal Church in the United States at Chicago in 1886 (The Chicago Quadrilateral).[65] The form in which the 1888 Lambeth Conference Committee on Home Reunion accepted them is as follows:

a The Holy Scriptures of the Old and New Testaments as 'containing all things necessary to salvation', and as being the rule and ultimate standard of faith.

b The Apostles' Creed, as the Baptismal Symbol; and the Nicene Creed, as the sufficient statement of the Christian Faith.

c The two Sacraments ordained by Christ Himself—Baptism and the Supper of the Lord—ministered with unfailing use of Christ's words of institution and of the elements ordained by Him.

d The Historic Episcopate, locally adapted in the methods of its administration to the varying needs of the nations and people called of God into the unity of His Church.[66]

Succeeding Lambeth Conferences reaffirmed the Quadrilateral. It was the fourth point which received the greatest criticism from Protestant churches. It was felt to be inviting Nonconformists to reunion on condition that they should surrender one of the main points for which they had contended.[67] It was reframed in the 'Appeal to All Christian People',[68] sent out by the 252 Anglican bishops who attended the Lambeth Conference of 1920, to read:

> A ministry acknowledged by every part of the Church as possessing not only the inward call of the Spirit, but also the commission of Christ and the authority of the whole body.

The Appeal continued:

> May we not reasonably claim that the Episcopate is the one means of providing such a ministry? It is not that we call in question for a moment the spiritual reality of the ministries of those communions which do not possess the Episcopate. On the contrary, we thankfully acknowledge that these ministries have been manifestly blessed and owned by the Holy Spirit as effective means of grace. But we submit that considerations alike of history and of present experience justify the claim which we make on behalf of the Episcopate. Moreover, we would urge that it is now and will prove to be in the future the best instrument for maintaining the unity and the continuity of the Church.

If the desired end is the union of all Christian people, the claim is a reasonable one, for the churches of at least four-fifths of Christendom possess episcopacy, and value it as much more than merely an accidental inheritance and a convenient form of administration. It is to be noted that the Quadrilateral leaves open the questions of the theology of episcopacy and the form which it might take in a united Church. 'The Anglican Communion has never officially endorsed any one particular theory of the origin of the historic episcopate, its exact relation to the apostolate, and the sense in which it should be thought of as God-given, and in fact tolerates a wide variety of views on these points.'[69] Anglicans also are aware that in the past, both in England and elsewhere, the historic episcopate has taken many different forms,[70] and make no claim that their own form represents an ideal pattern.

The Lambeth Quadrilateral, made more widely known through the 'Appeal to All Christian People' which was sent to the heads of all churches throughout the world, stirred up wide interest, and has been an influential factor in the ecumenical movement of the twentieth century. The acceptance of episcopacy in some constitutional form has, in fact, been part of all plans for union which have advanced any distance between churches which have the historic episcopate and those which have not.

Part 6

THE TWENTIETH CENTURY

19

The Ecumenical Movement

In entering upon a study of the developments in ecclesiology during the twentieth century, the writer becomes aware that here a new volume should begin. Never before has such close attention been paid to the question of the nature of the Church. The number of books, major articles, and reports of conferences on the subject is immense. In this final section two things will be attempted: first, to discern the factors which have led to this close study of our subject; and second, to present the ecclesiology of some influential, but widely differing, twentieth-century theologians.

The factors which have brought the doctrine of the Church into the foreground arise partly from the life and activity of the churches themselves (the subject of this and the next chapter), and partly from the vastly changed, and swiftly changing, world in which the churches are situated (chapter 21).

THE CHURCH'S MISSION, AND CHRISTIAN DISUNITY

The nineteenth century saw a great expansion of missionary endeavour. Missionary societies were formed in many European and North American churches, from which dedicated men and women went out to evangelize in all the continents of the world. In large and increasing numbers nationals accepted the Christian faith, and churches were established. Before long these young churches began to see the divisions between the churches, largely regarded as normal in the 'home' countries, in their true light—as a shameful contradiction of the nature of the Church of the one Lord. Differences and rivalries which originated centuries before in the ecclesiastical and political history of Europe were being perpetuated among new Christians who could have had little understanding of them. Such divisions were a stumbling-block to the advance of the Christian mission. Divided

Christians were unconvincing messengers of the Prince of peace and the Spirit of fellowship.

In many places the churches and missionary societies tried to mitigate the damage in the situation. 'Comity' agreements were made by which a territory was regarded as exclusively the field of a particular denomination. Elsewhere there was co-operation in education and social work, and sometimes in joint worship. But many felt the need for a more radical solution.

In Europe and North America national organizations were formed to provide representatives of the various missionary societies with a forum for the discussion of missionary problems. International gatherings also began to be organized, at intervals of about ten years, in London (1878 and 1888), New York (1900), and Edinburgh (1910). The World Missionary Conference in Edinburgh was in many ways a turning-point in what has come to be known as 'the ecumenical movement'.[1] Its main concern, however, was with the evangelism of non-Christian peoples. It aimed at providing means by which the missionary agencies of the churches could continue to take counsel and plan together, conscious of a common task to be performed in the name of Christ. One of the Conference's eight commissions was designated to study co-operation and the promotion of unity. Questions of faith and Church order, however, were felt to be outside the competence of a missionary conference. But Bishop Charles Brent of the Protestant Episcopal Church of the United States of America voiced the feeling of delegates when he said that Christians could not be content with arrangements for co-operation, and that there was need of a forum in which the churches could study the causes of Christian divisions with the purpose of removing them. He was to be the chief instrument in bringing into being the Faith and Order Movement.

The Edinburgh Conference was strengthened by the presence of members of the young churches of Africa and Asia. Its weakness was the absence of Roman Catholic and Orthodox representation. More than one speech alluded to this. Dr R. Woodlaw Thompson, a Free Churchman and officer of the London Missionary Society said, 'I long for the time when we shall see another Conference, and when men of the Greek Church and the Roman Church shall talk things over with us in the service of Christ'.[2]

The Conference unanimously voted for the creation of a standing International Missionary Council. Preparations for its establishment were hindered by the 1914–18 war, but it came into existence in 1921 under the chairmanship of John R. Mott. Its functions were to foster and co-ordinate the work of the various missionary societies, and to promote co-operative or united action wherever this was seen as desirable. Study of the doctrinal issues between the churches was not seen as part of its work.

BIBLICAL SCHOLARSHIP AND THE CHURCH'S UNITY

An important contributing factor in creating a favourable atmosphere for a renewed examination of the question of the Church's unity was the increasing collaboration of Christian scholars across denominational lines. The scientific theories of the nineteenth century and the application of literary and historical criticism to the Scriptures posed challenges to some of the fundamental tenets of the Christian religion—the doctrine of creation, the uniqueness of man, the integrity of the Scriptures—and in answering them scholars were increasingly drawn together across confessional lines, and this century has witnessed a fruitful collaboration between them. The denominational barriers behind which many theological schools had previously worked were being lowered. For example, the abolition of religious tests at the English universities in 1871 opened the way to the holding of theological chairs by non-Anglicans in the twentieth century. Endowed lectureships, often the closely guarded prerogatives of scholars of a particular church, were now opened to others. Academic eminence was beginning to transcend denominational lines. This cross-fertilization was greatly expedited by more rapid means of communication and travel, and by a quicker pace in translating important theological works. These ecumenical exchanges brought to light two facts which had been hitherto ignored, or unsuspected: that doctrinal differences which had been thought of as distinguishing features between churches were often present within a single church; and that misunderstanding of the other's position was at the bottom of some important theological differences. The possibility of removing at least some of the root causes of disagreement through dialogue began to appear.

Collaboration in the field of biblical scholarship has been especially significant. In 1870 the Convocation of Canterbury resolved upon a revision of the Authorized (King James) Version of the English Bible (eventually published in 1881). The work was to be undertaken by members of its own body, but they were to be 'at liberty to invite the co-operation of any eminent for scholarship, to whatever nation or religious body they may belong'.[3] This liberty was taken. The American Standard Version (1885) and the American Revised Standard Version (1952) were the work of scholars of several American churches. Roman Catholic scholars have increasingly collaborated with others, both in biblical studies and translation, since the encyclical of Pope Pius XII, *Divino Afflatu Spiritus* of 1943 gave a large measure of encouragement to the use of modern critical methods of biblical study and to the production of new vernacular translations.[4] There is today a lively commerce between Catholic and Protestant scholars in the exchange of papers, at conferences on biblical studies, and by mutual consultation in the production of new translations. Roman Catholic observers sat with the commission which produced the New English Bible.[5]

THE QUICKENING OF THE ECUMENICAL MOVEMENT: FAITH AND ORDER

The desire for Christian unity so strongly expressed in mission fields and the greater freedom of discussion among theologians together gave impetus to the ecumenical movement. Its history is intricate, and the reader is referred for fuller details to the standard work on the subject, the two volumes of *A History of the Ecumenical Movement*.[6]

At Edinburgh in 1910, Bishop Brent announced his intention of working to establish an interchurch and international forum in which the doctrinal causes of Christian disunion could be examined. Under his leadership the Protestant Episcopal Church of the United States took the initiative, sending letters and deputations to other churches, proposing the setting-up of a commission to prepare for a world conference. A meeting in New York in 1913, at which fifteen churches were represented by commissions, set out three principles. First, a world conference should provide opportunity for the study not only of points of difference, but also of the values of the beliefs characteristic of the various churches. Second, 'that while organic unity is the ideal which all Christians should have in their thoughts and prayers, yet the business of the Commissions is not to force any particular scheme of unity'. Third, that the questions to be considered by a world conference should be formulated in advance by committees of competent representatives of the churches.[7]

The First World War interrupted these plans, but in 1919 a deputation from the Protestant Episcopal Church travelled widely in Europe and the Near East, visiting heads of churches to propose the plan for a world conference. A favourable response was received from several Orthodox churches. The deputation was received in audience, with great friendliness, by Pope Benedict XV, but on its departure received the following statement which summarizes succinctly the attitude of the Roman Catholic Church of the day towards the kind of conference proposed:

> The Holy Father, after having thanked them for their visit, stated that as successor of St Peter and Vicar of Christ he had no greater desire than that there should be one fold and one Shepherd. His Holiness added that the teaching and practice of the Roman Catholic Church regarding the unity of the visible Church of Christ was well known to everybody and therefore it would not be possible for the Catholic Church to take part in such a Congress as the one proposed. His Holiness, however, by no means wishes to disapprove of the Congress in question for those who are not in union with the Chair of Peter; on the contrary, he earnestly desires and prays that, if the Congress is practicable, those who take part in it may, by the Grace of God, see the light and become reunited to the visible Head of the Church, by whom they will be received with open arms.[8]

The First World Conference on Faith and Order was held at Lausanne in 1927, attended by 387 delegates of 108 churches from many countries, representing Anglican, Baptist, Congregational, Disciples of Christ, Lutheran, Methodist, Old Catholic, Orthodox, and Reformed Church traditions. The Conference was divided into sections in order to discuss topics such as the meaning of Christian unity, the nature of the Church, the ministry and the sacraments, and to produce draft reports. These reports were then discussed and revised by the whole Conference with a view to commending them to the churches. The Orthodox delegation, which took a full part in discussion, refrained from voting on most of the reports, but voted in support of that on the Church's Message to the World.

The problems and difficulties experienced by many in a conference of this kind are well summarized by Dr Tissington Tatlow in an account of the proceedings of section 4 on 'The Church's Common Confession of Faith'.

> Some vigorously worded opinions were heard during the first meeting and a good deal of heat was generated. 'We must declare our loyalty to the Nicene Creed,' said an Orthodox, to which a Congregationalist replied,

'Well, I think we should clear all that old lumber out of the way.' Many differences were expressed on the authority attaching to the Scriptures, the creeds, tradition, and various confessions of the Reformation period. During an interval one member approached another and asked, 'Can you tell me of any volume in which I could read one of these old creeds they have been talking about?' He was delighted at the immediate loan of a Book of Common Prayer.[9]

There were also misapprehensions about the purpose of the Conference. Some feared that its aim was to suggest a union of churches on the basis of no more than collaboration in mission and service with scant attention to unity in faith and order. Others assumed, while yet others feared, that the intention was to produce a blueprint for a universal united Church, something which was manifestly impossible in the absence of a Roman Catholic delegation. Bishop Brent and others endeavoured to clarify matters: the Conference did not aim at complete agreement, still less at a united Church, but was an occasion on which 'both agreements and disagreements were to be carefully noted'.[10] The Faith and Order Movement, like the World Council of Churches later, has always maintained that although the world conferences and committees can do much to provide opportunities for discussion, clarify issues, and identify misunderstandings, it is only the churches themselves that can unite.

At Lausanne a Faith and Order Continuation Committee was appointed to promote joint study groups to prepare material for another conference. The subjects proposed were (1) The Grace of our Lord Jesus Christ, (2) The Church of Christ and the Word of God, (3) The Church of Christ: Ministry and Sacraments, (4) The Church's Unity in Life and Worship. The Second World Conference on Faith and Order met in Edinburgh in 1937 under the presidency of William Temple, then Archbishop of York. It was attended by 344 delegates, representing 123 churches. Three points in the proceedings of the Conference must be noted here:

First, the report of the section on 'The Grace of our Lord Jesus Christ' began with the words: 'There is in connection with this subject no ground for maintaining division between churches.'[11] The Conference agreed.

Second, the report of the section on 'The Ministry and Sacraments' showed, as was expected, great differences between the delegates. Yet Professor Donald M. Baillie (Church of Scotland), in presenting it, could say: 'We have come to discover our nearness to one another, and agreements were reached, not by compromise, but by genuine rapprochement. .... If it can happen on this ground of ministry and sacraments, it can happen on any ground; and if it can happen in a conference such as this, it can happen also in the churches themselves.'[12] Succeeding decades, however, have proved that this does not quickly happen. The disagreements identified in the conference in Edinburgh, on the nature of the Church, on authority, and on the ministry, are still the major areas of dissension wherever conversations on Church union take place.

Third, the Conference approved, without dissentients,[13] a statement which called on all Christians 'to co-operate in the concerns of the Kingdom of God', to learn from one another and seek to remove the obstacles to the furtherance of the gospel which are caused by Christian divisions. It was recognized that these divisions were rooted in different understanding of Christ's will for the Church. Nevertheless, they are contrary to his will. It asserted an awareness of 'a unity deeper than our divisions', a unity based on the common acknowledgement of one Lord, Jesus Christ, and of the one Spirit, a unity in that all are 'the objects of the love and grace of God, and called by Him to witness in all the world to His glorious gospel'. It declared also the conviction 'that our unity of spirit and aim must be embodied in a way that will make it manifest to the world, though we do not yet clearly see what outward form it should take'.[14] The difficulty of envisaging the outward form of the one Church of Christ has increased rather than diminished since 1937, as we shall see.

LIFE AND WORK

Contemporaneously with the Faith and Order Movement there proceeded the Life and Work Movement, for which Nathan Söderblom, the Lutheran Archbishop of Uppsala provided the same kind of leadership as had Bishop Brent for Faith and Order. Its purpose was to relate the Christian faith to social, political, and economic problems. After a preparatory conference at Geneva in 1920, the first Universal Conference on Life and Work took place at Stockholm in 1925, and the second in 1937 at Oxford. The Oxford Conference was concerned with the Church and its function in society and its relation to the community, the State, and the economic order. Throughout, its reports showed awareness that the primary duty of the Church to the State is to be the Church, namely to witness for God, to preach His Word, to confess the faith before men, to teach both young and old to observe the divine Commandments, and to serve the nation and the State by proclaiming the Will of God as the supreme standard to which all human wills must be subject and all human conduct must conform. These functions of worship, preaching, teaching, and ministry the Church cannot renounce, whether the State consent or not.[15]

'Let the Church be the Church' has been said to be the essential message of the Conference.

THE WORLD COUNCIL OF CHURCHES

Within both the Faith and Order and the Life and Work Movements an awareness grew that the concerns of each were so intimately related that they needed to be brought together in a single council. The Oxford and Edinburgh Conferences of 1937 both passed resolutions recommending the uniting of the two movements in a World Council of Churches. This, however, was not to be achieved until after the Second World War. That it could take place as early as 1948 testifies to the devotion of those who continued to work for this end despite the difficulty of communication during the war years. At Amsterdam in 1948 the World Council of Churches[16] was inaugurated as 'a fellowship of churches which accept our Lord Jesus Christ as God and Saviour';[17] 351 delegates were present, representing 145 churches. A representative central committee was set up to meet annually, and with power to appoint an executive committee. Geneva was chosen as the headquarters of the Central Committee, and a secretariat was set up there. The Second World Assembly was held at Evanston, U.S.A., in 1954; the third at New Delhi, 1961; and the fourth at Uppsala in 1968. At Uppsala 704 delegates represented 235 churches, and 14 Roman Catholic observers were present.

The work of the F. and O. and Life and Work Movements has been incorporated with that of the W.C.C., and the integration of the International Missionary Council was effected at the New Delhi Assembly in 1961. The work of F. and O. is conducted by a commission which has initiated studies, produced reports, and continued to arrange world conferences, the third being held at Lund in 1952, and the fourth at Montreal in 1963. The social, economic, and political concerns of Life and Work have been prominent on the agenda of the

Central Committee and of the World Assemblies. After the Second World War acute problems for the churches arose from the rapid social changes being experienced in most parts of the world, the persistence of racialism, the emergence from colonial status of some countries, and revolutionary situations in others. The W.C.C. has incurred much criticism in conservative quarters for its involvement in such matters. Its condemnation of the South African policy of apartheid in 1960 occasioned the withdrawal from membership of three Dutch Reformed Churches of South Africa.

THE W.C.C. AND ECCLESIOLOGY

From the outset the W.C.C. has stated that it 'is not and must never become a Super-Church'.[18] Membership does not call for acceptance of a particular ecclesiology. That churches are members of the W.C.C. implies recognition 'that the membership of the Church is more inclusive than the membership of their own church body'. They may or may not regard other member churches as churches in the full sense of the word, but they recognize them as serving the same Lord and as possessing 'elements of the true Church'. The W.C.C. sees itself as instrumental to the union of the churches, enabling them to speak and act together, hoping to provide conditions in which they may move towards a unity which is both inward and outward. Union between particular churches can only be initiated from within the churches themselves. The W.C.C. recognizes that its own existence is strictly anomalous.

Study of the doctrine of the Church and the nature of unity has been the special task of the F. and O. Commission. In preparation for the Lund Conference it produced a volume entitled *The Nature of the Church*,[19] edited by R. Newton Flew. This is an informative collection of essays by representatives of different churches setting out what each considered essential in its ecclesiology. Its effect was to make clear that visible unity was unlikely to be achieved by 'ecclesiastical joinery'. The Lund Conference (1952) admitted: 'We have seen clearly that we can make no real advance towards unity if we only compare our several conceptions of the nature of the Church and the traditions in which they are embodied.'[20] But it also asserted that the unity of the Church must find visible expression,[21] and this was reiterated by the Third World Assembly in New Delhi (1961) in the following words:

We believe that the unity which is both God's will and his gift to his Church is being made visible as all in each place who are baptized into Jesus Christ and confess him as Lord and Saviour are brought by the Holy Spirit into one fully committed fellowship, holding the one apostolic faith, preaching the one Gospel, breaking the one bread, joining in common prayer, and having a corporate life reaching out in witness and service to all and who at the same time are united with the whole Christian fellowship in all places and all ages in such wise that ministry and members are accepted by all, and that all can act and speak together as occasion requires for the tasks to which God calls his people.

It is for such unity that we believe we must pray and work.[22]

The statement was well received, but it was pointed out that it gave no indication of the way in which such unity might be found, and was silent about the marks by which 'the whole Christian fellowship in all places and all ages' may be recognized.

It was beginning to be thought that the way of advance might be found through a study of the Church in relation to the purpose of God in creation and redemption.[23] The Montreal Conference (1963), which had a strong Orthodox delegation, and in which Roman Catholic observers shared in the discussion, devoted one section to the subject of 'The Church in the Purpose of God'. From the outset, however, dissatisfaction with the prepared papers was expressed, and disagreement developed in several areas: on the relationship of the Church to creation and redemption, on the proper balance between emphasis on the death of Christ (*theologia crucis*) and on the resurrection (*theologia gloriae*), and on the relationship of the authority of Scripture to that of tradition. The report of the Conference[24] speaks of 'elements of tension which we neither minimize nor disguise', and describes the Conference as 'promising chaos'. It was now recognized that comparative study of the differing conceptions of the nature of the Church could by no means be neglected, but the Conference recommended further study of the Church in the light of God's creative and redemptive purpose, in response to which the F. and O. Commission undertook a study of 'Creation, New Creation, and the Unity of the Church'.[25]

It has generally been recognized that among the factors which divide the churches are those which are not strictly theological, but have to do with sociological and cultural influences. In different places and times the Church necessarily and rightly adopts institutions suitable for those places and times. F. and O. published a report on this subject in 1961.[26] Outward institutions, it asserted, are implied by the incarnational nature of the Church, but it recognized that institutions created strong attachments, sometimes of a sentimental kind, and sometimes arising from vested interest. It acknowledged also the difficulty of distinguishing in all cases between 'constitutive and permanent and, on the other hand, derivative and historically variable features'.[27] Is, for example, a particular form of ministerial order of the essence of the Church, or is the form of the Church's ministry something which may and should be varied in response to the needs of the Church in a particular place or time? This has proved to be one of the thorniest questions encountered in Church union conversations.

In undertaking this study F. and O. found itself entering the field of the comparatively new science of sociology. The post-Second World War years have produced a number of essays in applying sociological principles to the 'phenomenon' of the Church, a method which was pioneered by Ernst Troeltsch[28] early in the century. Since the Church is a society which claims to have a mission to the world, the study of the relationship between the Church and the society in which it finds itself is by no means to be regarded as irrelevant to ecclesiology.

The Fourth World Assembly of the W.C.C. at Uppsala in 1968 assigned to its first section the subject of 'The Holy Spirit and the Catholicity of the Church'. The section took firm hold of a question which had always been beneath the surface in ecumenical encounter: is there hope of union, or even of sincere co-operation between churches so widely different as Roman Catholic, Orthodox, and Anglican on one hand, and Evangelical and Pentecostal on the other? Can the one Church be both Catholic, and all that this word has come to stand for—time-honoured institutions, continuity with the past, appointed channels of grace—and at the same time be the creation of the Spirit who, as the wind, blows where he wills?[29] A preliminary document[30] provided a useful study of the issues involved, clarifying the term 'catholicity', exploring the doctrine of the Holy Spirit as the source of the Church's catholicity, defining the relation between the local church and the universal Church, examining the meaning of continuity, the problem of apparent discontinuity and the concept of unity in diversity. The final report of the Assembly insists that unity is not synonymous with uniformity, that a diversity in love may enhance unity, that apparent discontinuity may be, and has in the past been, the way in which the Holy Spirit leads the Church to a truer continuity with the one Christ who is over all; that 'catholicity' and the Holy Spirit must not be set in opposition, as they are not in the New

Testament: 'The Church is faced by the twin demands of continuity in the one Holy Spirit and of renewal in response to the call of the Spirit amid the changes of human history.'[31] Renewal and the preservation of essential continuity are each functions of the Holy Spirit in the Church as in the world.

The Assembly also faced the question, which it knew to be in the minds of many, whether 'the struggle for Christian unity in its present form is irrelevant to the immediate crisis of our times'. Should not the Church 'seek its unity through solidarity with ... forces in modern life, such as the struggle for social equality, and ... give up its concern with patching up its own internal disputes?'[32] The Assembly indeed saw the Holy Spirit at work in civil rights movements and protests against discrimination, and the Christian as called to bear his witness in these contexts. But the urgency of this should not entail the neglect of the other (Matt. 23.23).

> The purpose of Christ is to bring people of all times, of all races, of all conditions, into an organic and living unity in Christ by the Holy Spirit under the universal fatherhood of God.[33]

The overcoming of division in the Church is not irrelevant to that.

THE CHURCHES AND UNION

Officials, committees, and assemblies of the W.C.C. have constantly declared that the initiative in effecting union between separated Christian groups must be taken by the churches themselves. Such initiative has not been lacking. The twentieth century has seen the coming together of many churches and groups by incorporation or organic union, or, more loosely, by federation, or by establishing concordats. A list of those which occurred between 1910 and 1952 is given by Rouse and Neill in *A History of the Ecumenical Movement*.[34] Examples of organic union are that between the Presbyterian Church in the United States of America and the Welsh Calvinistic Methodist Church in the U.S.A. (1920), retaining the name of the former; and that in England of the Wesleyan Methodist Church, the United Methodist Church, and the Primitive Methodist Church to form the Methodist Church (1931); the formation in France (1938) of the Reformed Church of France from the Union of Reformed Churches, the Union of Reformed Evangelical Churches, the Evangelical Methodist Church, and the Union of Evangelical Free Churches; and in Canada (1925) the Union of Presbyterians, Methodists, and Congregationalists to form the United Church of Canada.

Examples of federations, in which the contracting churches retain their own structure, are the Federation of Swiss Protestant Churches (1920) which includes the Reformed Churches of the cantons and the Methodist Church in Switzerland; and the Evangelical Church in Germany (1948) comprising twenty-seven autonomous regional churches of both Lutheran and Reformed tradition.

Examples of the concordat are that between the Old Catholic churches of Holland, Germany, Austria, and Switzerland and the Church of England (1931); and that between the Protestant Episcopal Church of the U.S.A. and the Polish National Catholic Church (1946). These concordats established terms of full intercommunion, and Anglican churches in other countries have entered into them since.

Along a different line there has been another ecumenical movement, namely the drawing together of Protestant churches of the same 'family' or confession, but existing in different countries, into World Alliances.[35] These alliances have provided opportunities for the member churches to take counsel together in periodic world conferences, and through their representative permanent staffs. The larger federations are the World Alliance of Reformed Churches (the first to be founded, in 1875), the Baptist World Alliance, the International Congregational Council, the World Convention of the Churches of Christ (Disciples), the Mennonite World Conference, and the Friends' World Committee for Consultation.

Both before and immediately after the creation of the W.C.C. in 1948 fears were expressed that the continued existence of these worldwide confessional organizations might discourage the local churches of the confessions from co-operation and seeking union with other churches. At Amsterdam it was decided that membership of the W.C.C. should be on the basis of churches, not of confessions, seats however being allotted with a view to adequate confessional and geographical representation. The importance of the confessional groups to the ecumenical movement was recognized in that they provided means for the churches of the confessions better to understand their own traditions. Many of these world federations have set up headquarters in Geneva, and since 1957 there have been regular meetings between their staffs and that of the W.C.C.

THE CHURCH OF SOUTH INDIA

The unions, concordats, and world alliances which I have been describing have provided no example of agreement between episcopal churches and those whose order of ministry is presbyteral or congregational. The first such instance was the union effected in 1947 between certain dioceses of the (Anglican) Church of India, Burma, and Ceylon, the South India United Church (itself a union of Presbyterians, Congregationalists, and the Basel Evangelical Mission) and the Methodist Church of South India, to form the Church of South India.[36] This union provided a model from which both positive and negative lessons have been drawn by those who have since been engaged in conversations between episcopal and non-episcopal churches.

Standards of faith were agreed upon without great difficulty: the Scriptures as the supreme authority for faith, the Nicene Creed as the authoritative summary of Christian teaching, and the sacraments of baptism and the eucharist as sacraments of the gospel. The question of ministry was not so easily settled. Anglicans, many of whom held that the episcopate within the historical succession belongs to the essence of the Church, and therefore that non-episcopal ministries lacked validity, were unwilling that there should be no more than a mutual acceptance of one another's ministers. Non-Anglicans were unable to accept the suggestion that their ministers should agree to episcopal ordination or conditional ordination, for this would either have denied, or thrown doubt upon, the reality of the ministry which they had previously exercised. Anglicans and non-Anglicans alike were unhappy with the proposal that all should receive supplemental ordination. The solution reached was a compromise, namely that from the inauguration of the Church of South India all new ministers should be episcopally ordained, but that all who were ministers at the time of inauguration should be accepted with equal rights and status without further commissioning or conditional ordination. It was expected that within about thirty years all ministries within the Church of South India would have been episcopally ordained. Meanwhile, this has meant that episcopally and non-episcopally ordained ministers have been working side by side. This is undoubtedly an anomaly, but, it is claimed, not so serious an anomaly as that of separate and competing churches attempting to present the gospel of the one Lord to a hostile or apathetic world.[37]

THE PROBLEM OF MINISTRY IN UNION CONVERSATIONS

The South India scheme throws into prominence the difficult problems which are encountered when episcopal and non-episcopal churches enter into negotiations.

On the one hand are those who are convinced that episcopacy is essential to the Church, and that the bishops who have received consecration in the historic line of succession from the apostles have the oversight (*episkope*) of the Church and are its ordaining ministers. From this position it follows that the ministry of those who are not episcopally ordained is invalid.

On the other hand are those who, while agreeing that *episkope*, in the sense of properly constituted oversight, is necessary to the church and in accordance with the will of Christ, claim that particular forms of *episkope* must be adapted to the needs of the Church and its mission. There have been and may be situations in which by the guidance of the Holy Spirit it is necessary to discover new forms. The condition of the Church on the eve of the Reformation was one such situation. The ministries of the Reformed Churches were constituted by the Spirit, have been blessed by God, and have borne the fruit of countless devoted Christian lives.

The two positions are diametrically opposed. Yet there are indications of willingness to overcome the opposition. Many who hold the first position admit gladly that the ministries of non-episcopal churches are effective in the sense that God has used them to impart grace to the lives of their members. Yet because those ministries must be deemed to be invalid—or, at the least, irregular—they invite those churches to embrace episcopacy, and their ministers to accept the laying on of hands by bishops. It should be noted that those who adopt this position raise for themselves some difficult questions. If a ministry and sacraments are *effective* without validity, what meaning does the word 'validity' have in this context? If a ministry and sacraments which are irregular are *effective*, may not the irregularity be justified?

It is a remarkable witness to the deep desire for Christian unity on the part of many non-episcopal churches now engaging in conversations that they are prepared to accept episcopacy 'in some constitutional form'.[38] But they are unwilling that the inauguration of a union with an episcopal church should include any rite which could be interpreted as casting doubt on the reality of the ministry which they have already exercised.

In the dialogue between these various positions, questions both of an historical and a theological nature arise, of which the following are examples:

1 What is the strength of the evidence that episcopacy in the same sense that Roman Catholics, Orthodox, and Anglicans understand it today was universally the ministerial order of the Church between N.T. times and the middle of the second century?

2 What is the significance of the fact that episcopacy was undoubtedly universally accepted by the beginning of the third century, and that today the great majority of Christians recognize the episcopal order of the Church?

3 Does apostolic succession mean only ministerial continuity conveyed by bishops, in succession from the apostles, consecrating other bishops in each generation? Are there not other senses of the words which are equally, perhaps more, important: an apostolic succession in faith and true doctrine, in fellowship and service? Should not the phrase properly refer to the continuity of the whole Church in the apostolic vocation and mission?

4 It being granted that due order, and the exercise of oversight are Christ's will for the Church, is it an unsurmountable cause of division that in some places and times oversight has been exercised by a body of presbyters while elsewhere it has been vested in the bishop alone? Is *no* rapprochement possible here?

These and similar questions continue to be discussed. In them are implicit some of the most obstinate barriers to union between episcopal and non-episcopal churches. It is by no means impossible, indeed there are some signs to suggest, that a way through may be pioneered by that church which has most lately entered the ecumenical movement: the Roman Catholic Church. To its relationship towards other Christian bodies, and to movements such as F. and O. and the W.C.C., I now turn.

20

The Roman Catholic Church
Vatican II and its Significance

In the first half of the twentieth century there was little to suggest that the Church of Rome had in any way moved from its position that the 'problem' of Christian divisions can only (but very simply) be solved by submission to the papacy, since the Roman Catholic Church is identical with the One Holy Catholic Church. Other Christian communions, confessions, and groups (with the sole exception of the Orthodox Churches) were officially referred to as societies, not churches. Pope Leo XIII in the Bull *Apostolicae Curae* (1896) had declared Anglican ordinations to be invalid, the implication being that the Church of England and its sister churches of the Anglican Communion are not part of the true Church of Christ. The polite but firm rebuff of Pope Benedict XV in 1919 to the invitation to the Roman Catholic Church to participate in a world conference on problems of faith and order made it clear that for him the unity of the Church meant the acceptance of the papacy.[1]

POPE PIUS XII

The encyclical *Mystici Corporis* (1943) of Pius XII was equally firm. It affirms that the doctrine of the mystical body is implicit in the very idea of the Church. It rejects all vague senses of the phrase. 'Mystical body' denotes the visible hierarchical body whose head is Christ, whose soul is the Spirit, and whose members may be saints or sinners. It signifies a unity which is not physical nor, on the other hand, merely metaphorical. It is a real unity which is constituted by regeneration in the waters of baptism, profession of the true faith, and adherence to the structure of the body. That structure is identified with the Roman Catholic Church and its hierarchy, since Christ rules on earth through his vicar, the Roman pontiff. Its members alone are effectively members of the mystical body. Of others, however, whether baptized or not, it is said that they may be ordained[2] to the mystical body 'by a kind of unconscious desire and will'. This opens the way for an interpretation of 'no salvation outside the Church' less rigid than was traditional.

A later encyclical, *Humani Generis* (1950), sharply attacked certain tendencies among liberal Roman Catholics, including that of distinguishing between the mystical body and the Church of Rome. In 1950 Pius XII took the step of defining *ex cathedra*, and therefore infallibly, the doctrine of the bodily assumption of the Blessed Virgin Mary, a doctrine which, though popularly accepted by Roman Catholics, was admitted by many theologians not to be contained in holy Scripture. This action was interpreted by many as an intentional closing of the door to any dialogue with other churches. Even the Orthodox were to receive a sharp reminder of their schismatic condition. Pius XII's encyclical *Sempiternus Rex* (1951) contains the words:

> Let those who, because of the inequity of the time, especially in Eastern lands, are separated from the bosom and unity of the Church, follow the teaching and example of their forefathers and not hesitate to render duly reverent homage to the Primacy of the Roman Pontiff.[3]

A brake was thus applied to ecumenical dialogue which had been undertaken by Roman Catholic theologians here and there.

POPE JOHN XXIII AND THE SECOND VATICAN COUNCIL

The accession of John XXIII in 1958 quickly brought a change of climate. The summoning in January 1959 of an Ecumenical Council,[4] the first since Vatican I of 1869–70, was unexpected even in circles close to the papacy. It quickly became clear that the doctrine of the Church was likely to be the main subject of the Council. The brake applied by Pius XII was felt to be eased, alike by non-Roman Catholics and by those within the Roman Catholic Church who believed that the way to Christian unity lay in the renewal of the Church and through dialogue rather than by a demand for submission. In the months following, many articles and books were written by Roman Catholic theologians on Church renewal and new possibilities of dialogue among the churches. During this period the Pope established a Secretariat for Promoting Christian Unity with Cardinal Augustin Bea as its first president. It saw its immediate task as to keep non-Roman churches informed about the Council. At the same time the relations with the W.C.C. were improved. A constructive meeting took place between Cardinal Bea and the General Secretary of the W.C.C., Dr W. A. Visser 't Hooft. Five Roman Catholic observers attended the Third Assembly of the W.C.C. at New Delhi in 1961. Moreover, some months before the Council met, it was decided that observers from other churches should be invited: Orthodox, Anglican, and the churches with world confessional organizations, as well as representatives of the W.C.C. About 150 observers in fact attended the Council for longer or shorter periods.

The Council assembled on 12 October 1962. There were four sessions, concluding on 8 December 1964, the last three sessions being presided over by Pope Paul VI after the death of John XXIII in 1963. Sixteen documents were promulgated. The doctrine of the Church is involved in all of them, but three in particular clearly reveal what the Church of Rome was moved to say at a time of unprecedented expectation on the part of Roman Catholic clergy and laity for renewal, and on the part of other Christians for an ecumenical gesture. These are the 'Dogmatic Constitution on the Church', the 'Pastoral Constitution on the Church in the Modern World', and the 'Decree on Ecumenism'.

VATICAN II: THE DOGMATIC CONSTITUTION ON THE CHURCH[5]

This Constitution, known as *Lumen Gentium* ('Light of All Nations') from its first words in Latin, begins by describing the Church as 'a kind of sacrament or sign of intimate union with God, and of the unity of all mankind',[6] and proceeds to speak of its divine foundation:

[The Eternal Father] planned to assemble in the holy Church all those who would believe in Christ. Already from the beginning of the world, the foreshadowing of the Church took place. She was prepared for in a remarkable way throughout the history of the people of Israel and by means of the Old Covenant. Established in the present era of time, the Church was made manifest by the outpouring of the Spirit. At the end of time she will achieve her glorious fulfilment. . . .

The Son, therefore, came on mission from His Father. It was in Him, before the foundation of the world, that the Father chose us to become adopted sons. . . . Christ inaugurated the kingdom of heaven on earth and revealed to us the mystery of the Father. By His obedience He brought about redemption. The Church, or, in other words, the kingdom of Christ now present in mystery, grows visibly in the world through the power of

God ('Dogmatic Constitution on the Church' i, 2–3; Abbott, op. cit., pp. 15–16).

The work of our redemption is carried on, and the growth of the Church in the unity of the one body of Christ is nourished by the constant celebration, in the eucharist, of Christ's sacrifice on the cross.

Chapter I goes on, with constant reference to biblical passages, to speak of the Holy Spirit's work of sanctifying, guiding, and renewing the Church, and to draw out briefly the significance of the various N.T. images of the Church: flock, vineyard, household, temple, spouse, and body of Christ.[7]

Christ established the Church as a visible structure through which he communicates grace to all. It is a single, visible structure:

> The society furnished with hierarchical agencies and the Mystical Body of Christ are not to be considered as two realities, nor are the visible assembly and the spiritual community, nor the earthly Church and the Church enriched with heavenly things. Rather, they form one interlocked reality which is comprised of a divine and a human element. For this reason, by an excellent analogy, this reality is compared to the mystery of the incarnate Word. ...
>
> This Church ... subsists in the Catholic Church, which is governed by the successor of Peter and by the bishops in union with that successor, although many elements of sanctification and of truth can be found outside her visible structure. These elements, however, as gifts properly belonging to the Church of Christ, possess an inner dynamism towards Catholic unity (ibid. i, 8; op. cit., pp. 22–3).

This is the Constitution's first reference to non-Roman Catholic Christians.

That Chapter II is devoted wholly to a consideration of the Church as the people of God is said by Father Avery Dulles[8] to have 'met a profound desire of the Council to put greater emphasis on the human and communal side of the Church'. The Church is not to be equated with the hierarchy. Nevertheless, we are reminded that the people of God which as a whole exercises a priestly, prophetic, and kingly function, includes the hierarchical ministry whose priesthood differs from that of the whole people 'in essence and not only in degree'.[9]

Some passages which are reminiscent of F. D. Maurice[10] occur in a section which speaks of all men being called to belong to the new people of God:

> Among all the nations of earth there is but one People of God, which takes its citizens from every race, making them citizens of a kingdom

which is of a heavenly and not an earthly nature. . . . The Church or People of God takes nothing away from the temporal welfare of any people by establishing the kingdom. Rather does she foster and take to herself, in so far as they are good, the ability, resources, and customs of each people. Taking them to herself she purifies, strengthens, and ennobles them (ii, 13, p. 31).

Maurice might also have written: 'Within the Church particular Churches hold a rightful place',[11] but the words following show that the Constitution does not relax the claim to papal primacy: 'These Churches retain their own tradition without in any way lessening the primacy of the Chair of Peter.' Consequently,

they are fully incorporated into the society of the Church who, possessing the Spirit of Christ, accept her entire system and all the means of salvation given to her, and through union with her visible structure are joined to Christ, who rules her through the Supreme Pontiff and the bishops (ii, 14, p. 33).

What, then, of other Christians, those of whom the Constitution says that 'they do not profess the faith in its entirety, or do not preserve unity of communion with the successor of Peter'? With them, it is said, the Church is linked in many ways. They honour the Scriptures, believe in God and in Christ, are consecrated by baptism which unites them with Christ, recognize and receive other sacraments in 'their own Churches or ecclesial communities'.[12]

Likewise we can say that in some real way they are joined with us, in the Holy Spirit, for to them also He gives His gifts and graces, and is thereby operative among them with His sanctifying power (ii, 15, p. 34).

It is to be noted that this constitutes a rejection of the view advanced by Augustine during his controversy with Donatists,[13] that in Christian groups separated from the Catholic Church the Holy Spirit does not operate, so that their sacraments have no efficacy and their lives are bereft of grace—an opinion which has been widespread among Roman Catholics until very recent times.[14]

We have here, then, a declaration that 'in some real way' other Christians are joined to the one Church of Christ. The strong desire of all sincere Christians 'to be peacefully united in the manner determined by Christ'[15] is noted. While it is not here actually stated that the manner determined by Christ is to 'render duly reverent homage to the Primacy of the Roman Pontiff', this is clearly expected of all who would 'be fully incorporated into the society of the Church'. *Lumen*

Gentium offers little reason for the non-Roman Catholic Christian to hope for a change of mind on this point on the part of the Church of Rome.

Chapter III, 'The Hierarchical Structure of the Church, with Special Reference to the Episcopate', takes up the work which the First Vatican Council had left undone. That Council, having defined the papal primacy and infallibility, was interrupted by the political up-heavals of 1870 before it could consider the authority of the bishops in relation to the pope. This chapter now enunciates the principle of episcopal collegiality. The Lord called the apostles, whom 'He formed after the manner of a college or fixed group, over which He placed Peter'.[16] The apostles 'took care to appoint successors in this hierarchically structured society',[17] among whom 'the chief place belongs to the office of those who, appointed to the episcopate in a sequence running back to the beginning, are the ones who pass on the apostolic seed'.[18] The account here given of the emergence of the episcopate is very sketchy, and many ambiguities in the early history of the development of Christian ministry are passed over.

As St Peter and the other apostles formed one apostolic college, so do the Roman pontiff and the bishops. This collegiality has found expression in the linkage of the bishops with one another all over the world and with the bishop of Rome, by 'bonds of unity, charity, and peace', in the decisions of conciliar assemblies, and ecumenical coun-cils, and is marked by the practice by which several bishops take part in the consecration of a new bishop.[19] It is stressed that the word 'college' in this context is not to be understood as 'a group of equals who entrust their powers to their president'.[20] Hence:

> The college or body of bishops has no authority unless it is simultaneously
> conceived of in terms of its head, the Roman Pontiff, Peter's successor,
> and without any lessening of his power of primacy over all.... For in vir-
> tue of his office, that is, as Vicar of Christ and pastor of the whole
> Church, the Roman Pontiff has full, supreme, and universal power over
> the Church. And he can always exercise this power freely (iii, 22, p. 43).

The difference between this understanding of collegiality and that of Cyprian in the third century[21] should be noted. *Lumen Gentium*'s definition, and the ways in which it can be made practically effective, are matters of sharp debate within the Roman Church.

Chapter III then discusses the prophetic, priestly, and kingly func-tions of the bishops (paras. 25–7) in relation to the ministries of priests and deacons (paras. 28–9).

Christ ... through His apostles, made their successors, the bishops, par-
takers of His consecration and His mission. These in their turn have
legitimately handed on to different individuals in the Church various
degrees of participation in this ministry. Thus the divinely established
ecclesiastical ministry is exercised on different levels by those who from
antiquity have been called bishops, priests, and deacons (iii, 28, pp. 52–3).

Professor Hans Küng notes[22] that the claim is not here made that
these three orders of ministry have existed from the apostles' time. The
phrase used is 'from antiquity' (*ab antiquo*), not 'from the beginning'
(*ab initio*). Yet the suggestion that there was everywhere a smooth
devolution of authority from apostles to bishops and then to ministers
of a lower order 'who do not possess the highest degree of
priesthood'[23] is again too simplistic a description of the early development of the Christian ministry, and begs several historical questions.

Chapter IV, 'The Laity', ascribes to the laity a positive ministry in
the Church and to the world in virtue of their calling and commissioning through baptism and confirmation. This ministry is
described as a share in the prophetic, priestly, and kingly work of
Christ and of the whole people of God. The subject of Chapter V is
'The Call of the Whole Church to Holiness', and Chapter VI, entitled
'Religious', deals with the particular call to holiness of those who enter
the religious Orders.

Chapter VII, 'The Eschatological Nature of the Pilgrim Church and
her Union with the Heavenly Church' presents the Church in a new
perspective. In Chapter III, despite some hints of a greater openness to
non-Roman Catholic Christians and to the non-Christian world, we
were given much the same picture of the Church as had been painted
in the Catholic West for centuries: the hierarchical structure, itself
containing the whole of Christian truth, inerrant, majestic, triumphant,
unshakably stable, presented almost as a statuesque image of perfection. In Chapter VII, however, although the Church is 'the universal
sacrament of salvation', it is depicted as in progress on a pilgrim way.
The restoration of all things is promised, and has indeed begun in
Christ, so that on this earth the Church is marked with a genuine
holiness. But it is an 'imperfect holiness'; it 'takes on the appearance of
this passing world'. The note of triumphalism is muted; that of the
need for renewal rises in crescendo. Joined with Christ in the Church
its members are truly sons of God but 'have not yet appeared with
Christ in the state of glory'. There is need, therefore, 'to live more for
Him, who died for us and rose again', to strive 'to please the Lord in

all things', to put on God's armour as a protection against evil.[24] Such words call forth an affirmative response from those of other churches in a way which the earlier chapters of the Constitution do not.

THE PASTORAL CONSTITUTION
ON THE CHURCH IN THE MODERN WORLD

This Constitution,[25] known also as *Gaudium et Spes* ('Joy and Hope') from its first words in Latin, is, significantly, the longest of the documents of Vatican II. It deserves, and is receiving, close attention. Here the Fathers of the Council show themselves to be fully aware that the Church is now in the twentieth century, a century which confronts a world with problems different from and more difficult than those of the past. And they declare the Church to be in, for, and open to the world, not above, against, and closed to it. More than any other Council document *Gaudium et Spes* has promoted renewal in the Roman Catholic Church—and involved it in the risks and tensions between the old and the new which inevitably accompany a determined effort at reformation. It is not possible here even to summarize how the Council Fathers draw out in detail the relation of a Church which sees itself as 'truly and intimately linked with mankind and its history'[26] to modern society in its cultural, economic, and political dimensions. I shall content myself with a quotation from an introduction to the Constitution by Father D. R. Campion, S.J., and some reference to comments of Dr Robert McAfee Brown.

Father Campion reminds us[27] that the preparatory commissions had not envisaged any document on the Church and the modern world. *Gaudium et Spes* was prompted by an intervention from the floor towards the close of the first session by the Belgian primate, Cardinal Suenens. He suggested that the Council should do more than concern itself with internal reform and should address itself to a question which the world was asking: Church of Christ, what do you say of yourself? Any answer to that must include an account of how the Church sees its relation to the contemporary world. The Pastoral Constitution is the Council's answer to the question. Father Campion holds that

the most distinctive note sounded in the text ... is that of the Church putting itself consciously at the service of the family of man. It may well be that in generations to come men will read this as a highly significant step towards a rethinking of conventional ecclesiological images, e.g. that of the Church viewed as a 'perfect society' standing over against the perfect society of the *Civitas*.[28]

Robert McAfee Brown, an American Protestant commentator, declares[29] that it is 'highly significant' that the Council, besides concerning itself with internal affairs, 'turned outward to examine the ways in which a Church subject to "reform and renewal" should relate to those beyond its walls'. The Constitution, he says, 'is an immeasurably important first word on a subject to which Catholicism has given far too little attention in the past'. He particularly welcomes its positive attitude to 'the world' in contrast with the negativism, sometimes perilously close to a denial of the goodness of creation, which has been characteristic of much Christian thought, both Catholic and Protestant. Recognition and understanding of the world, readiness to learn from it and to co-operate with all men, within and outside the Church—even with its avowed enemies—for the betterment of the human lot are corollaries of the new positive attitude which the Constitution itself draws out.[30]

He also sees as important the admission that the Church bears part of the responsibility for the present plight of the world, and the recognition that 'rather than striving to rule in the affairs of men, the Church must offer herself as a servant to men'. The Constitution's statement that the right of religious freedom is due to the dignity of the human person; the stress on lay activity and even initiative in the work of the Church; and the recognition of the social nature of man which 'renders untenable the frequent attempt to describe Christian ethical responsibility in purely individual terms' and calls for 'corporate human action on a large scale' are also singled out as encouraging signs of new and outward-looking attitudes on the part of the Roman Catholic Church.[31]

In the first stages of the implementation of 'The Pastoral Constitution on the Church in the Modern World', the Roman Catholic Church has not only engaged itself in conversations and in some measure of co-operation with other Christian bodies, but also has made contacts with representatives of other religions and with Marxists.

THE DECREE ON ECUMENISM[32]

Chapter I is entitled 'Catholic Principles of Ecumenism'. Prior to the final draft it had been headed 'Principles of Catholic Ecumenism'.

Father W. M. Abbott's note on this[33] explains that 'the change implies that the Council recognizes ecumenism as one movement for all Churches and Communities. The goal for all is the same, unity in the Christian faith, but the way of conceiving that unity and faith may vary, and so one may speak of a Church having its own principles of ecumenism'. The chapter begins by stating the beliefs which Roman Catholics bring to the ecumenical dialogue, summarizing what has been said in *Lumen Gentium*.

From the beginning rifts arose in the one and only Church. In later centuries large communities have separated from full communion with the Catholic Church. Often there was blame on both sides. Those who are born into separated communities cannot have the sin of separation imputed to them:

> The Catholic Church accepts them with respect and affection as brothers. For men who believe in Christ and have been properly baptized are brought into a certain, though imperfect, communion with the Catholic Church. Undoubtedly, the differences that exist . . . do indeed create many and sometimes serious obstacles to full ecclesiastical communion. These the ecumenical movement is striving to overcome. Nevertheless, all those justified by faith through baptism are incorporated into Christ. They therefore have a right to be honoured by the title of Christian, and are properly regarded as brothers in the Lord by the sons of the Catholic Church ('Decree on Ecumenism' i, 3, p. 345).

As in *Lumen Gentium*[34] it is admitted that within the separated churches there are many elements of true Catholic faith and practice. Many of their sacred actions engender the life of grace, and can truly be described as 'capable of providing access to the community of salvation'.[35] But these churches do not have that unity which Christ wishes to bestow upon the faithful, a unity which is found in the Catholic Church alone.

Roman Catholics are exhorted to participate in ecumenism intelligently. There should be dialogue in which each side presents its position fully, avoiding provocative statements and actions. This is intended to lead to a greater appreciation of the teaching and religious life of each communion, to co-operation where conscience allows, to common prayer 'where this is permitted', to an examination of their own faithfulness to Christ, and to the undertaking of renewal and reform wherever necessary.[36]

Chapter II, 'The Practice of Ecumenism', lays down further guidelines for ecumenism. These are often cautious, as the warning that common worship is not an instrument to achieve unity, but rather signifies a unity already present.[37] Chapter III, 'Churches and Ecclesial Communities separated from the Roman Apostolic See', examines the relationship of the Roman Catholic Church and other churches under two headings: 'The Special Position of the Eastern Churches', and 'The Separated Churches and Ecclesial Communities in the West'. The conviction that the unity of the Church demands the return of the separated churches to papal obedience is never far below the surface. Yet at the same time there shows through a new openness both towards these other churches and to the guidance of God. It is expressed in the admission that sins against unity are not all on the side of 'the separated brethren':

> Thus, in humble prayer, we beg pardon of God and of our separated brethren, just as we forgive those who trespass against us (ii, 7, p. 351).

And the Decree concludes with the words:

> This most sacred Synod urgently desires that the initiatives of the sons of the Catholic Church, joined with those of the separated brethren, go forward without obstructing the ways of divine Providence and without pre-judging the future inspiration of the Holy Spirit. Further this Synod declares its realization that the holy task of reconciling all Christians in the unity of the one and only Church of Christ transcends human energies and abilities. It therefore places its hope entirely in the prayer of Christ for the Church, in the love of the Father for us, and in the power of the Holy Spirit. 'And hope does not disappoint, because the charity of God is poured forth in our hearts by the Holy Spirit who has been given to us' (iii, 24, pp. 365–6).

AFTER THE SECOND VATICAN COUNCIL

The years since the close of the Council in 1965 have been difficult for the Roman Catholic Church. The period of the Council had been a time of self-examination, of expression of dissatisfaction with many features of the Church's life, of questioning even the nature of the Church's authority expressed through the magisterium, both on the part of the Church at large and in the Council itself. Many of the decisions of the Council arose out of this heart-searching and questioning. The question now, writes Dr Lukas Vischer, was: 'Would it be possible to restore an order comparable with that of the pre-conciliar period? Or would the questioning and seeking which had marked the sessions of the Council henceforth be a feature of the life of the Church as a whole?' He goes on:

> The Council had given rise to a new image of the Church. The very fact that for several years vital questions had been discussed openly before the whole Church, indeed before the whole world, had clearly demonstrated that the Church is most alive when it is moving forward, when it proclaims the gospel while at the same time asking itself questions about the gospel. Had not the Council itself planned with this movement in mind? Had it not continually stressed the Church's readiness for dialogue with the world? But could the Church face the problems of the modern world without also continuing its questioning and seeking?[38]

It is too early to answer the main question here, which is whether the Church of Rome will return to the self-understanding which prevailed from the time of Bellarmine to the accession of John XXIII. But in the years since the Council the questioning and seeking have continued.

Much has been done to implement the intention of the Council concerning ecumenism. The Secretariat for Unity has been continued in being, and through it official dialogue has been established with a number of churches. Discussion with the Lutheran World Federation began in 1965, with the Anglican Communion in 1966, and with the World Methodist Council in 1967. The practice has been to set up joint committees of theologians to study particular theological subjects and to prepare agreed statements for referral to the churches concerned. The Anglican Roman Catholic International Commission has issued statements on the eucharist, ministry, and authority in the Church which have been well received both by the Anglican and Roman Catholic Churches, and by others. They have not, however, been officially endorsed. The conferences of Roman Catholic bishops in several countries have set up ecumenical committees and centres which are fostering dialogue with other churches on the national level. By 1973 in the United States, for instance, conversations were being sponsored with the American Baptist Convention, the Christian Church (Disciples of Christ), the Episcopal Church (Anglican), Southern Baptists, Orthodox, Lutherans, Methodists, and Presbyterians.

Relations with the W.C.C. are closer. The Joint Working Group of the Roman Catholic Church and the W.C.C., established in 1965, has met twice a year for periods of several days. Its main task has been to discover whether a common understanding of the meaning of ecumenism can be reached, and to discuss possibilities of co-operation. The underlying question, whether the Roman Catholic Church may become a member of the World Council, is still unresolved. Fourteen Roman Catholic observers attended the Uppsala Assembly of the W.C.C. in 1968, and in the same year permission was given for Roman Catholic theologians to become full members of the Faith and Order Commission.

During these years the Roman Catholic Church has begun to experience difficulties which other Christian churches, with the exception of the newest evangelistic and pentecostal groups, have encountered for decades, and which have their roots in the materialistic, pluralistic, and anti-authoritarian society which has emerged with quickening pace as the century has advanced. There is declining membership in many places, and a shortage of clergy caused both by resignation of orders and by absence of vocation on the part of younger men (and for similar reasons a great reduction in membership of religious Orders, both of men and women). Many large buildings, monasteries, and seminaries stand empty. The Roman Catholic Church is reacting positively to these exigencies. For instance, the Synod of Bishops is currently addressing itself to the question of evangelization. A document[39] issued from the Vatican in 1973 calls on the conferences of bishops in the different countries to co-operate in this study and to help establish practical guidelines for evangelization. It abounds in questions. They are open-ended questions on which the corporate wisdom of the bishops is sought; and they are based on frank recognition of the world as it is:

> The world of today is in full evolution. Individuals and communities by their own activity are constructing their individual and social lives; a new way of life is coming into being, as a consequence of industrialization, urbanization, the independence of new nations, etc., indeed the very judgement and scale of values in men's consciences are undergoing change.[40]

Certain elements in the situation are seen as favouring evangelization. This part of the document deserves to be quoted in full:

a People are seeking a new life style, freedom from all types of servitude, and the development and promotion of the whole man.

b In human society individuals as well are seeking the meaning of life and are daily becoming more involved in the discussion of the matter.

c Dissatisfaction springs not only from lack of progress; it also increases with the advent of progress itself.

d The Church has become progressively less identified with society's political structures, and is able to manifest her religious nature more clearly.

e There is an evident reaction against conformism and immutable traditions. This reaction manifests itself in the questioning of structures imposed from without.

f New community forms of every kind arising everywhere demonstrate people's urge to foster mutual solidarity.

g There is an increase in the sense of personal responsibility.

h The less elevated forms of religious practice are coming to be recognized as lacking in substance and are being either rejected or corrected. A more genuine religious experience is prized and sought after.

i The various religious and world ideologies are coming together in the quest for peace and justice.[41]

A list of possible hindrances to evangelization follows: 'possible', because it is asked whether they are all to be regarded as obstacles, and not rather as providing fruitful ground for evangelization. The list includes: concepts of man and interpretations of human life which are not open to the gospel, and which are assumed as axiomatic in some currents of psychological, sociological, and anthropological thought and often accepted by the masses; the prevalence of atheism; the secularization of schools and hospitals; rapidly changing social conditions through urbanization and migration; the speedy dissemination of news by modern means of communication; the challenge to traditional values, e.g. of the family, and the questioning of ethical principles long held to be absolute. Under the heading 'Obstacles within the Church' are mentioned the shakiness of faith of many Christians; 'certain currents of thought, which find expression in the "death of God" and "religionless Christianity" theories' which gained much prominence in the 1960s; uncertainty about 'central teachings of the Gospel (Christ's identity, his true divinity, the Resurrection . . .)'. With reference to the Roman Catholic Church itself are mentioned disagreements about moral standards in relation to the individual, the family, and the State; the difficulty of communicating the faith 'in a language understood by our contemporaries'; the accusation that the Church co-operates 'with certain organs of economic and political power which are perhaps unjust' for the sake of material support; a certain emphasis on plurality within the Church which tends towards 'diversity in customs, discipline, liturgy, and sometimes even in the way the faith is formulated'.[42]

How evangelism may be promoted in these circumstances is the question which this paper asks the conferences of bishops. The document is significant in various ways. It is part of the implementation of the doctrine of episcopal collegiality as defined by the Second Vatican Council. It is significant of a Church, fully aware of the kind of world in which men now live, which urgently seeks renewal in the light of this understanding. It reveals also that the Church is undergoing 'a crisis in authority'; 'disagreement concerning the interpretation of the moral demands made by the gospel' can only mean that the magisterium is being challenged. That this is so became clear when Pope Paul VI's encyclical, *Humanae Vitae* ('Of Human Life'), was published in 1968.

The Church of Rome no longer presents a monolithic image to the world.[43] The conservative-liberal tension is felt perhaps more strongly than in any other church. Objections to the introduction of the new and simplified liturgy in the vernacular in accordance with Vatican II's 'Constitution on the Sacred Liturgy' are as vehemently outspoken as the protests against the official adherence to traditional teaching on birth control in *Humanae Vitae*.[44] In ecclesiology a vigorous debate goes on. The nature of the Church is receiving much attention from a number of Roman Catholic scholars, all independent thinkers, and some of whom (Hans Küng and Rosemary Ruether perhaps) are more radical than others.[45] Chapter 24 will discuss Küng's ecclesiology. Here I shall briefly mention some of the others.

SACRAMENTUM MUNDI: THE CHURCH AS SERVANT

In these contemporary Roman Catholic ecclesiologists two themes are constant, both inspired by the documents of Vatican II. One is the idea of the Church as *Sacramentum mundi*, the Sacrament of the world; the other is the concept of the Servant Church. The phrase *Sacramentum mundi* is not found in the Vatican II documents, but *Lumen Gentium*'s first paragraph contains the words:

By her relationship with Christ, the Church is a kind of sacrament or sign of intimate union with God, and of the unity of all mankind. She is also an instrument for the achievement of such union and unity ('Dogmatic Constitution on the Church' i, 1, p. 15).

In Chapter VIII, 48, also, the Church is said to be the 'universal sacrament' of salvation. The Constitution did not develop these ideas, but here is the seed for a fruitful doctrine of the Church, and one which, although using different terminology, is very close to the doctrine of the mystical body.

A sacrament is a gift of God: something earthly is set aside for holy use, a sign and representative of what all things earthly are meant to be, and an instrument of sanctification of all that is earthly. In the idea of the Church as the sacrament of the world, then, we have the concept of a society instituted by God which is itself in microcosm what the world must be, and which exists to enable it to be that which itself is, the body of Christ. Thomas O'Dea in a recent article[46] explores what such a concept implies for the Church's structures and activity in the world of today. In the light of the technological revolution, the unsolved social problems it has created, and the consequent 'worldwide destructuration of traditional forms and the often chaotic search for new forms and structures of thought and relationship', O'Dea believes that the Church which has stood 'aloof and defensive for several centuries now becomes part of the quest of modern men, now as a "Pilgrim Church" takes its position in the ranks of evolving humanity', and asks: 'How shall it be a sacramental sign and a facilitating means in these circumstances?'[47] This article, with others in the same volume, 'The Church: Sign and Instrument of Unity' by Richard McBrien,[48] and 'Structures of the Church's Presence in the World of Today—through the Church's own Institutions' by Robert Rodes, attempts to suggest what the 'restructuration' of the Church demands in terms of canon law, diocesan and parochial organization (the question whether the territorial parish is outdated is raised), relationship to the State, education, and social service.

Edward Schillebeeckx, a Dutch theologian, also develops the idea of the Church as the sacrament of the world.[49] Taking up another hint from *Gaudium et Spes*,[50] he relates this aspect of the Church to the dialogue which he sees as a newly understood and accepted 'principle', 'basic attitude', and 'inner demand':[51]

The Church's new understanding of herself and her new understanding of the world, form the basis of the Church's change from monologue to dialogue. The whole of this fundamental change of emphasis can be summarized in the key-idea which inspired this change, even though it was not so used in any of the documents of the Council. This is the idea of the Church as the *Sacramentum mundi*. *Mundus* ('world') in this context means the confraternity, or other-orientated existence, of men in the world—man's mode of existence in dialogue with his fellow-men. The Church must, according to the Council, really be the sacrament of this brotherhood: ... the Church is 'the sign of that fraternity which permits and strengthens sincere dialogue'.[52] As such the Church really fulfils the 'ministry of communication' in the world. Wherever there are impediments to communication, the Church must lead the way in overcoming them. As Gibson Winter has said so succinctly, the Church 'has the task of re-opening communication'.[53] He went even further, saying that 'the ministry of reconciliation of the Servant Church is the restoration of communication to society'[54]. .... The Church is the sacrament of dialogue, of communication between men (*God the Future of Man*, pp. 123–4).

This does not, he maintains, necessitate abandoning the Church's 'claim to exclusiveness', which previously seemed to make dialogue impossible. On the contrary, dialogue demands that the truth which each has should be brought into relation with the truth of others. Moreover, Schillebeeckx claims, however it has appeared in history, the Church does not claim to possess all truth and to be always right:

> The Church has a religious mission in the world and *thus*, in this mission, also a humanizing task. But for the task of humanizing the world as it is she receives from divine revelation no light other than that of all men and their experiences, and she has therefore to search tentatively for solutions. Furthermore, her *religious* claim, her 'claim to exclusiveness' on the basis of Christ's promise, is made relative by the fact that she is eschatologically orientated—still on the way, in history, towards the kingdom of God and not yet identical with the kingdom of God (ibid., pp. 124–5).

Whether this is consonant with the still official doctrine of the infallibility of the Church and of the pope is debatable. But on this basis Schillebeeckx is convinced that the Roman Catholic Church can, and must, as *Sacramentum mundi* enter into dialogue with the world, as a church which is a servant church[55] and one which 'will always need reform and purification'.[56]

Professor Gregory Baum of St Michael's College, Toronto, and editor of *The Ecumenist*, is a theologian who, both by his writing and by taking many opportunities of interchurch and interfaith dialogue, shows himself in agreement with Schillebeeckx's contention that the Roman Catholic Church has a mission to the world which must now manifest itself in dialogue.[57] He too is concerned to interpret the position of the Church of Rome in a way which will not stifle dialogue from the start. Its claims can, he admits, no longer be based on the traditional argument about identity through continuity with the Church of the New Testament,[58] nor on the argument that it alone manifests in any fullness the four credal 'marks' of the Church: 'Remembering the four marks of the Church, we discover in how many ways we are *not* united, *not* universal, *not* holy, and *not* faithful to the original gift.'[59]

The uniqueness of the Roman Catholic Church, Gregory Baum believes, rests rather on the fact that it is the only church which has maintained the tension between local and universal unity, and the tension between past and present. The former tension is built into the structure of the Church: 'Episcopacy affirms the unity and relative autonomy of the local community and the papacy affirms the unity of the universal Church, in which the local communities participate.'[60] Because the tension is maintained, 'the Catholic Church is able to come to consensus on the meaning of her own life of faith, which is acknowledged as authoritative by the faithful'.[61] The tension between past and present is that between belief 'that everything God has done for the salvation of man has happened in Jesus Christ and hence lies in the past' and the belief 'that the divine work of redemption, revealed in Christ, is still going on and hence is present to us'.[62] 'The Catholic Church, because of its concept of "tradition", is capable of retaining the two poles of this tension between past and present'[63] without falling into primitivism on the one hand or modernism on the other. Tradition is 'a process in which the Spirit is creatively involved'. Knowing this, the Church is not bound to the past, but open in the present and to the future, and is able to reinterpret its teaching 'in obedience to God's Word in the present',[64] or, to put it another way, it is able 'to refocus' the gospel upon the spiritual-cultural situation of today and of every day.[65] To summarize: the Roman Catholic Church, according to Baum, because of its papal-episcopal structure and its grasp of the true meaning of tradition, is able to arrive at doctrinal agreement and to make the gospel relevant to the contemporary world. In this it is unique, and in these terms its exclusive claims must be made. This is the contribution it must make to the Ecumenical Movement.[66]

But it has to be asked whether the bases for the claim to uniqueness which Baum expounds bear any more weight than the criteria he has rejected. The papal-episcopal hierarchy simply has not reached a consensus 'received as normal' by the Church's members, for example on infallibility and birth control: different matters indeed, but both of great relevance to the church-world relation. Moreover, it is not self-evident that the Roman Catholic Church alone has grasped the concept of the Holy Spirit as interpreter of the gospel and Christian tradition to every age.

Rosemary Radford Ruether appears to be the most radical of recent Roman Catholic writers on the Church. The phrase 'appears to be' is used advisedly since she herself in the Introduction to her book, *The Church Against Itself*, warns the reader against shock and tells us that it was written to test the spirit of openness to the world and the future which has been claimed for Vatican II.[67] She reacted, moreover, very sharply to a critical review by another Roman Catholic woman theologian, claiming that the reviewer had not understood the dialectical nature of her argument and consequently had attributed to her inconsistencies where none existed.[68] The book contains a trenchant criticism of institutionalism in the Church, and indeed in all churches, and asserts that it is only by discontinuity with its own past that the Church can keep continuity with the gospel, and therefore be true to the gospel in the present. Its institutional forms (the Scriptures, the episcopal succession, the sacraments are included) are means by which the Church has maintained itself in history. They were not instituted by Christ, or by the apostles, for they expected the near approach of the End, but by history: 'Only the Church as an eschatological community is "from Christ".'[69] The institutional office of the Church 'can put itself back into a positive relationship with the Spirit when it understands that it was *not* instituted by Christ, but was instituted by history',[70] and 'the Holy Spirit does not underwrite any finalized historical structures or dogmas, but rather breaks apart and brings to an end such history'.[71] Mrs Ruether, it seems, does not share Gregory Baum's confidence in the institution of pope and bishops. Not that she wishes to sweep all ecclesiastical institutions away, but 'all this is a secondary reality, not without its usefulness if properly understood, but which distorts and even betrays the inner nature of the Church when it is given a hypostatic reality of its own'.[72] The following paragraph brings out clearly the important point she is making:

> The role of the external institution is both indispensable and limited in power. For the institutional church to accept this limit to itself is at the

same time to keep itself in that open situation whereby the eschatological reality of the Church can again and again become real in history for the Christian community. Therefore, in order for Church office to fulfil its task authentically, it must know its own conditioned and relative nature. Its polity is always given by the political and social forms of the times, not appointed by God and invested with absolute validity in itself. It can truly be a fertile bed for the seed sown by the divine sower, or a rocky patch which withers and destroys it, depending on whether it takes an open and self-abnegating, or a closed and self-absolutizing, view of itself (*The Church Against Itself*, pp. 139–40).

Rosemary Ruether, then, is convinced that the Church must be recognized to be an eschatological community. 'To be in the Church is to be already, in principle, within that kingdom of the Christ, that new creation of God which brings this "evil aeon" to an end. . . . We need to recover that vivid sense of the Church as an eschatological community that was so characteristic of primitive Christianity.'[73] But the *koinonia*, whose true mode of being is future, has allowed itself to become naturalized in history and has claimed ultimate significance for its historically induced institutions.[74]

Yet this *koinonia* is also an everyday mode of being for man here and now.[75] *Koinonia* and *diakonia*, therefore, belong together. Chapter 10, 'Christian Ministry as Encounter', is a compelling exposition of the nature of ministry:

> We are not called to play church games, but to put our whole existence on the line, to lay down our whole selves for our fellow-man in a way that leaves no aspect of our person untouched and which penetrates into every corner of human and cosmic reality (ibid., p. 193).

In the writings of all these contemporary Roman Catholic authors the second theme which we mentioned as inspired by Vatican II is prominent, namely that of the Church as servant. This is apparent in the case of Rosemary Ruether from the quotation immediately above. Edward Schillebeeckx declares that service in and to the world is implicit in the Church's nature as a sacrament of dialogue:

> The Church . . . is certainly not present in the world for her own sake, but is there to give Christ's Good News of the kingdom of God which is to come. That is why the Church's dialogue must not be self-centred—it is rather a ministry or service of the Church. . . . It is, moreover, an essential aspect of sincere dialogue that one is not thinking of oneself, but of the other. . . . In this dialogue, the Church is *omnium bono serviens*, serving the well-being of all (*God the Future of Man*, pp. 127–8).

He goes on to describe the content of such a dialogue: 'It may take the form of encouragement and confirmation, help, collaboration, or the taking of initiatives. It may also consist of criticism and protest.'[76] There are 'experiences which evoke the protest "No! it can't go on like this; we won't stand for it any longer!" ' and which compel the Church to 'protest against war, various forms of social injustice, racial discrimination, large landholding, colonialism'.[77] The Church's dialogue is not primarily 'a reflexive dialogue, but rather the existential involvement of Christians in the world'.[78]

Gregory Baum proposes[79] a sociological model for the institutional life of the Church which he believes corresponds to the new understanding of an 'open Church' whose mission is to unify and reconcile the whole human family. The model is 'the outer-oriented movement'. He sees the Church as a movement which 'wants to involve the whole of society in conversation . . . is in solidarity with the human community in which it lives . . . wants to bear the burden with others . . . wants to help solve the problems from which people suffer'.[80] He envisages cities in which there are various centres of Christian life, where worship is celebrated, and educative and active programmes are arranged, centres whose influence will be such that the social conscience of the city will be awakened, programmes of reform initiated, and people generally made 'more sensitive to what is precious and important in life'. Catholics will 'become more dedicated members of the secular society in which they live', and men will be drawn 'more deeply into the mystery of redemption present in human life'.[81]

> The Church as movement makes people conscious of what community means in the lives of men. At the institutional centre of the Church, Christians learn the mystery of community in the eucharist and in the teaching of Christ; they learn this, not to form a closed community about the visible centres but, rather, to become community-creators themselves and move into society, the places where they live and work, to form community with people there (*The Credibility of the Church Today*, p. 209).

Baum believes that in the cities in Roman Catholic Church is already being transformed into such an 'outer-oriented movement', a Church which both serves its Lord and serves the community in which it is situated.

We shall see (Chapter 24) Professor Hans Küng also placing emphasis on the servant aspect of the Church, on the ground that *diakonia* is intrinsic to the idea of the Church in the New Testament.

21

The Twentieth Century
Church and World

Since the work of Max Weber (1864–1920) and Ernst Troeltsch (1865–1923) it has been recognized that Christianity, the Church and the churches, whatever else must be said of them, are sociological phenomena, and can be studied as such. Weber distinguished two forms in which Christianity has manifested itself in history: the Church-type and the sect-type. Troeltsch added a third, the mystical-type.

Troeltsch distinguishes the first two types in this way:

> The Church is that type of organization which is overwhelmingly conservative, which to a certain extent accepts the secular order, and dominates the masses; in principle, therefore, it is universal, i.e. it desires to cover the whole life of humanity. The sects, on the other hand, are comparatively small groups; they aspire after personal inward perfection and they aim at a direct personal fellowship between the members of each group. From the very beginning, therefore, they are forced to organize themselves in small groups, and to renounce the idea of dominating the world. Their attitude towards the world, the State, and Society may be indifferent, tolerant, or hostile, since they have no desire to control and incorporate these forms of social life; on the contrary, they tend to avoid them; their aim is usually either to tolerate their presence alongside of their own body, or even to replace these social institutions by their own society. Further, both types are in close connection with the actual situation and with the development of Society. The fully developed Church, however, utilizes the State and the ruling classes, and weaves these elements into her own life; she then becomes an integral part of the existing social order; from this standpoint, then, the Church both stabilizes and determines the social order; in so doing, however, she becomes dependent upon the upper classes, and upon their development. The sects, on the other hand, are connected with the lower classes, or at least with those elements in Society which are opposed to the State and to Society; they work upwards from below, and not downwards from above (*The Social Teaching of the Christian Churches*, vol. i, p. 331).[1]

Examples of the church-type are the medieval western Church, the Russian Orthodox Church of pre-Revolution days, the Lutheran churches of Europe, the Church of England, the Reformed Church of Geneva, the Church of Scotland. Although the precise relationship with the State differs, in each case it is implied that Church membership and citizenship are two sides of the same coin.

Examples of the sect-type are the Waldensians, the 'Spiritual' Franciscans, the Lollards and the Hussites prior to the Reformation, the English Independents of the seventeenth century, the Congregational churches, and many modern Pentecostal churches. These differ greatly from each other in doctrine and practice, but are one in their rejection of the world and its culture and in their desire to form a 'gathered' church of voluntary believers, providing for their own leadership and discipline, and acknowledging no authority outside the congregation itself but Christ.

Earlier in this work I have treated of these two types and of most of the examples mentioned. It should, however, be noted that in the post-Reformation period there has occurred a combination of the two.[2] Many North American denominations have emerged as 'free churches' in which 'the church-type has become joined to the voluntarist principle'.[3] Both types and the combined type have deeply influenced society, whether it be by acquiescence and adoption, or by resistance and rejection. They have all, conversely, been moulded to a considerable degree by the society and culture in which they have emerged. Troeltsch's monumental historical survey makes this abundantly clear. Few can disagree that between the Church, in its various manifestations, and society a mutual interaction, a shaping and being shaped, has continuously been at work. Not even the most rigidly exclusive of sect-type churches have in fact succeeded in insulating themselves completely from the world.

Brief reference must be made to Troeltsch's third type, which he refers to as mysticism and spiritual idealism.[4] It is, he says, 'a very difficult matter to distinguish between this type of mysticism and the sect-movement'.[5] It has roots in primitive and medieval Christianity, but 'is far more closely connected with Luther's original main ideas, and is therefore still more strongly rooted within Protestantism'.[6] It is marked by 'insistence upon a direct inward and present religious experience', and either a reaction against 'the objective forms of religious life in worship, ritual, myth, and dogma', or an attempt to supplement them 'by means of a personal and living stimulus'.[7] He cites as examples of this third type, among others, Thomas Münzer, Karlstadt, Sebastian Franck, and Jacob Böhme, and notes that its characteristics appear in movements like the Quakers, Methodism, and Pietism. But the type itself, as Troeltsch describes it, seems essentially to be that of the sincerely religious individual, mystically inclined, who cannot easily or for long find fulfilment within a structured group.[8]

Towards the close of a discussion of the 'penetrating and comprehensive' social influence in western Europe and America of what he calls Ascetic Protestantism or Puritan Calvinism, Troeltsch writes:

> To what extent they [i.e. Puritan Calvinism and the 'purified' communities of the sects] will be able to dominate the modern civilized world permanently in a Christian manner is another question. This school of thought is still a power in world history. But it is clear on all hands that to a great extent the State, Society, and economic life will no longer allow themselves to be dominated by it, and in their present position cannot possibly be dominated by it any longer (ibid., vol. ii, p. 816).

This was written in 1911. Nearly seven decades later it must be said that those last words have been proved true. Even in the few remaining countries where there is a close relationship between Church and State, the question of the Church's domination of society no longer arises. The question rather is whether the Church now exercises, or can exercise, any effective influence upon modern society.

The process of secularization, whose pace quickened in the eighteenth century, now advances at a gallop. Men's minds are oriented to this world, this present age (*saeculum*). Modern society, having become increasingly pluralistic, acknowledges no divine right of kings or rulers, no divinely promulgated laws, relates everything to man himself. The process has kept pace with the scientific and technological advances which made possible the industrial revolution which began in the late eighteenth century and whose momentum is now changing the face of the earth. The aeroplane is now a more familiar sight than the horse. 'Agrarian' or 'mercantile' are no longer appropriate descriptions of any western state. Agriculture and trade still go on, to be sure, but these activities are being transformed by highly efficient agricultural machines and computers. Technology reaches even to those countries which western nations have come to call undeveloped, or underdeveloped, for it is from them that, to a very considerable extent, the raw materials are drawn which are necessary to sustain the higher standards of living which the technological revolution has engendered.

The pace of all this has been such that the world suddenly finds itself confronted with new problems. Technology has created urban populations so vast that it proves increasingly difficult to provide for essential services or for law and order. Technology has made it possible to utilize raw materials so rapidly that supplies for future generations are in jeopardy. Only recently has there dawned a general awareness of the problems of ecology: the atmosphere and the waters of the world are becoming so polluted by the waste products of industry that a threat is posed alike to plant, animal, and human life. The population of the world, nevertheless, increases rapidly, while the area of arable land is encroached on by sprawling cities, wide arterial roads, airports, industrial plants, and mining operations. Technology, moreover, has given to man instruments of destruction which, if touched off, could result in the destruction of the human race.

Although it is difficult to compare one age with another in matters of ethical behaviour, it can confidently be said that twentieth-century man is no less prone to acts of violence and to defiance of authority than were his ancestors. It is unsafe to walk alone at night in an increasing number of cities. Despite the factors which might be expected to foster mutual understanding and co-operation between nations (improved communications, greater knowledge of the needs and aspirations of others, cultural exchanges) national rivalry has scarcely abated. There are wars, and where there are not, peace is uneasy.

Technology has advanced in the name of progress and development. Yet many people, not unappreciative of very much that has been achieved, are asking the questions: progress towards what? Development of what, and for whom?

The subjects briefly touched on above (technology, urbanization, ecology, pollution) need no further elaboration here. The literature on them is enormous. Every issue of a daily newspaper illuminates some aspect of them. Obviously mankind faces a whole set of problems which, if not all new in kind, are new in the urgency they now assume, and in that they have arisen not singly, but simultaneously. Man seems to be standing at one of the crossroads of his history, and he wonders whether any of the possible turnings is anything but a cul-de-sac.

It would be deplorable if, in this situation, Christian thinkers and writers were not asking the question of the Church's *raison d'être*.

What significance has the Church, what possible function has it in the crisis of today's world? What *is* the Church? Will former answers to this question suffice? Does the secularization of the age prove the Church's failure? Has it become an anachronism, useful in its day, but now no more than an archaeological curiosity?

Dietrich Bonhoeffer, one of the first theologians to express awareness of the fact, and the challenge, of secularization, began to ask these questions.[9] In a letter written from prison to a friend, Eberhard Bethge, he said:

> What is bothering me incessantly is the question what Christianity really is, or indeed who Christ really is, for us today.... We are moving towards a completely religionless time; people as they are now simply cannot be religious any more. ...
>
> The questions to be answered would surely be: What do a church, a community, a sermon, a liturgy, a Christian life mean in a religionless world? ... How do we speak (or perhaps we cannot now even 'speak' as we used to) in a 'secular' way about 'God'? In what way are we 'religionless–secular' Christians, in what way are we the *ek-klesia*, those who are called forth, not regarding ourselves from a religious point of view as specially favoured, but rather as belonging wholly to the world? (*Letters and Papers from Prison* 30 April 1944).

In this letter Bonhoeffer first introduces several theological 'seed-thoughts' which have since become influential.[10] He recognizes the fact of the secularization of the western world, and *welcomes* it. He speaks of it as the world coming of age:

> The movement that began about the thirteenth century ... towards the autonomy of man (in which I should include the discovery of the laws by which the world lives and deals with itself in science, social and political matters, art, ethics, and religion) has in our time reached an undoubted completion. Man has learned to deal with himself in all questions of importance without recourse to the 'working hypothesis' called 'God' (ibid., 8 June 1944; op. cit., p. 325).

It is not to be supposed that Bonhoeffer himself had found it impossible or unnecessary to believe in God. His argument is that man has always tended to 'use' God as the explanation of what he himself cannot yet explain, as a solver of problems or a crutch in times of distress. As science and technology have solved more and more problems, God has been 'increasingly pushed out of the world that has come of age'.[11] Bonhoeffer's complaint is that the Church has accommodated itself to this development by a feverish attempt to find gaps in man's knowledge where God is still needed as an explanation, and to prove that in the inner areas of man's life (his guilt feelings and fears, for instance) God is also needed: 'There still remain the so-called "ultimate questions"—death, guilt—to which only "God" can give an answer, and because of which we need God, the church, and the pastor.'[12]

Bonhoeffer believes that such an apologetic is an attack on the adulthood of the world 'which is pointless, ignoble and un-Christian'.[13] Such tactics involve two theological errors: 'First, it is thought that a man can be addressed as a sinner only after his weakness and meannesses have been spied out.'[14] He speaks of 'clerical snuffing-around-after-people's-sins in order to catch them out'; and in an earlier letter he had written about the efforts of existential philosophers and psychotherapists 'who demonstrate to secure, contented, and happy mankind that it is really unhappy and desperate and simply unwilling to admit that it is in a predicament about which it knows nothing'.[15] This was not Jesus' way: 'When Jesus blessed sinners, they were real sinners, but Jesus did not make everyone a sinner first. He called them away from their sin, not into their sin.'[16]

Second, it is thought that a man's essential nature consists of his inmost and most intimate background ... his 'inner life', and it is precisely in those secret human places that God is to have his domain![17] But, Bonhoeffer points out, the Bible does not make this distinction between the outward and the inward. It is concerned with the whole man.[18]

Bonhoeffer believes that the Church should address modern man in a very different way:

> I therefore want to start from the premise that God shouldn't be smuggled into some last secret place, but that we should frankly recognize that the world, and people, have come of age, that we shouldn't run man down in his worldliness, but confront him with God at his strongest point (ibid., 8 July 1944, p. 346).

In the letter of 30 April 1944, he had written similarly:

> I should like to speak of God not on the boundaries, but at the centre, not in weaknesses but in strength; and not in death and guilt but in man's life and goodness (ibid., p. 282).

Not enough time was to be allowed to Bonhoeffer to develop the answer to his question about the meaning of the Church in his day. A few phrases only give us hints of how he might have done so. 'Jesus claims for himself and the kingdom of God the whole of life in all its manifestations.'[19] Consequently, the Church receives the vocation of claiming 'the whole of life in all its manifestations' for Christ. 'The Church stands, not at the boundaries where human powers give out, but in the middle of the village.'[20] 'The Church must come out of its stagnation. We must move out again into the open air of intellectual discussion with the world, and risk saying controversial things, if we are to get down to the serious problems of life.'[21]

In the 'Outline for a Book' which he sketched in August 1944, he includes a condensed criticism of the German Protestant churches, among them the 'Confessing Church', which had stood boldly against Hitler's domination of the Church in the pre-war years:

> The Protestant church: Pietism as a last attempt to maintain evangelical Christianity as a religion; Lutheran orthodoxy, the attempt to rescue the Church as an institution for salvation; the Confessing Church; the theology of revelation; a *dos moi pou sto* ['give me a place to stand'] over against the world, involving a 'factual' interest in Christianity; art and science searching for their origin. Generally in the Confessing Church: standing up for the Church's 'cause', but little personal faith in Christ. 'Jesus' is disappearing from sight. Sociologically: no effect on the masses—interest confined to the upper and lower middle classes. A heavy incubus of difficult traditional ideas. The decisive factor: the Church on the defensive. No taking risks for others (ibid., p. 381).

The outline for the third chapter tells us what kind of risks he means:

> The Church is the Church only when it exists for others. To make a start, it should give away all its property to those in need. The clergy must live solely on the free-will offerings of their congregations, or possibly engage in some secular calling. The Church must share in the secular problems of ordinary human life, not dominating but helping and serving. It must tell men of every calling what it means to live in Christ, to exist for others. . . . It must not underestimate the importance of human example . . . it is not abstract argument, but example, that gives its word emphasis and power . . . it is something that we have almost entirely forgotten (ibid., pp. 381–2).

Bonhoeffer is insistent that it is the Christian's vocation to suffer. God came in Christ to address men in their vigour and strength, but he also came in weakness and to suffer. So it must be with Christ's follower, because the world *is* godless:

> He must therefore really live in the godless world, without attempting to

gloss over or explain its ungodliness in some religious way or other. He must live a 'secular' life, and thereby share in God's sufferings. He *may* live a 'secular' life (as one who has been freed from false religious obligations and inhibitions). To be a Christian does not mean to be religious in a particular way ... on the basis of some method or other, but to be a man—not a type of man, but the man Christ creates in us. It is not the religious act that makes the Christian, but participation in the sufferings of God in the secular life (ibid., 18 July 1944, p. 361).

Three days later he writes:

By this-worldliness I mean living unreservedly in life's duties, problems, successes and failures, experiences and perplexities. In so doing we throw ourselves completely into the arms of God, taking seriously not our own sufferings, but those of God in the world—w?   ; with Christ in Gethsemane. That, I think, is faith; that is *metanoia* [repentance] (ibid., 21 July 1944, p. 370).

He adds: 'I think you see what I mean, even though I put it so briefly.' Perhaps we do not completely grasp his meaning. His letters provide us with very little guidance about *how* one may live as a Christian in the world in a 'religionless way'. He seems not to mean that the Church and the Christian must refrain from speaking of God and Christ. He tells us that he found it easier to speak openly and naturally of God with those who have no religion[22] than with religious people. Nor does he envisage the neglect of prayer, worship, the sacraments. The letters reveal Bonhoeffer as one who prayed and read the Bible daily, who hummed remembered hymns, who kept track of the holy days of the Christian year. It does seem, however, that in the Church's situation in a godless world, he saw this kind of observance as a vital source of strength for Christians, but as not to be prominent in the Church's address to the world. Perhaps he feared that men would be encouraged again to believe that such observances were means of self-salvation—one aspect of the 'religion' which Bonhoeffer criticizes. Men must know God to be at the centre of their lives, and then they would see the need for prayer, worship, and sacrament. But Bonhoeffer is certain that he himself, and the faithful Christian, must not let go of prayer, worship, the study of the Bible, and the observance of traditions. This seems to be the thrust of the phrase 'secret discipline' (*disciplina arcani*) which he uses in the letter of 30 April: 'What is the place of worship and prayer in a religionless situation? Does the secret discipline ... take on a new importance here?' And in the letter of 5 May he writes: 'A secret discipline must be restored by which the mysteries of the Christian faith are protected against profanation.'[23]

We may not be far from the truth in suggesting that Bonhoeffer saw the situation of the Church in his day as close in many respects to that of the Church in its earliest days in the world of the Roman Empire, an environment of superstition mixed with scepticism. The same options were open. They included a policy of retreating from the world into small enclosed groups for the cultivation of holiness, an option which was taken by some in the early centuries, and again by some in the crises of the Renaissance and the Reformation. It is being taken by some today.

Bonhoeffer presents another option: 'The Church is the Church only when it exists for others.'[24] The Church must live on the one hand courageously and joyfully, but without triumphalism, in the world; and on the other, in the spirit of the man for others, agonize with him in the world's suffering. For this the Church and its faithful need to be enabled by holding fast to the truths and practices of Christian faith, endeavouring without any ostentation to make them understandable and relevant to others, and always ready, humbly and thankfully, to receive those others into the fellowship of faith.

RENEWAL

Bonhoeffer's last writings make frequent reference to the shortcomings of the Church. The need for repentance and renewal on the part of the Church is a note frequently struck in recent ecclesiology. *Gaudium et Spes* of Vatican II recognizes that Christians themselves have much to do with the rise of modern atheism,[25] that too many Christians have been content with 'a merely individualistic morality',[26] and that the social conscience of the Church needs strengthening.[27] Moreover: 'It does not escape the Church how great a distance lies between the message she offers and the human failing of those to whom the gospel is entrusted.'[28]

Among Protestant churches there is a similar recognition that their own attitudes have helped to produce the modern situation and its problems.[29] Liberal Protestantism gave its blessing to the 'progress' and 'development' which were the outcome of the prevailing scientific and humanistic spirit as the twentieth century dawned, as if they were signs of the coming of the Kingdom of God. The major Protestant churches have come to recognize that they have identified themselves too closely with the middle-class values of success in business and respectability, and have lost touch with the great mass of industrial workers.

This note of repentance is accompanied by a realization that the Church's organization and methods of ministry are now outdated. The geographical parish system, appropriate for rural areas and towns of moderate size, and the congregational system which assumes a settled population within easy distance of the church building and within reach of the personal ministrations of the pastor, are anachronistic in relation to the vast metropolitan areas of today and to a society which is increasingly mobile. Difficulties arise for the parish priest and minister of a congregation from the facts that the wage-earner of a family rarely works, the housekeeper rarely shops, and the children rarely go to school where they live; that a higher standard of living and the availability of transport make it easy for families to spend weekends away from home; that the business and industrial world is such that families are with increasing frequency uprooted in order to follow the wage-earners where employers send them. Rare nowadays are instances of people being baptized, married, seeing their children marry, and their grandchildren grow up within the same community. Yet the parochial and congregational organization of the churches and their forms of ministry are based on the assumption that this is the norm. How, then, can the Church be the Church, and how can it minister effectively in the world today? There is increasing sensitivity to the need to take cognizance of social realities, of the nature of industrialized and technological society, of the unlikelihood of decrease in the size of metropolitan areas, and of the highly mobile state both of the metropolitan and rural population.

In recent years many studies have been published relating to the problems of the Church in the modern situation. Here I shall speak of two of the best known: Professor Gibson Winter's *The Suburban Captivity of the Churches* (1962),[30] and Professor Harvey Cox's *The Secular City* (1965).[31]

GIBSON WINTER: THE SUBURBAN CAPTIVITY OF THE CHURCHES

Gibson Winter begins with a sociological study of the development of the modern city and of the movements of population within the growing metropolitan areas. He writes of the North American city, but his analysis applies to many cities elsewhere. Industrial plants, railway stations and yards, and centres of all kinds of business were first established in or close to the centre of the city. Owners, managers, and workers lived close at hand. As the city prospered and became more crowded, wealthier citizens moved out from the centre, establishing new residential areas. As soon as they could afford to do so, the middle classes and those workers who had advanced themselves began to do the same. Thus the city becomes encircled by 'residential rings' for the upper and middle classes and skilled workers. Unskilled workers remain in the centre, living in the deteriorating dwelling-houses of former generations. Meanwhile, successful industrialization creates a demand for more workers which is met by immigration from rural areas, other countries and, in the United States especially, of blacks. These different groups tend naturally to live in close proximity, and thus ghettos are created. Such cities have become divided into separate areas whose residents are 'homogeneous'. The suburban dwellers find their personal fulfilment in their families and among friends in their neighbourhood, and do their utmost to protect the homogeneity of their suburb from the encroachments of others. The city centre becomes more crowded and less able to provide the services to make life tolerable. The resources of the wealthy are now primarily used to preserve their own communities, and the cost of providing adequate services in the city centre is beyond the means of those who live there.

Winter maintains that the churches (and he writes principally of the Protestant churches) have failed to adapt to the new situation. The situation is that in the metropolitan areas, instead of heterogeneous parishes or pastoral charges in which people of every social class live and work in close proximity, there now exists a conglomeration of homogeneous residential areas, ranging from the ghettos of the centre to the rich neighbourhoods of the outer ring. In those wealthy suburbs exclusiveness is carefully guarded, and relationships outside the community are on a strictly impersonal level.

> Since churches have traditionally anchored their communal life in residential areas, they inevitably become victims of the pathology that assails neighbourhood life.... How can an inclusive message be mediated through an exclusive group, when the principle of exclusiveness is social-class identity rather than a gift of faith which is open to all? (*The Suburban Captivity*, pp. 32–3).

Winter deplores the fact that the churches' leaders, 'confronted with a dilemma between organizational expansion and responsibility for the central city',[32] have too often concentrated on the middle-class suburbs:

> Denominational leaders have watched the new residential areas surrounding the central cities with greedy eyes. These are largely middle- and upper-class residential areas; they have adequate resources for constructing church buildings; their residents are responsive to religious programs; in fact, denominational leaders call these 'high potential areas'. . . . In recent decades almost exclusive attention has been given to establishing churches in suburban areas (ibid., p. 35).[33]

Although there are notable exceptions, ministry in central city areas has been left to a diminishing number of the churches of the main denominations, understaffed and with steadily decreasing congregations as members 'better' themselves and move out, and to small sectarian churches. The churches have been concerned about survival rather than ministry.[34] Yet by identifying themselves with the middle classes and failure to minister to the whole metropolitan area, they have cut themselves off from a much larger membership.[35]

Thus the social inclusiveness of the early church has been exchanged for the exclusive church of the metropolis.[36] Society has established a pattern by which 'residential association is . . . built almost exclusively around similarity in economic rank', and churches which 'organize their congregations or parishes primarily around residential neighborhoods' inevitably find that their congregations are 'a cluster of people of like social and economic position'.[37]

> A new image of the Church is emerging in the contemporary world, an image created by the domination of contemporary life by economic activities. The Church is now a reflection of the economic ladder (ibid., pp. 76–7).

Congregations have become primarily economic peer groups, and only secondarily believing and worshipping communities.[38] Inclusiveness, which is an important aspect of catholicity and therefore intrinsic to the nature of the Church, is forgotten.[39] The organizational activity of the suburban church is so closely geared to the maintenance of the exclusive residential group that the concept of mission and reconciliation reaching to the whole metropolis is lost.[40] The suburban church becomes introverted:

> The introverted church is one which puts its own survival before its mission, its own identity before its task, its internal concerns before its

apostolate, its rituals before its ministry ... [it] stresses the Church as structure at the expense of the mission and task of the Church. . . . Undue emphasis on the static structure of the Church has led to the disappearance of a significant lay ministry in denominational Protestantism. Loss of dynamic form and surrender of mission undercut the lay ministry, for it is the Church as mission which rests its case upon the laity and their outreach to the world. The more introverted the Church, the more it becomes subject to priestcraft and routinized activities. The introverted Church substitutes celebrations of its own unity for witness in the metropolis. An introverted church is an apostate body, for it denies the essential quality of Church—the testimony of reconciliation in the world (ibid., pp. 120–21).

In the middle-class areas which are distant from the place of work of the residents, the churches' ministry is almost entirely confined to the family concerns and leisure interests of their members. In allowing their ministry to be circumscribed in this way, the churches withdrew from the context of public accountability.[41] It is not that pastoral concern for people's private and family lives is wrong; but exclusive identification of ministry with the private sphere encourages the widespread idea that Christianity is irrelevant to all other areas of man's life and activity. The churches need a new vision of the metropolis and of their mission to it.

'To be the Church is to be involved in mission. To be the Church in the metropolis is to be rooted in the missionary task to inner city and suburb as an interdependent process.'[42] Ministry to fragments of society,.and those the most comfortably placed, is to ignore that 'there is strong warrant in Scriptures for beginning with the areas of greatest personal, physical, and social need—the poor of the earth—as the decisive point for estimating the form appropriate to the task' of ministry.[43]

Winter is convinced that the Church must minister to the whole metropolis. He sees certain experimental ministries which are often of an ecumenical nature, and which cut across parochial boundaries and transcend traditional congregational concerns as pointing a way forward. But his main suggestion[44] is that, so far as metropolitan areas are concerned, the basic unit of ministry should be not the parish or congregation as we have known it, but a sector of the city stretching from its heart to the outer edges, 'from blight to suburb, Negro to White, blue collar to white collar, down-and-out to privilege'.[45] A council of representatives drawn from the whole area would make the decisions about use of money and buildings, and the kind of ministries to be engaged in, according to developing needs. Some such development of organic interdependence between neighbourhoods and ministries he sees as a way in which the Church may be renewed. It would provide opportunities and a challenge to lay men and women to engage in a ministry much more Christian than the round of activities which are invented for the consolidation and perpetuation of an exclusive suburban enclave.

> Until men and women are drawn into the missionary enterprise of the Church, they do not discover the meaning of their baptism. . . . The sector ministry, or any other interdependent form of Christian community, is essential as a context of ministry and Christian experience; everyone who joins the Christian Church should have an opportunity to serve in the lay ministry, when he can answer for the faith that is in him and discover his true identity in Christ through sharing in His reconciling work. The breakthrough from a local enclave to a public platform of ministry and worship is essential for the renewal of the churches and for the recovery of the lay apostolate (ibid., pp. 179–80).

The parish and the congregation *as units for the Church's ministry* represent, Winter contends, 'an arrested form of development'. In most cases they do not provide an opportunity for people to become both a receiving and a giving community, a ministering and missionary fellowship. Evolution, therefore, must be towards an organically interdependent ministry which transcends the social barriers of life in the city, whatever may be the structural details necessary to bring this about in different places. 'The Church is deformed by the struggle to survive and reformed only as ministry and mission.'[46]

Although his book concentrates on the Church's ministry to the modern city, Winter is not unmindful of the Godward life of the Church, expressed in faith and worship. The Church has many privileges and graces bestowed upon it by the Holy Spirit. But they are given to it on behalf of the world. Ministry is obedience to Christ, so that, in demonstrating the meaning of community to the metropolis, the Church is no mere servant of the world, but the servant of Christ and his Spirit.[47]

HARVEY COX: THE SECULAR CITY

Professor Harvey Cox's *The Secular City* has two sub-titles: 'Secularization and Urbanization in Theological Perspective' on the inside title page, and 'A Celebration of its Liberties and an Invitation to its Discipline' on the cover. The latter indicates that Professor Cox welcomes the evolution of the secular city, that same metropolitan area about which Winter writes. Some readers[48] have felt that, although he distinguishes between the kingdom of God and the secular city, the two are very close together in Cox's thought. 'The idea of the secular city supplies us with the most promising image, by which *both* to understand what the New Testament writers called "the kingdom of God" *and* to develop a viable theology of revolutionary social change.'[49] He sees in the secular city 'a present-day sign of the kingdom of God'.[50] The anonymity of the city, its opportunities for mobility and its technology offer the citizen privacy, freedom, and happy leisure respectively, and these things he regards as good and the will of God.[51] The same sub-title shows that Cox, however, knows that the secular city calls for discipline. All is not well with the secular city. There are 'urban fractures'. There is a crisis, a challenge which man must accept.

With Bonhoeffer he regards secularization[52] as a maturing process in the history of man, and as 'basically a liberating development'.[53] The process, he suggests, stems from the biblical literature. The Hebrew doctrine of creation desacralizes nature; the exodus from Egypt, being a revolt against a duly constituted monarch, points to the desacralizing of politics ('no one rules by divine right in secular society');[54] the prohibition of 'graven images' in the Sinai Covenant desacralizes and relativizes all human values ('for the ancients, gods and value systems were the same thing').[55] Under biblical and Christian influence, though slowly and with many hesitations, secularization has proceeded to the point at which the technopolis, made possible by modern technology, has emerged:

> Our task should be to nourish the secularization process, to prevent it hardening into a rigid world-view (viz., secularism). Furthermore, we should be constantly on the lookout for movements which attempt to thwart and reverse the liberating irritant of secularization (*The Secular City*, p. 36).

The few years which have elapsed since Cox wrote have made it clear that there are indeed such threats. The anonymity which he regards as a liberating characteristic is also a cloak for crime. Statistics show a rapid increase of serious crime in most big cities. Mobility is the last word which would occur to a commuter in any large city of the western world between 4.0 and 6.0 pm. Despite technology some public services have deteriorated, notably postal services and street-cleaning. The opinion grows that the particular expression of technological advance which Cox calls 'technopolis' is a mistake. Be that as it may, our concern is with Cox's doctrine of the Church.

THE CHURCH AS GOD'S *AVANT-GARDE*

'The starting-point for any theology of the Church today', Cox writes, 'must be a theology of social change. The Church is first of all a responding community, a people whose task it is to discern the action of God in the world and to join in His work.'[56] But the Church which should, therefore, be responding to social change is still working with definitions of itself which belong to the past. A Church which recognizes the significance and challenge of the process of secularization must be prepared to be reshaped continuously by God's action. It must be God's *avant-garde*.

The Church is the people of God. God in Christ went, and goes, before the Church into the world, and the Church must follow him where the action is. The action, Cox is convinced, is in the secular city, the sign of the coming kingdom of God, of the new régime. Only when Christian people recognize where God is at work, and discern what their function must be, can their institutional forms be decided. In fact, he suggests, 'a doctrine of the Church is a secondary and derivative aspect of theology which comes *after* a discussion of God's action in calling man to co-operation in the bringing of the kingdom'.[57] The institutional forms must be such as to enable the people of God to locate and participate in the mission of God, to continue the ministry of Jesus as he described it in his reply to John the Baptist (Luke 4.18–19). In traditional terms it is a ministry of *kerygma* (proclamation), *diakonia* (reconciliation, healing, service) and *koinonia* (fellowship).

'Because the new régime breaks in at different points and in different ways, it is not possible to forecast in advance just what appearance the Church will have.'[58] Nor, because cities differ, is it possible to describe a missionary strategy appropriate for all places. But everywhere the task must be *kerygmatic*, *diakonic* and *koinoniac*: to proclaim 'that a revolution is under way and that the pivotal battle has already taken place'.[59]

The *kerygma* is the message that 'God has defeated the

"principalities and powers" by Jesus and has made it possible for man to become the "heir", the master of the created world'.[60] The 'principalities and powers' of this age of the secular city are those forces which still cripple and corrupt human freedom. Cox cites as examples the concepts of the *id*, of the collective unconscious, of the dialectic of history, of statistical probability and economic pressures. These were not meant to control man. God's action, made known in Jesus, calls man to freedom from the 'principalities and powers' and to responsibility in controlling them. Men must accept responsibility in and for the city of man.

The Church's diakonic ministry is best defined as healing or reconciling, and must be directed to the 'urban fractures', the cleavage between city centre and suburbs, rich and poor, racial groups and political parties. Like Gibson Winter, Cox regards the desertion of the city centre by the Protestant churches as shameful, and not to be rectified by planting mission churches or patronizing incursions from outside. It is rather a matter of Christian suburbanites participating in a revolution aimed at decreasing the power of the suburbs in relation to the less privileged sections. To work for changed banking practices, new zoning laws, more equitable school financing and tax structures calls for sacrifice on the part of suburbanites. But it is *diakonia*.[61]

The Church's koinoniac function is to make visible 'a kind of living picture of the character and composition of the true city of man'. The Church is already what Rudolf Bultmann calls the eschatological community, and what Karl Barth describes as 'God's providential demonstration of his intention for all humanity'. The Church 'occurs' where its three functions occur, and where 'a new inclusive human community emerges'.[62] It must include 'all the elements of the heterogeneous metropolis'. If it is divided along ethnic, racial, or denominational lines it is not performing its koinoniac function. It is not a Church at all, but a group of antichurches, unable to break out of the past. The true eschatological nature of the Church will be shown when it is recognized that

> |Jesus Christ| is always ahead of the Church, beckoning it to get up to date, never behind it waiting to be refurbished. Canon and tradition function not as sources of revelation but as precedents by which present events can be checked out as the possible *loci* of God's action (ibid., p. 148).

THE CHURCH AS CULTURAL EXORCIST

Cox believes that the three functions of the Church come together in its role as 'cultural exorcist'. The casting out of demons was central in Jesus' ministry. The N.T. demoniacs really believed that they were possessed by demons. The culture and society which surrounded them persuaded them of it. Modern man is no less prone to irrationalities caused by his own repressions or by the projection of others on to him. Modern society, even in the secular city, is riddled by attitudes, prejudices, and norms which belong to the past. Exorcism in the twentieth century is 'that process by which the stubborn deposits of town and tribal pasts are scraped from the social consciousness of man'.[63] To set men free to see things as they really are 'was what Jesus was always doing, and it represents an indispensable element of the Church's function in the secular city'.[64]

> The ministry of exorcism in the secular city requires a community of persons who, individually and collectively, are not burdened by the constriction of an archaic heritage. It requires a community which, if not fully liberated, is in the process of liberation from compulsive patterns of behavior based on mistaken images of the world. In performing its function the Church should be such a community and should be sensitive to those currents in modern life which bear the same exorcizing power. The Church should be ready to expose the fallaciousness of the social myths by which the injustices of a society are perpetuated and to suggest ways of action which demonstrate the wrongness of such fantasies (ibid., p. 155).

Such an idea of the Church is seen by many as an intolerable threat to the forms of Church life which they have known. It is Cox's opinion that the real ecumenical crisis today is not between Catholic and Protestant, but between those who are ready to explore new structures and modes of Church life and those who are not.[65] The structural changes and new forms of ministry which he goes on to suggest are along lines similar to those proposed by Gibson Winter; and in Part Three of his book he discusses the work of the Church as cultural exorcist in the contexts of work and leisure, sexual relations, and the secular university.

As we have seen, Cox's delineation of the Church and its functions is largely drawn from the realm of political action. He is, however, convinced that his conception rests on biblical foundations.

It is important to remind ourselves of another important feature of the biblical view of the Church [i.e. other than the description of the Church as *avant-garde* and exorcist]: *only faith can discern the Church of Jesus Christ*. It is not an entity which can be empirically detected and located by a bulletin board or a sociological survey. Only God knows the name of His saints. Furthermore, the Greek word for church, *ecclesia*, is a word of motion. It refers to those on the way, responding to the herald's announcement. The Church is what such diverse theologians as Karl Barth, Rudolf Bultmann, and Gerhard Ebeling have called 'an event'. It *happens*. It occurs where the reconciling actuality of God's work in human history comes to fulfilment and is brought to human speech. ... The Church is the word-event by which reconciliation across the divisive lines of race, nation, belief, sex, age, and social status occurs, and men live, if only provisionally, in the new age (ibid., pp. 225–6).

To say that the Church is an object of faith is not to say that it is invisible. Yet it is 'not a building, a budget, a program, an organization. It is a people in motion, an "eventful movement" in which barriers are being struck down and a radically new community ... is emerging'.[66]

22

The Ecclesiology of Karl Barth

There is little doubt that Karl Barth (1886–1968) was the most outstanding Protestant theologian of the first two-thirds of the twentieth century. Born in Berne, Switzerland, he studied there and in Germany, and following twelve years in pastoral ministry became a professor successively at Göttingen (1921), Münster (1925), and Bonn (1930). When Hitler came to power in 1933, Barth was among the foremost of those who resisted the attempt to subjugate the Evangelical Church to National Socialism, and was the principal draftsman of the courageous Barmen Declaration (1934). On refusing to take an oath of allegiance to Hitler, he was deprived of his chair at Bonn in 1935, and returned to Switzerland, becoming Professor of Theology at Basel, a post which he held until he retired in 1962. His greatest work was the four huge volumes of *Church Dogmatics (Die Kirkliche Dogmatik)* begun in 1932, which occupied him for well over twenty years.[1]

Barth's Commentary on the Epistle to the Romans (*Der Römerbrief*), published in 1919 with an enlarged edition in 1921,[2] first gained him prominence. It was a sharp rejection of the liberal theology which had dominated German Protestantism since the time of Schleiermacher. His study of Romans convinced him that liberal theology had neglected the great themes of N.T. theology. With an optimistic estimate of man and reliance on the capability of human reason, it had brushed aside the Pauline insistence on the sovereignty and righteousness of God, the sinfulness of man, and God's initiative in man's salvation through revelation and by grace. Barth utterly rejects 'natural theology'. If man searches for God by the light of his reason he will find only an idol of his own creation, and not the God who can only be known as he reveals himself. God is not an object of man's search. There is an 'infinite qualitative difference' between God and man—a phrase which Barth takes from Kierkegaard. God is transcendent, wholly other, always Subject and never Object.

Students of Barth have noted development in his theology, something not unlikely during a writing career of some fifty years. Barth himself readily admitted in an address delivered in 1956[3] that there were certain exaggerations in his early theology, but maintained that its forthrightness was necessary in the decade following the First World War. He had not retreated from his earlier basic affirmations of the otherness, priority, and freedom of God and his graciousness in revelation. It was rather a question of revision, 'a new beginning and attack in which what previously has been said is to be said more than ever, but now even better'.[4] Barth by then had ceased to use terms like 'the infinite qualitative difference' between God and man. The address mentioned above was, indeed, on 'The Humanity of God', which 'rightly understood,' he says, 'is bound to mean God's relation to and turning towards man'.[5] This is not to deny God's sovereignty, for it is in his divine freedom that he wills to be the God of man, to be for man, entering into history and into dialogue with man. 'It is precisely God's *deity* which, if rightly understood, includes his *humanity*.'[6] We know this through his revelation, his Word, in Jesus Christ. The theme (although the phrase 'the humanity of God' does not appear) is worked out at length in *Church Dogmatics*, volume iv, 'The Doctrine of Reconciliation', part 1, published in 1953.

Some have discerned also a development in Barth's doctrine of the Church. Emilien Lamirande, a Roman Catholic scholar, distinguishes four periods in its evolution:[7] the period of the commentary on Romans, characterized by a very negative attitude to the Church; an intermediate period of some ten years to the beginning of the *Church Dogmatics* (1932), which he describes as 'the period of the Word of God and of the Church as pure event'; third, the period of the *Church Dogmatics* 'which brings out more explicitly the link between the Church and the Incarnate Word'; and finally a period inaugurated by the 1956 lecture on 'The Humanity of God'.

Lamirande says that in the first period Barth 'envisages the Church as an attempt to humanize the divine, to comprehend it, to secularize it. ... The Church was seen as a form of the religion of the world, a form of sin, in opposition to revelation, but also as a way to the gospel, in this sense at least, that she reveals what we are: sinners and darkness'.[8] H. R. Mackintosh in his *Types of Modern Theology* (1937)[9] notes some of the more radical things which Barth says in the *Römerbrief*: 'The work of the Church is the work of men: it can never be God's work'; 'In the Church the hostility of man against God is brought to a head; for there human indifference, misunderstanding, and opposition attain their most sublime and also their most naive form.' But Mackintosh, like Lamirande, notes that Barth declares that the Church is not to be forsaken: 'It would never enter our heads to think of leaving the Church. For in describing the Church we are describing ourselves.'[10] At this stage Barth lays stress on the Church as an institution, subject to the weaknesses of every human organization. Yet it is the community of justified sinners, 'the place of fruitful and hopeful repentance'[11] and an instrument of God for man's salvation.

THE CHURCH AS 'EVENT'

Lamirande denotes the second period of Barth's ecclesiology as that of the Church as 'pure event'. But this is a concept which endures in Barth's thought, being closely linked to his unswerving insistence on the sovereignty and free grace of God. It has been called his 'actualism'. Man as such is and possesses nothing that is not God's gift. His life as man, the Word of revelation, his faith, his communityness in the Church are God's continuing gifts. Man has these things only *in actu*, by an act of God, an event. It is a dynamic as opposed to a static concept of the relationship between God and man. The faith of a Christian, then, is an event.[12] So is the existence of the Church. The Word given to the Church to be proclaimed must continually be received and proclaimed. Otherwise whatever word the Church spoke would not be the Word of God and the Church would not be the Church. The Word is always an act of God, an event. The Church, therefore, which exists to proclaim the Word of God, is also an act of God, an event.[13] To some this has suggested an idea of the Church as fluctuating between existence and non-existence according as it does or does not proclaim the Word of God. Thus Lamirande writes:

> Barth persistently insisted that the Church is pure event, that she has nothing of her own, that her very being is the being of God and of Christ. The Church appeared as the transient, discontinuous, the event which occurs in the institution and is thus made visible to the eyes of faith. Through God's sovereign action, the Church is at every moment actualized, she is a totally dynamic event. Thus Barth apparently failed to acknowledge her objective permanent reality. To the eyes of a Roman Catholic, his position was still, in this period, radical actualism, tantamount to a mere negation of the Church.[14]

There seems to be inconsistency in this paragraph, for how can the Church be both 'transient, discontinuous' and 'at every moment actualized'? But Lamirande is voicing a criticism which others[15] have raised against Barth's actualism and his consequent denial that there is a *state* of being a Christian and that the Church is a *static* entity. But, as Dr Herbert Hartwell has pointed out,[16]

> Barth's actualism does not mean ... that his theology leaves no room for the idea of a 'state' of things. It only denotes that there can be no 'state' which does not arise out of God's constant giving. ... Act and being are linked up in Barth's theology in such a way that there is no 'being' apart from God's continued action, and this action takes place in the freedom of the divine grace.

Barth's actualism is another way of insisting on the principle of 'grace alone' and of rejecting triumphalism in the Church or in the Christian individual.

BARTH'S DEVELOPED ECCLESIOLOGY

Lamirande speaks of the third period in the development of Barth's ecclesiology as that of the *Church Dogmatics*. This is somewhat misleading, since the two halves of volume iv, part 3, were not published in Switzerland until 1959, three years after the lecture which he suggests inaugurates the fourth period! Lamirande probably means to indicate the period from 1932 to 1955, the date of publication of *CD* iv, 2, after which four years elapsed before the appearance of iv, 3. Just as we noted[17] that there is reason to doubt whether a distinction can properly be made between a second and a third period in Barth's ecclesiology (at least in quite the way Lamirande wishes to make it), so we may doubt whether the lecture on 'The Humanity of God' marks a new development in his doctrine of the Church. However this may be, although the Church is discussed in many contexts in the earlier volumes of *CD*, it is in volume iv, 'The Doctrine of Reconciliation', that we find Barth's fullest treatment. Part 1, published in 1953, has a section on 'The Holy Spirit and the Gathering of the Christian Community', and part 3, second half (1959) has a section on 'The Holy Spirit and the Sending of the Christian Community'. To these sections I now turn.

THE HOLY SPIRIT AND THE GATHERING OF
THE CHRISTIAN COMMUNITY

Barth prefaces this section with a summary:

> The Holy Spirit is the awakening power in which Jesus Christ has formed
> and continually renews His body, i.e. His own earthly-historical form of
> existence, the one holy, catholic, and apostolic Church. This is Christen-
> dom, i.e. the gathering of the community of those whom already before all
> others He has made willing and ready for life under the divine verdict
> executed in His death and revealed in His resurrection from the dead. It is
> therefore the provisional representation of the whole world of humanity
> justified in Him (*CD* iv, 1, p. 643).

The Church has its being in the divine *actus* of God in the Word of
his revelation in Jesus Christ. It is the true Church only as Jesus
Christ, the risen Lord, is present and acting in and through its
members. This he does through the power of the Holy Spirit.

> It is still God Himself in this work, in the strict sense in which the same
> must be said of the work of creation and the objective realization of the
> work of Atonement in Jesus Christ (ibid., pp. 645–6).

> In everything that we have to say concerning the Christian community
> and Christian faith we can move only within the circle that they are
> founded by the Holy Spirit and therefore that they must be continually
> refounded by Him, but that the necessary refounding by the Holy Spirit
> can consist only in a renewal of the founding which He has already ac-
> complished (ibid., p. 647).

> Fundamentally and in general practice we cannot say more of the Holy
> Spirit and His work than that He is the Power in which Jesus Christ
> attests Himself effectively, creating in man response and obedience (ibid.,
> p. 648).

The Church, then, has its being in a new and continuous creative
work of God. In describing its being, Barth says that we must aban-
don the usual distinctions between being and act, status and dynamic,
essence and existence:

> Its act is its being, its status its dynamic, its essence its existence. The
> Church *is* when it takes place that God lets certain men live as His ser-
> vants, His friends, His children, the witnesses of the reconciliation of the
> world with himself as it has taken place in Jesus Christ, the preachers of
> the victory which has been won in Him over sin and suffering, the heralds
> of His future revelation in which the glory of the Creator will be declared

to all creation as that of His love and faithfulness and mercy (ibid., pp. 650–51).[18]

Barth insists on the visibility of the Church ('no sect, however spiritual, can completely escape it'[19]). A doctrine that the Church is invisible is an ecclesiastical docetism which is as impossible as a Christological docetism. God is for the world, and His Church is for the world. Christ was the incarnate Word of God in the world, and His Church is in the world. 'The Christian community as such cannot exist as an ideal commune or universum but—also in time and space—only in the relationship of its individual members as they are fused together by the common action of the Word which they have heard into a definite human fellowship; in concrete form, therefore, and visible to everyone.'[20] There is, indeed, an 'invisible aspect which is the secret of the visible',[21] and this is that 'the community is the earthly-historical form of existence of Jesus Christ Himself'.[22] Knowing this, the Church cannot but be involved visibly in the conflicts and dangers of history.

Barth then discusses[23] the Pauline doctrine of the Church as the body of Christ which he takes to be neither symbolic nor metaphysical, but a statement of the reality that the Christian community is the earthly-historical form of Christ's existence. He then turns to the four credal notes of the Church: 'I believe one holy, catholic, and apostolic Church.' The principle of interpretation is that these marks belong to the Church in so far as it is the earthly-historical form of existence of the one living Lord, and that they can only be recognized by faith. Barth's discussion is lengthy, and I shall here refer to his main points, and as much as possible, through quotation, allow him to speak for himself.

THE CHURCH IS ONE

The Church in its visible and invisible aspects is one: 'The one is the form and the other the mystery of one and the self-same Church.'[24] Likewise the Church militant and the Church triumphant are one. The people of Israel both before and after Christ and the Christian Church initiated on the day of Pentecost are two forms and aspects of the one inseparable community.[25] Barth speaks of the existence of a Judaism which does not believe in Jesus Christ as something which makes even the Church's own existence problematical, 'an ontological impossibility', 'a gaping hole in the body of Christ, something which is quite intolerable'. The Jewish question, if Paul is right in Romans 9–11, is the Christian question.[26]

The existence of Christian communities in different places does not damage the unity of the Church, but the existence of different and opposing churches does:

> It is an impossible situation that whole groups of Christian communities should exhibit a certain external and internal unity among themselves and yet stand in relation to other groups of equally Christian communities in an attitude more or less of exclusion (ibid., p. 676).

Recognizing that separate churches sincerely claim Jesus Christ for themselves, each believing that his real presence is among them, Barth's plea is that they should act upon their belief that he really is the present, living, and speaking Lord,[27] and listen to him:

> In the realization of faith in the one Church in face of its disunity, the decisive step is that the divided churches should honestly and seriously try to hear and perhaps hear the voice of the Lord by them and for them, and then try to hear, and perhaps actually hear, the voice of others. Where a church does this, in its own place, and without leaving it, it is on the way to the one Church. It is clear that in so doing it has already abandoned its claim to be identical with the one Church in contrast to the others, and in this sense to be the only Church. The claim has been dashed out of its hand by the One who is the unity of the Church . . . and if it lets Him open the question of its individual existence, then it will automatically be open to the other churches in the sense that it will be willing and ready to let them say something to it, thus renouncing, in fact, its isolation as the only Church, its exclusion of all other churches (ibid., p. 684).

THE CHURCH IS HOLY

> Holy means set apart, marked off, and therefore differentiated, singled out, taken (and set) on one side as a being which has its own origin and nature and meaning and direction—and all this with a final definitiveness, decisively, inviolably and unalterably, because it is God who does it. The term indicates the contradistinction of the Christian community . . . to the other gatherings and societies which exist in the world (ibid., p. 685).

'It is God who does it', and God does it by the calling of his Word and the gathering of his Holy Spirit:

> What else can the holiness of the Church be but the reflection of the holiness of Jesus Christ as its heavenly Head, falling upon it as He enters

into and remains in fellowship with it by His Holy Spirit? ... In the existence of the community we have to do with the earthly-historical form of His existence. As it is gathered and built up and commissioned by the Holy Spirit it becomes and is this particular part of the creaturely world, acquiring a part of His holiness, although of and in itself it is not holy, it is nothing out of the ordinary, indeed as His community within Adamic humanity it is just as unholy as that humanity, sharing its sin and guilt and standing absolutely in need of its justification (ibid., pp. 686–7).

The Church is holy only as the body of Christ, because He, the Head is holy; holy only in its community with Him, gathered to Him by the Holy Spirit. It is not a question of an individual acquiring holiness and *therefore* becoming a member of the Church. In the N.T. the 'partner' of Jesus Christ is the community. 'The community lives in Christians, Christians live in the community, and in this way Jesus Christ lives in the world. In this way they are holy in Him and with Him.'[28] Barth remarks that this is to say something very like *extra ecclesiam nulla salus*. Yet he will not restrict the freedom of God to save outside the Church. It must, however, be said that outside the Church there is no revelation, no faith, no knowledge of salvation, and no holiness. 'There is no legitimate private Christianity', for the Holy Spirit leads the individual 'directly into the community and not into a private relationship with Christ.'[29]

Barth in no way avoids the fact that the holy community, indestructible because it is the body of Christ and possesses his promise (Matt. 16.18), has constantly failed and fallen into error: 'When has it been the case that men could simply see the good works of Christians and had to glorify their Father which is in heaven?'[30] The Church is always in need of reformation, always needs to pray 'forgive us our trespasses'.

The Creed says 'I believe one holy, catholic Church', not 'I believe *in* ...'. We can only believe *in* God, Father, Son, and Holy Spirit. We believe the existence of the holy Church because of the promise of the Holy God. It is a matter of the perception of faith, and therefore: 'We all do well to begin with the question how it is with ourselves', with a readiness to allow to count in favour of others what we believe to be in our own favour, which, stripped to its essential basis, is that 'the Holy One of his free grace has called us into his Holy community'.[31]

THE CHURCH IS CATHOLIC

'Catholic' means general, comprehensive. Applied to the Church it speaks of 'a character in virtue of which it is always and everywhere the same and always and everywhere recognizable in this sameness, to the preservation of which it is committed'.[32] The term 'catholic' implicitly raises the question of a Church which is false, heretical, even apostate. *Credo catholicam ecclesiam* means 'I believe in the existence of a community which in the essence which makes it a Christian community is unalterable in spite of all its changes of form, which in this essence never has altered and never can or will alter. And negatively, I do not believe that a community which is different in essence is the Christian community'.[33]

Catholicity is not negated by geographical and cultural variety: 'In essence the Church is the same in all races, languages, cultures, and classes, in all forms of State and society',[34] and it must not accept any kind of dependence on any other society. Every church must always seriously ask whether it is merely a respectable expression of local culture; whether it is an instrument of the ruling class; whether it is simply tolerated because its moral stance is considered useful for the State. In short it must ask: 'Does it exist of its essence and in faithfulness to its essence? We must never think that we can arrive at a position where we will not be disturbed by this question' (ibid., pp. 703–4).

'Catholic' also indicates a temporal dimension for the Church. It exists in history: 'It is in a way which is surrounded by a continually changing landscape and in which it is itself subject to change—but in which it can never be anything other than itself.'[35] Barth here criticizes both 'ecclesiastical romanticism' and 'flirtation with the new'. The Church is the true and catholic Church, 'only to the extent that in its own age it participates in the essence of the one Church, being faithful to it and knowing how to do it justice in its visible expression'.[36] What counts is not progress—a highly doubtful idea as applied to the Church—but continual reformation.

The Church is also catholic, general, and comprehensive, in its relationship to individual members. Again Barth insists that 'the Christian is first a member of the Christian community and only then, and as such, this individual Christian in his particular Christian being and nature and presence'.[37] He insists strongly on the priority of the Church over its members, something which, he says, has been flagrantly neglected in modern Protestantism. He devotes a long note[38] to the 'depressing phenomena' of churches which, even in official documents, assume that individuals first become Christians and *then*, out of community of interest, join themselves into a church. He concludes his treatment of catholicity by acknowledging that too frequently the Church has failed to maintain it: 'There is hardly a church which in this respect has not been seriously, perhaps very seriously, damaged.'[39] In particular, 'where a church thinks that it cannot and should not merely believe its catholicity but should be able—in its own form—to see and maintain it, then in its arrogance and unreadiness to repent, this church shows itself to be a-catholic'.[40]

As with its unity and holiness, so with its catholicity, the Church has no control over it. The Church is the earthly-historical form of the existence of Christ, and its catholicity is grounded in him as its Head. The community is catholic only as he lives, speaks, and acts within it and as it listens and is obedient. The mark of catholicity is only to be recognized and realized by an active faith in Jesus Christ as its Head.[41]

THE CHURCH IS APOSTOLIC

Barth contends that 'apostolic', introduced in the creed of the Council of Constantinople in 381, does not add anything new to the three other predicates, but does provide the criterion by which a judgement can be made whether 'in this or that case we have or have not to do with the one holy, catholic Church'. This criterion is spiritual (to be understood only, like the Church's oneness, holiness, and catholicity, by faith in the Head of the Church),[42] but it is also concrete:

> Apostolic means in the discipleship, in the school, under the normative authority, instruction, and direction of the apostles, in agreement with them and accepting their message. The Church is the true Church and therefore the one holy Church in the fact and to the extent that it is apostolic in this sense, and by this fact it can and should be distinguished from the false Church (ibid., p. 714).

Apostolicity especially emphasizes the being of the Christian community as an event. A relationship to the apostles can only take place in a history between the community and the apostles. He who wishes to recognize the community as apostolic must himself take part in this history:

> He cannot be a neutral and decide its apostolicity from outside. He must be a living member, and as such must know its basis in the apostles, himself standing in their discipleship, in their school, under their authority and direction, himself hearing their witness, himself being taught and

questioned by them. He must be put by them in a definite movement, in the movement in which they found themselves, in which they still find themselves today—for in the New Testament they are still before us in living speech and action. To be in the community of Jesus Christ means to take part in this movement (ibid., pp. 714–15).

Barth rejects the idea that the Church's apostolicity can be sought on historical and juridical grounds. He refers to the claim that historical proof can support the notion that apostolic authority and office is transmitted successively to supreme office-bearers in the Church, 'e.g. from a bishop to his successor, and from this successor to the inferior ministers who will be ordained by him'.[43] This kind of apostolic succession may be as a 'welcome adornment' of the institution of a church. To prove the possession of it is a matter of historico-critical examination of a list of names—which has little to do with the Holy Spirit, or with faith. It does not, however, guarantee apostolicity[44] as Barth understands it. It seems, moreover, to involve an unscriptural doctrine which asserts that the Holy Spirit can be controlled, and his presence and action confined:

> How can apostolic authority, and power and mission, how can the Holy Spirit be transferred, when obviously apostolicity is His work and gift?—as though the Holy Spirit were a legal or technical or symbolical It (ibid., p. 717).

Barth maintains that the apostolicity of the Church belongs with its character as the earthly-historical form of the existence of Jesus Christ in which he gives himself to be known to the community and through it to the world. The earthly-historical medium of his self-manifestation is those who knew him as the Word made flesh in the form of a servant and then in his glory—namely, the apostles. These he chose, called, ordained, and sent out as his direct witnesses. They are the rock on which he builds his Church. They do not build his community. He is the builder, they his servants. It is in this serving that their normative significance lies, and that they are the holy apostles. He speaks through them. He who hears them hears him. He himself and the awakening power of his Holy Spirit have no other earthly-historical form than the apostles' witnessing power. Only when their witness is proclaimed, received, accepted, and reproduced is the community present.[45]

> Thus the existence of His community is always its history in its encounter with this witness—the history in which it is faithful or unfaithful to it in its

exposition and application. There is, therefore, a legitimate apostolic succession, the existence of a Church in the following of the apostles, only when it takes place in this history that the apostolic witness finds in a community discipleship, hearing, obedience, respect, and observance. But it is in the fact that they serve that the apostles follow the Lord Himself and precede the community. It would, therefore, be very strange if the community for its part tried to follow them in any other authority, power, and mission than that of their service (ibid., p. 719).

There is but one true apostolic succession, and it is a succession of service, of the *ministerium verbi*, not of *dominium*.

Barth points out that this interpretation of apostolicity is identical in substance with a term used, in a different context, 'to describe the authority of the Bible as the source and norm of the existence and doctrine and order of the Church—the "Scripture-principle" '.[46] The apostles are the original disciples of the evangelical records, the eye-witnesses of the Messiah of Israel. Consequently, the apostolic Church is that which bears the apostolic witness of the N.T., which reads the Scriptures as the direct witness to Jesus Christ alive yesterday and today, which is constantly in encounter with the biblical witness, which allows the Holy Spirit to direct it to look in the direction in which Scripture looks, to the living Jesus Christ:

> As Scripture stirs up and invites and summons and impels the Church to look in this same direction, there takes place the work of the Spirit of Scripture who is the Holy Spirit. Scripture then works in the service of its Lord, and the Church becomes and is apostolic and therefore the true Church (ibid., p. 723).

THE CHURCH AS SERVANT

In his treatment of apostolicity, Barth has emphasized the note of service which we have seen to be prominent in twentieth-century ecclesiology. In the second half of *CD* iv, 3 he devotes a section to this subject under the heading 'The Holy Spirit and the Sending of the Christian Community'.[47] There are four sub-headings: (1) The People of God in World-Occurrence; (2) The Community for the World; (3) The Task of the Community; (4) The Ministry of the Community. It is a long section of 220 pages in which he frequently reintroduces former themes. Here I shall draw attention to the new material.

THE PEOPLE OF GOD IN WORLD-OCCURRENCE

Here Barth is at his most profound, and his most difficult:

> [Jesus Christ] is the man in whose person God has ... elected and loved from all eternity the wider circle of humanity as a whole, but also, with a view to this wider circle, the narrower circle of a special race, of His own community within humanity (*CD* iv, 3 (second half), p. 682).

Thus the Church is in the world and must know that its Lord is Lord also of the world. 'The community would be guilty of a lack of faith and discernment if it were to see and understand world history as secular or profane history.'[48]

Barth recognizes that the world is ruled *hominum confusione* (by man's confusion); but it is also ruled *Dei providentia* (by God's providence). He faces frankly the grim results of man's confusion, even the possibility of world destruction (atomic sin). But God has decided for mankind, and 'the community of those to whom Jesus Christ has entrusted the word of reconciliation ... cannot possibly accept either human confusion or a cosmic confusion ... as the final meaning of world-occurrence'.[49] The world is also the theatre of the glory of God 'in all its explored and unexplored dimensions, with all its known and as yet unknown or only suspected possibilities and powers, with a nature God Himself has given no less than in the case of men'.[50] Barth acknowledges the mystery of the relationship between man's confusion and God's providence. But he is certain that it is not to be explained in the manner of Hegel as a matter of thesis and antithesis which are one day to be brought together in a synthesis, for this would be an eventual justification of man's rebellious confusion:

> What does the people of God see in world-occurrence around it? To be sure, up above it sees first and last the glorious spectacle of its God, the Creator of the world and man, who as such is the Lord and Ruler of this occurrence. To be sure, down below it sees the dreadful spectacle of the man who has fallen away from God and fallen out with his neighbour and himself. To be sure, it sees the contradiction, the conflict, the *diastasis*, the riddle of this occurrence. And accordingly, to be sure, it sees no real synthesis resolving the riddle, no harmony between above and below, no relation between the positive will of God and the confusion of man, no possibility of understanding the one as the basis of the other, or the other as grounded in it. It accepts the twofold view. But it also sees that there is more to be said (ibid., p. 708).

This additional thing to be said is 'a new thing' which the community knows on the basis of its own existence. The 'new thing' is that God has revealed himself as for the world, and has spoken his Word to it. 'The new thing which the people of God perceives in world-occurrence is the new unique person, Jesus Christ. It is the grace of God addressed to the world in Him.'[51] The community knows that it is entrusted with the task of attesting this new thing to the world. It is therefore 'concerned not only with God but also directly with humanity ... with the very impure, historical, and sinful humanity which has fallen away from God and fallen out with itself, with the "flesh of sin" (Rom. 8.13), and therefore with the subject of the great confusion of world history'.[52] Since God in Jesus Christ has decided for men, the Church can only be for men. If the community truly believes in the living Christ, it accepts this role 'in the resoluteness of a definite hope for world-occurrence':[53]

> It is a resolute confidence even in relation to the future, to the goal of the totality of world history. The Christian community dares to hope for the world. It waits for Him who came once and for all yesterday, and who is and lives always and therefore tomorrow. In relation to Him it knows that the form of the world which now confronts it cannot last but will one day perish and be seen no more, and that its new reality will then appear and alone be seen by itself and all men—the world reconciled to God, the covenant fulfilled by Him, the order reconstituted by Him. It waits for Jesus Christ. It waits for Him to emerge from His concealment in world-occurrence and to show Himself to it and to the men of every age and place as the One He already is as its Lord. It yearns for this. It rejoices in it (ibid., p. 720).

World history for the people of God is the sphere in which it has to live with this resoluteness. It is the time between Easter and the final coming of Christ.[54] It is the time of which Barth said in a series of lectures given in 1946:

> In the resurrection of Jesus Christ the claim is made, according to the New Testament, that God's victory in man's favour in the person of His Son has already been won. Easter is indeed the great pledge of our hope, but simultaneously this future is already present in the Easter message. It is the proclamation of a victory already won. The war is at an end—even though here and there troops are still shooting, because they have not heard anything yet about the capitulation. The game is won, even though the player can still play a few further moves. Actually he is already mated. ... It is in this interim time that we are living: the old is past; behold, it has

all become new. The Easter message tells us that our enemies sin, the curse and death, are beaten. Ultimately they can no longer start mischief. They still behave as though the game were not decided, the battle not fought. We must still reckon with them but fundamentally we must cease to fear them any more . . . one thing still holds . . . that Jesus is the Victor . . . we are invited and summoned to take seriously the victory of God's glory in this man Jesus and to be joyful in Him (*Dogmatics in Outline*).[55]

This interim time is given to the world as a time for human response, a time for the community to proclaim the gospel of reconciliation in Christ and to elicit faith.

Therefore the Christian community exists in the world as an empirical phenomenon, in the sphere of visibility, even in a sense, as Bellarmine said, 'like the kingdom of France or the republic of Venice'.[56] Again Barth rejects a doctrine of the Church as solely invisible as 'ecclesiastical docetism'.[57] Like its Lord, Jesus Christ, the Word who became flesh, the Church must be directed *ad extra* (towards the outside world), visible, like the world and in solidarity with it. But at once it must be said that like its Lord who is visibly true man and invisibly true God, the Christian community too is not merely visible as one group among others, but invisible as the people of Jesus Christ, called by God. 'It is both visible and invisible in the one essence.'[58] The Church is invisible, i.e. not plainly seen by all, because it is the community of Jesus Christ and the people of God in world-occurrence. Indeed, without God's calling and election it would not exist at all, even visibly. But by the power of the divine decision the Church exists, not only visibly, but also 'from within, uniquely and therefore invisibly, i.e. in a way which is visible to some, though not all'.[59] They who perceive its invisible aspect are those who know that the community is grounded in the being of Jesus Christ, and that 'what it is from within is what calls for expression *ad extra*. What it is invisibly wills as such to become generally visible, and has the promise that one day it will do so.'[60]

Its being, then, is invisible, but its impulse is from within outwards, from invisibility to visibility, from particularity to universality. Even as visible, it bears the promise of invisibility within it. This means, however, that, even though it is like the world and in world-occurrence, yet it is distinct from the world and different, individual and unique in relation to it, being set over against and in confrontation with world-occurrence. The existence of the Christian community thus corresponds to the existence of Jesus Christ to the extent that He first came in the flesh, so that in His human nature He is the eternal Son of God, and as such different from the world in spite of His solidarity with it, confronting world-occurrence unequivocally as its Lord even while He inconspicuously integrates Himself into it. His community follows Him as it must understand and therefore express its own being as one which is wholly worldly and yet also as a being in encounter with world-occurrence (*CD* iv, 3, p. 728).

THE COMMUNITY FOR THE WORLD

The community of Jesus Christ is for the world, i.e. for each and every man. ... In this way it also exists for God. ... First and supremely it is God who exists for the world. And since the community of Jesus Christ exists first and supremely for God, it has no option but in its own manner and place to exist for the world. How else could it exist for God? (ibid., p. 762).

Barth finds that there is a gap at this point in the patristic, scholastic, Reformation, and post-Reformation doctrine of the Church. No answer, or at the most an unsatisfactory answer, is given to the question concerning the meaning and purpose of the existence of the Christian community. The impression is given that the Church is 'an end in itself in its existence as the community and institution of salvation'.[61] 'What', he asks, 'has become of the decisive New Testament saying in 2 Corinthians 5.19 that it was the world which God reconciled to Himself in Jesus Christ?'[62]

The community exists for the world. It is the fellowship in which it is given to man to know the world as it is, to know man as he is, seeing, addressing, and treating him in the light and on the basis of God's covenant with all men, concluded in Jesus Christ. It is the society in which it is given to men to know and practise their solidarity with the world (which does not imply conformity), and to be under obligation to the world. It is not given to it to rule the world (that is God's work), but it is called to co-operate with God in his work.[63]

It is not a matter of any activity in the world, but of that which is required, of that which corresponds to its commission, of that for which it is empowered by the One who gives it. In no circumstances, however, may it or should it try to evade this task. In discharging it, it will always need the forgiveness of the sins which it commits, and therefore correction, and therefore constant self-criticism. But even the most stringent self-criticism must never be a reason or occasion for prudently doing nothing. Better something doubtful or over bold and therefore in need of correction and forgiveness than nothing at all! If even in the most holy reserve and modesty and prudence it prefers to fold its hands and therefore to rest itself, it is certainly not the true Church. The true Church may sometimes engage in tactical withdrawal, but never in strategic. It can never cease wholly or basically from activity in the world (ibid., pp. 779–80).

THE TASK OF THE COMMUNITY

The community's task is very definite. It is to exist for the world: 'If it had not been given it, it would not have come into being.'[64] The content of the task is to confess Jesus Christ: 'To use the simplest and biblical formulation: "Ye shall be witnesses unto me" (Acts 1.8).'[65] 'Jesus Christ signifies God Himself become man's Neighbour and Brother, akin and alongside in order in his stead to redeem his ruined cause.'[66] Therefore: 'Man cannot be omitted either for a single instant or in a single respect from the content of the message entrusted to the community.'[67]

Although there are differences in the vocation of members of the community, and various kinds of service,

> there are no differences within the community and in the execution of its task which can possibly throw doubt on the unity and totality of its content, i.e. of that which is at issue in it, the Gospel. . . . Its concern will be with the total content and therefore unconditionally with Jesus Christ, with the great Yes, with the goodness of God, and with man ennobled by God's goodness (ibid., p. 801).

The man who is addressed in this task is not man as understood by any particular anthropology or analysis of 'modern' man (which may or may not be relevant), but man as he is known and addressed by God Himself acting and revealed in Jesus Christ.[68]

> We have to distinguish between what the Gospel sees man to be in himself in virtue of his ignorance, and what it also sees him to be in virtue of the work of God and the Word of God addressed to his ignorance . . . this ignorant and suffering and unloving and loveless man in all the historical forms, in all the twists and turns, in which he tries to be rid of his need and anxiety, is the man whom God loves as His creature, whom He has elected in His Son . . . and whom He has called once and for all in His incarnate Word to Himself, to fellowship with His life, to eternal life (ibid., p. 809).

The Church does justice to its task only if it addresses every man as 'one who will be within even though he is now without', as one who is called to the service of God and is open to this future. It does not do justice to its task if it gives up one whom God does not give up.[69]

Barth proceeds to discuss the ways in which the community may fail, and has in the past failed in its task. He speaks of the temptation and danger of distorting the gospel into 'general timeless truth' which men are invited to consider favourably in comparison with competing theories of world-occurrence; of failing to recognize that God has a concrete and decisive Word for every time and situation; of the temptation and danger of falsifying the gospel by dressing it in the philosophical and ethical notions of the age (which is to treat the gospel as an object over which the community has control); of neglecting those for whom the community exists (with the excuse, perhaps, that there are so many tasks to be done for the 'inner circle'); or, on the other hand, of patronizing them, which means to treat them as so much material for one's own benevolence, ability, or superior knowledge. In all these ways the community fails in its task and negates its *raison d'être*.[70]

THE MINISTRY OF THE COMMUNITY

The ministry of the community is concretely defined as 'a ministry to God and man by its institution and ordination as such in the discipleship of Jesus Christ'.[71] It is a ministry of witness to the Word and reconciling work of God, spoken and accomplished in Jesus Christ, the primary Witness, the Mediator between God and man. This ministry is sustained, as it needs to be because the community shares the weakness of humanity, by the promise of God that its ministry is fulfilled in Jesus Christ.[72]

The *nature* of the ministry is the declaration of the gospel, its explanation or explication, and 'evangelical address', i.e. the application of the gospel to the situation in time and place of those who are addressed. Whatever forms the ministry may take, this is its essential nature.[73]

The *forms* of ministry are multiple: 'The Holy Spirit does not enforce a flat uniformity';[74] the community is one body, but has many members, and these are called by the Spirit to special forms of ministry and endowed for them by grace. On the basis of texts like Mark 6.12–13 and Luke 9.6, 'preaching the gospel and healing everywhere', Barth makes a distinction, though not a division, between ministries of speech and action:

> There can be no doubt that in the light of its origin, of the Giver of its task who is also its content, [the community's] ministry and witness have always to move along these two lines ... no less along the one than the other, but with equal seriousness and emphasis along both. ... There is a work of the lips and also of the hands. There is speech and also action, proclamation, and also healing; though it must be remembered, of course, that the direction given by Jesus to His disciples displays a clear sequence, the speech always preceding the action (ibid., p. 863).

Paul, who placed prophecy, the word of wisdom and knowledge, and the ministry of apostles and prophets first in his lists of various ministries (Rom. 12.6; 1 Cor. 12.8; Eph. 4.11), also evidently regarded the bearers of the ministry of the Word as the principal members of the whole body.[75]

The *'speech' forms of ministry* are described by Barth as (within the community): (1) to praise God; (2) the proclamation of the gospel in the assembly; (3) instruction of the community; and (directed outwards to the world): (4) evangelization in the immediate surroundings of the community; (5) mission to non-Christian lands. He adds also (6) the ministry of theology.[76]

ACTION FORMS OF MINISTRY

Forms of ministry which are predominantly action are (7) prayer; (8) the cure of souls; (9) personal example of Christian living; (10) diaconate in the sense of bringing relief to the needy in and outside the community; (11) prophetic action, by which Barth means action based on perception into the meaning of the current situation both of the community and of the world, and apprehension of what the Word of God has to say in this situation; and (12) the establishment of fellowship between nations, races, cultures, and economic classes.[77]

Baptism and the Lord's Supper are the community's significatory actions which establish fellowship:

> In baptism we have the once-for-all and conscious entry and reception, manifested in the sign of purification, of the individual man into membership of the people of those who are called by God in free grace to be His witnesses, to participate in the work of His witness. And in the Lord's Supper we have the repeated and conscious unification of this people, manifested in the sign of common eating and drinking, in new seeking

and reception of the free grace which it constantly needs and is constantly given in its work of witness. There is more to be said concerning baptism and the Lord's Supper. But it certainly has to be said concerning them that they are significatory actions in which men, instead of being merely alongside or even apart, both come and are together. They are thus actions which establish fellowship. In baptism and the Lord's Supper an invisible action of God—the fellowship of the Father and the Son in the Holy Ghost, the fellowship of God and man in Jesus Christ, the fellowship of Jesus Christ the Head with His body and its members, and finally the fellowship of God with the world created by Him and reconciled to Him—is the prototype, the meaning and the power of the visible and significatory action of the community and therefore of the unification of men therein attested. But on this basis and as likenesses of this original, baptism and the Lord's Supper are not empty signs. On the contrary, they are full of meaning and power. They are thus the simplest, and yet in their very simplicity the most eloquent, elements in the witness which the community owes to the world, namely the witness of peace on earth among the men in whom God is well-pleased (ibid., p. 901).

Throughout his long description of the forms of ministry Barth is insistent that each form of ministry is laid upon the whole community. We find here no discussion of the ordained ministry. The nearest Barth comes to this subject is the assertion, in respect of those who are called to particular forms of ministry, that

> in virtue of their origin in God, in Christ and in the Holy Spirit, it is made impossible that any one of them ... shall break loose and swallow the others, finally making itself out to be the one ministry, or the one fellowship of ministry, and acting as such. All of them, i.e. of the few or many Christians who find themselves commonly called to this special action and equipped for it, have to serve together 'the edifying of the body of Christ' (Eph. 4.12) and have thus to be modest in their mutual relations.[78]

There is no indication that he has modified his earlier rejection of a hierarchy of office in the Church and of a distinction between clergy and laity, office-bearers and others: 'Strictly, no one has an office; all can and should and may serve; none is ever "off duty".'[79]

It was noted above[80] that some have discerned the beginning of a new development in Barth's ecclesiology in his address on 'The Humanity of God' in 1956. It has to be remembered that by this date *CD* iv, Parts 1 and 2 were already published, and the writing of iv, 3, published in 1959, must have been well advanced. In the few pages devoted to the Church at the end of the lecture he certainly admits that in 1920 he viewed the Church in an exaggeratedly negative way.[81]

He does not withdraw, however, his early teaching that God's judgement rests upon the Church, nor the concept that the Church is *event* before it is institution.[82]

He does now say very clearly that the Church is prior to the individual: 'Jesus Christ is the Head of His body and only so is He also the Head of its members.'[83] He does declare that 'what Jesus Christ is for God and for us, on earth and in time, He is as Lord of this community, as king of this people, as Head of this body and all its members'.[84] Despite the sins and failures of this 'strange communion of these strange saints', the Church is not too mean a thing for Jesus Christ, 'but, for better or for worse, sufficiently precious and worthy in His eyes to be entrusted with His witnessing and thus His affairs in the world—yes, even Himself. So great is God's loving-kindness!'[85] We have here a 'high', christologically grounded doctrine of the Church. But Barth had said most, if not all, of these things in the earlier *CD* iv, 1.

I have tried to let Barth speak for himself in this chapter, and it may fittingly close with the concluding words of this address:

> Our 'I believe in the Holy Spirit' would be empty if it did not also include in a concrete, practical, and obligatory way, the 'I believe one Holy, Catholic, and Apostolic Church'. We believe the Church as the place where the crown of humanity, namely, man's fellow-humanity, may become visible in Christocratic brotherhood. Moreover, we believe it as the place where God's glory wills to dwell upon earth, that is, where humanity—the humanity of God—wills to assume tangible form in time and here upon earth. Here we recognize the humanity of God. Here we delight in it. Here we celebrate and witness to it. Here we glory in the Immanuel, just as He did who, as He looked at the world, would not cast away the burden of the Church but rather chose to take it upon Himself and bear it in the name of all its members. 'If God is for us, who is against us?' (*The Humanity of God*).[86]

23

The Ecclesiology of
Paul Tillich

Paul Tillich (1886–1965) was deprived of his chair of Philosophy at the University of Frankfurt because of his opposition to the Hitler régime, and sailed for the United States in 1933. He became Professor of Philosophical Theology at Union Theological Seminary, New York, and later University Professor at Harvard (1955). He was one of the most influential theologians in the English-speaking world during the middle years of the century. His intimate acquaintance with philosophy, psychiatry, and many branches of the arts and sciences won him a respectful readership in and beyond the circle of professional theologians, and he was 'one of the most widely read and widely debated thinkers of his time'.[1]

SOME MAIN THEMES IN TILLICH'S THEOLOGY

His ecclesiology is developed in the third volume of his *Systematic Theology*.[2] In order to put his doctrine of the Church in its proper context, it is necessary to describe certain of his main themes. For Tillich, the function of theology is to declare and interpret the Christian message for each generation. It must elucidate the crucial questions which man asks in his situation in existence, and then show how the revelation of the New Being in Jesus as the Christ answers those questions. It must be an 'answering' or apologetic theology. Tillich calls this 'the method of 'correlation'; it 'explains the contents of the Christian faith through existential questions and theological answers in mutual interdependence'.[3] In his theological method, therefore, as in many other ways, Tillich's theology is in sharp contrast with that of his great contemporary, Karl Barth.

In pursuance of his aim, Tillich offers an acute analysis of man's situation. Man in existence is in 'a state of estrangement from his essential nature';[4] he 'is not what he essentially is and ought to be'.[5] He has fallen from his essence by actualizing the finite freedom which belongs to him, and which he had possessed in 'dreaming innocence' in union with the ground of his being—God. This is symbolized in the garden of Eden story of Genesis 2–3. This fall was the transition from essence to existence.[6] Man in existence is finite being, subject to the categories of time, space, causality, and substance, all of which threaten him with the possibility of his *not* being—not being somewhen, somewhere, somehow, somebody. He is anxious; he asks how he can continue to be, what basis there is for 'the courage to be' in his present. The answer of theology is the doctrine of God, which Tillich expounds in *Systematic Theology*, volume 1. The being of God is being itself. He is the ground of all being, and 'he is the power of being in everything and above everything'.[7] This power is the power of infinite love which desires the union of the estranged, and the fulfilment of all being.

But man in his existential situation has other urgent questions. There is not only the question of courage in the face of the threat of not being. Aware that his being is estranged from its essence and involved in inextricable contradictions, man asks about the possibility of salvation, the possibility of new being in which his essential being may be regained.

Being has a structure which, Tillich holds, has been disrupted for man in finite existence. Basically it is a subject–object structure. Every being is an individual, confronted by an environment, and man experiences this as a self-world relationship. Tillich analyses[8] the basic self-world structure of being into three elements, which are polarities: individualization and participation; dynamics and form; and freedom and destiny. Man who is a self participates in all other being (physical, biological, personal). But how can he do so without losing his individuality? Man as self has potentialities (*dynamis*) which must take some form, must in some way be actualized. But how can man employ his potentialities without on the one hand embarking on a chaotic life ('everything by starts and nothing long'), or, on the other hand, arriving at some rigid form which crushes all potentialities but one? Man as self has freedom, but his freedom is interdependent with his destiny, by which Tillich means that which a man is at any given moment, i.e. as formed by all the influences which have made an impact on him, ancestral and environmental, and by his own decisions. But how can man preserve his freedom without defying his destiny, so losing the meaning and direction of his life, and how can he preserve his destiny without losing his freedom?

Man in existence tends to assert his individuality, potentialities, and freedom against their opposite poles. On the other hand, stress on the other poles carries the danger of collectivization, rigidity, and loss of freedom. In either case the structure of man's being is thrown out of equilibrium. Tillich uses the word 'estrangement' to denote man's situation—estrangement from the ground of his being (God), from other beings, and from his essential self. Estrangement is, however, to use biblical terms, 'sin' (unbelief, *hubris* or self-elevation, and concupiscence) and a state of 'guilt'.[9]

Man's attempts at self-salvation must fail, because he can only act within the resources of his estranged being, and these are not sufficient to overcome the ambiguities of his estrangement and restore unity with his essential being. He therefore asks, and must ask, about the possibility of new being. Here, as elsewhere, Tillich upholds what he calls 'the Protestant principle'; the distance between God and man cannot be bridged by man; all is of God. The answer to this question of man is given in the appearance of the New Being in Jesus as the Christ. It is in *ST* 2 that Tillich expounds this theological answer. In Jesus as the Christ, essential being in 'undisrupted unity' with God appears under the conditions of finite existence. He preserves this unity while taking upon himself the self-destruction implicit in man's existence,[10] and thus conquers the gap between essence and existence. In him the power of the New Being is manifested. It grasped the disciples of Jesus, who, in the receiving act which every revelation needs, themselves grasped the New Being in their acceptance of him as the Christ. And in accepting him as the Christ they accepted that he had accepted them. That man must accept that he is accepted is another nuance of the 'Protestant principle'.

THE SPIRITUAL PRESENCE

Man's life, even the life of the man who has accepted that he is accepted, needs to be transformed (or, in more traditional language, salvation, initiated in justification by grace through faith, is a process which continues in sanctification). His life is still a 'mixture' of essence and existence, still has to come to terms with the polarities of individualization and participation, dynamics and form, freedom and destiny, and is still ambiguous. In *ST* 3 Tillich again analyses the ambiguities which confront man, this time in connection with the basic functions of life, namely self-integration, self-creativity, and self-transcendence.[11] These are the functions of human life which man expresses in morality, culture, and religion. In each of them the ambiguities and problems inherent in the self-world structure of being become apparent. Goodness, beauty, truth, holiness lie beyond man's grasp because he cannot bridge the gap between subject and object or overcome his estrangement from his essential being. What, then, can bring about for man the transcendent unity of life, union with his essential being and with God, unambiguous life? The answer that theology gives is the Spiritual Presence, i.e. 'the presence of the divine Spirit within creaturely life'.[12]

The Spiritual Presence was fully manifested in Jesus as the Christ:

> The divine Spirit was present in Jesus as the Christ without distortion. In him the New Being appeared as the criterion of all Spiritual experiences in past and future. Though subject to individual and social conditions his human spirit was entirely grasped by the Spiritual Presence; his spirit was 'possessed' by the divine Spirit, or, to use another figure, 'God was in him'. This makes him the Christ, the decisive embodiment of the New Being for historical mankind (*Systematic Theology*, vol. 3, p. 144).[13]

THE SPIRITUAL COMMUNITY

'Jesus, the Christ, is the keystone in the arch of Spiritual manifestations in history.'[14] His appearance is the central revelatory event. But revelation must be *received*, or there is no revelation:

> The Christ would not be the Christ without those who receive him as the Christ. He could not have brought the new reality without those who have accepted the new reality in him and from him (ibid., p. 149).

Two New Testament stories in particular illustrate the nature of the revelation of the Christ to those who have received him as such:

> The first one, which is most significant for the meaning of 'Christ', is also most significant for the relation of Christ to the Spiritual Community. It is the story of Peter's confession to Jesus that he is the Christ at Caesarea Philippi and Jesus' answer that the recognition of him as the Christ is a work of God; this recognition is the result not of an ordinary experience but of the impact of the Spiritual Presence. It is the Spirit grasping Peter that enables his spirit to recognize the Spirit in Jesus which makes him the Christ. This recognition is the basis of the Spiritual Community against which the demonic powers are powerless and which Peter and the other

disciples represent. Therefore we can say: As the Christ is not the Christ without those who receive him as the Christ, so the Spiritual Community is not spiritual unless it is founded on the New Being as it has appeared in the Christ (ibid., p. 150).

The second is the story of Pentecost and its immediate sequel (Acts 2–4) which reveal the ecstatic character[15] of the Spiritual Community, its grounding in a faith which had almost been destroyed by the crucifixion, its expression in love and service and its drive towards unity and universality.[16] Thus is constituted a community, grasped by the New Being, and responding to it, a community wherein the New Being may continue to manifest itself.

THE SPIRITUAL COMMUNITY IN ITS LATENT AND MANIFEST STAGES

The Spiritual Presence was present fully and without distortion in Jesus as the Christ. But throughout history mankind has been under the impact of the Spiritual Presence:

> Mankind is never left alone. The Spiritual Presence acts upon it in every moment and breaks into it in some great moments, which are the historical *kairoi* (ibid., p. 140).[17]

Wherever and whenever men have been open to the divine Spirit, there is the Church latent. The distinction between the Church latent and manifest is not to be confused with the classical distinction between the Church visible and invisible. Nor is it merely the temporal distinction between before and after Christ. Tillich is not simply repeating what many others have said, that there is a sense in which the Church existed before Christ. Rather, he is speaking of contemporary individuals and groups who have responded to the Spiritual Presence. He lists the communities of the world religions. 'Not even Communism', he says, 'could live if it were devoid of all elements of the Spiritual Community.'[18] In all these, and in many other religious and humanist movements 'there are elements of faith in the sense of being grasped by an ultimate concern, and there are elements of love in the sense of a transcendent reunion of the separated'.[19] But in so far as they have not yet accepted the New Being in Jesus as the Christ as the ultimate criterion of the Spiritual Presence, the Spiritual Community is still latent in them. The distinction, then, between the Church latent and manifest points to stages in the history of the Spiritual Community—before and after encounter with and acceptance of the New

Being in Christ. The Church latent and the Church manifest may and do exist contemporaneously:

It is most important for the practice of the Christian ministry, especially in its missionary activities towards those both within and without the Christian culture, to consider pagans, humanists, and Jews as members of the latent Spiritual Community and not as complete strangers who are invited into the Spiritual Community from outside. This insight serves as a powerful weapon against ecclesiastical and hierarchical arrogance (ibid., p. 155).

The manifest Church is the Spiritual Community of those who have found themselves grasped by the Spiritual Presence of Jesus as the Christ, the one who has conquered existential estrangement, and whose lives express this central revelatory experience. In them is initiated a movement which Tillich describes as 'ecstatic', in which man's spirit is driven out of itself towards the overcoming of the ambiguities of the functions of life (morality, culture, and religion) and towards transcendent unity. Faith and love are the content of this ecstatic movement, being the marks of the Spirit which was supremely manifested in Jesus.[20] The faith and love of the Spiritual Community drive towards its unity and universality under the impact of the Spiritual Presence:

The unity and universality of the Spiritual Community follow from its character as a community of faith and love. Its unity expresses the fact that the tension between the indefinite variety of the conditions of faith does not lead to a break with the faith of the community. The Spiritual Community can stand the diversities of psychological and sociological structures, of historical development, and of preferences as to symbols and devotional and doctrinal forms. This unity is not without tensions, but it is without break. It is fragmentary and anticipatory because of the limits of time and space, but it is unambiguous and, as such, the criterion for the unity of the religious groups, the churches of which the Spiritual Community is the invisible Spiritual essence (ibid., p. 156).

The Spiritual Presence drives towards universality:

The immense diversity of beings with regard to sex, age, race, nation, tradition, and character—typological as well as individual—does not prevent their participation in the Spiritual Community. The figurative statement that all men are children of the same father, is not incorrect, but it has a hollow sound, because it suggests mere potentiality. The real question is whether, in spite of the existential estrangement of the children of God from God and from each other, participation in a transcendent union is possible. This question is answered in the Spiritual Community and by the working of *agape* [love] as a manifestation of the Spirit in it (ibid., p. 157).

In the Spiritual Community, the Spiritual Presence, operating through faith and love, restores the unity of morality, culture, and religion. These functions of life, united in man's essential nature, have been separated under the conditions of existence. The Spiritual Community realizes their unity in that, when the Spirit is present, 'every act is an act of self-transcendence',[21] and the false separation between what is moral, cultural, and religious disappears: 'Culture is the form of religion, and religion the substance of culture',[22] and both are expressions of acceptance of the moral imperative which is implicit in 'the personal–communal character in which the New Being appears',[23] i.e. in the Spiritual Community itself.

Tillich constantly insists that the overcoming of ambiguities and the achievement of unity is only fragmentary, for while the churches participate in the unambiguous life of the Spiritual Community they also participate in the ambiguities of life in general. The life of the Spiritual Community is a process whose principles are an increasing awareness both of the ambiguities of life and of the power of the Spiritual Presence which can overcome them, increasing freedom, increasing relatedness to others, and increasing self-transcendence in the direction of the ultimate, i.e. participation in the holy.[24]

How these principles will unite in a new type of life under the Spiritual Presence cannot be described before it happens, but elements of such a life can be seen in individuals and groups who anticipated what may possibly lie in the future (ibid., p. 231).

The Christian life never reaches the stage of perfection—it always remains an up-and-down course—but in spite of its mutable character it contains a movement towards maturity, however fragmentary the mature state may be (ibid., p. 237).

THE SPIRITUAL COMMUNITY, THE CHURCH, AND THE CHURCHES

Tillich, as will have been noticed, prefers the term 'Spiritual Community' to Church. He explains:

The term 'Spiritual Community' has been used to characterize sharply that element in the concept of the Church which is called the 'body of

Christ' by the New Testament and the 'church invisible or Spiritual' by the Reformation. In the previous discussion[25] this element has sometimes been called 'the invisible essence of the religious communities'. Such a statement implies that the Spiritual Community is not a group existing beside other groups but rather a power and a structure inherent and effective in such groups, that is, in religious communities. If they are consciously based on the appearance of the New Being in Jesus as the Christ, these groups are called churches. If they have other foundations they are called synagogues, temple congregations, mystery groups, monastic groups, cult groups, movements. In so far as they are determined by an ultimate concern, the Spiritual Community is effective in its hidden power and structures in all such groups. In the language of the New Testament, the manifestation of the Spiritual Community in the Christian church is described in the following way: the Church in New Testament Greek is *ecclesia*, the assembly of those who are called out of all nations by the *apostoloi*, the messengers of the Christ, to the congregation of the *eleutheroi*, those who have become free citizens of the 'Kingdom of the Heavens'. There is a 'church', an 'assembly of God' (or the Christ), in every town in which the message has been successful and a Christian *koinonia*, or communion, has come into being. But there is also the overall unity of these local assemblies in the Church universal, by virtue of which the particular groups become churches (local, provincial, national, or after the split of the Church universal, denominational). The Church universal, as well as the particular churches included in it, is seen in a double aspect as the 'body of Christ', on the one hand—a Spiritual reality—and as a social group of individual Christians on the other. In the first sense, they show all the characteristics which we have attributed to the Spiritual Community. . .; in the second sense, all the ambiguities of religion, culture, and morality that were already discussed in connection with the ambiguities of life in general are present (ibid., pp. 162–3).

Tillich does not, however, advocate giving up the word 'Church' to denote the body of Christ. He believes, however, that his own terminology avoids some of the confusion which has surrounded it in connection with the distinctions between Church and churches, and Church invisible and Church visible. The Spiritual Community, he explains, is not something existing beside the churches. It is their spiritual essence. It is not an ideal constructed out of the positive elements in the life of the churches; nor is it an assembly of spiritual beings, angels, saints, and the saved from all ages. Rather, the Spiritual Community is to be interpreted 'essentialistically': it is the essential, which gives power and direction to the existential churches and 'is the source of everything which makes them churches'.[26] In scriptural terms it is the New Creation.

The churches exist in a paradoxical manner since they participate both in the unambiguous life of the Spiritual Community, which is their essential being, and in the ambiguities of their historical existence. Their paradoxical character is evident when one considers how the credal marks of the Church can be applied to the churches. The churches are holy, united, and universal (catholic) because of the holiness, unity, and universality of their foundation. These marks can be attributed to the churches as they exist historically only with the addition of an 'in spite of'.[27]

The same must be said of the faith and love of the churches. The Spiritual Community is the community of faith and love. It is the dynamic essence which makes the churches communities of faith and love. But in the churches the ambiguities of religion are not eliminated. They are conquered 'in principle', which Tillich, in accordance with the strict meaning of the Latin *principium*, interprets as 'the power of beginning, which remains the controlling power in a whole process'.[28] The ambiguities are conquered in the life of churches only in so far as they embody the New Being. Faith and love have often failed in the churches and their members, but in so far as they are truly grasped by the Spiritual Presence, and constantly refer to the original revelatory event of Jesus as the Christ, they possess faith and love unambiguously even while they struggle against the failures of faith and lack of love within and between their particular communities. Nevertheless, the victories, under the conditions of finite existence, can only be fragmentary.

CHURCH AND WORLD: THE FUNCTIONS OF THE CHURCHES

For Tillich, then, the Spiritual Community or the Church is the community of those who have received the revelation of the New Being in Jesus as the Christ, and have been grasped by the divine Spirit which was present without distortion in Jesus. This is the essential nature of the Church, and what imparts its essential character to each of the particular existential communities (churches) which are consciously based on the New Being in Christ. This essential nature is necessarily expressed in a number of functions, which Tillich categorizes as constitutive, expanding, constructing, and relating.

1 **The constitutive functions of the churches**[29] are concerned with the reception and mediation of the message which constitutes the Church—the message of the New Being in Jesus as the Christ. Receiving and mediating must go on continuously. Tillich includes pastoral care and counselling, worship, prayer, and contemplation among the churches' constitutive functions.

The mediation of the message implies the preservation of tradition (or the message would be lost); it also entails the application of the message to every new situation, and therefore readiness for reformation. In this the churches experience the tension between 'conservative' and 'liberal'.

2 **The expanding functions of the churches**[30] are mission, education, and apologetics as they strive to enlarge the borders of the Spiritual Community. Here arises the question to what extent the culture of those to whom the message is addressed is relevant to the way in which the message is given. Tension is experienced between those who hold that the integrity of the message must be preserved by insulating it from the culture of human groups, and those who hold that its integrity is precisely manifested in its ability to speak to men in and through their culture.

3 **The constructing functions of the churches**[31] have to do with the building of the life of the churches under the influence of the Spiritual Presence. In this they clearly cannot insulate themselves from human culture:

> The church can never be without the functions of construction and, therefore, cannot forgo the use of cultural creations in all basic directions. Those who indulge in contrasts of the divine Spirit with the human spirit in terms of exclusiveness cannot avoid contradicting themselves: in the very act of expressing this rejection of any contact between cultural creativity and Spiritual creativity, they use the whole apparatus of man's cognitive mind, even if they do it by quoting biblical passages, for the words used in the Bible are creatures of man's cultural development. One can reject culture only by using it as a tool of such rejection. This is the inconsistency of . . . the radical separation of the religious from the cultural sphere (ibid., pp. 196–7).

Tillich analyses the constructive functions into the aesthetic and cognitive (which belong to the realm of theory) and the communal and personal functions (which belong to the realm of practice). He discusses the use of art forms, painting, architecture, music, dance, and drama; the use of the discursive element of cognition in theology; the relation of the churches to social and political structures; and the relationship between asceticism, or Christian self-discipline, and humanity.

In the performance of all these constructive functions, the churches and individual Christians encounter dangers, tensions, and ambiguities. The questions must constantly be faced: 'How can the human spirit be prevented from replacing the impact of the Spiritual Presence by self-creative acts of its own? How can the life of the churches be prevented from falling under the sway of the profane element in the ambiguities of religion?'[32]

4　**The relating functions of the churches**[33] arise from the fact that the churches are sociological realities in continuous encounter with other social groups. Tillich discusses three ways in which this may happen. The first is silent penetration, 'the continuous radiation of the Spiritual essence of the churches into all groups of the society in which they live'.[34] But the churches must realize that the influence is mutual; they receive their forms from the surrounding society.

The second is the way of critical judgement, 'prophetic criticism of the negativities in ... society up to the point of martyrdom'.[35] Again, the churches must know that 'there is, on the part of society, a criticism directed towards the churches ... as justified as the churches' prophetic criticism of society. It is the criticism of "holy injustice" and "saintly inhumanity" within the churches and in their relation to the society in which they live.'[36]

The third way is that of political establishment. One task of church leaders is to gain from other social groups the acknowledgement of the right of the Church to exist and to exercise its functions. There are many ways in which this can be, and has in the past been, secured. But if churches have to act politically, they must do so in the name of the Spiritual Community, rejecting all means which contradict its spiritual character (force, false propaganda, trickery, the arousing of fanaticism):

> The character of the church as expression of the Spiritual Community must remain manifest. This is first endangered if the symbol of the royal office of the Christ and through him of the church, is understood as a theocratic–political system of totalitarian control over all realms of life. On the other hand, if the church is forced to assume the role of an obedient servant of the state, as if it were another department or agency,

this means the end of its royal office altogether and a humiliation of the church which is not the humility of the Crucified but the weakness of the disciples who fled the Cross (ibid., p. 215).

In all these functions the churches find themselves in paradoxical situations. They act in the name of the Spiritual Community which is founded on the New Being in Jesus as the Christ, but they inevitably act also as sociological groups subject to the ambiguities of life. Tillich holds strongly, however, that the churches cannot be separated from the world: that world into which the Church is sent 'is not simply not-church but has in itself elements of the Spiritual Community in its latency which work towards a theonomous culture'.[37] The world is open to the Spiritual Presence. 'The divine Spirit is not bound to the media it has created, the churches.'[38] The divine Spirit is present in all human culture, morality, and religion. Within the various cultures there arise prophetic individuals and groups who see the need of the union of the secular and the holy, and point towards man's ultimate concern. This creates the latent church. The function of the Spiritual Community which is the manifest church is, in the power of the Spiritual Presence, to overcome the ambiguities which inhere in all culture, morality, and religion, and, by love, which is the creation of the Spiritual Presence, to unite all life and being in transcendent unity. This transcendent unity has appeared in the New Being in Jesus as the Christ. It appears, although fragmentarily, wherever the divine Spirit creates the Spiritual Community.

THE CHURCH AND THE KINGDOM OF GOD

Tillich's ecclesiology is similarly developed in the course of his treatment of the Kingdom of God.[39] There are, he asserts, three main symbols for the theological answers to the questions raised by the ambiguities of life. These symbols of unambiguous life are: Spirit of God (or Spiritual Presence), Kingdom of God, and Eternal Life.[40] Of these, he says, Kingdom of God is the most inclusive symbol for salvation. It includes both the vision of the Hebrew prophets of this-worldly, inner-historical renewal, and the other-worldly, trans-historical reference which the later Jewish apocalyptists emphasized.[41] Moreover, 'the New Testament adds a new element to these visions: the inner-historical appearance of Jesus as the Christ and the foundation of the church in the midst of the ambiguities of history'.[42] The symbol, 'Kingdom of God', therefore has both an immanent and a transcendent reference, and may be said to include both the symbols of the Spiritual Presence and Eternal Life.

There can be no identification of the Church, still less of the churches, with the Kingdom of God. The churches, and the Spiritual Community itself in its historical dimension, are in a situation of finitude. The finite must not be elevated to infinite value and meaning. 'This self-elevating claim to ultimacy is the definition of the demonic.'[43] The claim of any church to have brought into being 'the ultimate towards which history runs',[44] or to be the Kingdom of God, is demonic. But the churches do represent the Kingdom of God, although this representation is as ambiguous as their embodiment of the Spiritual Community in that they both reveal and hide the holy. Despite this ambiguity, the churches remain churches:

> Just as man, the bearer of spirit, cannot cease to be such, so the churches, which represent the Kingdom of God in history, cannot forfeit this function even if they exercise it in contradiction to the Kingdom of God. Distorted spirit is still spirit; distorted holiness is still holiness (ibid., p. 375).

Tillich acknowledges here, as elsewhere, that in many places and times the churches have failed grievously.

In this section, Tillich again introduces[45] the distinction between the manifest and the latent Church. The manifest Church exists wherever there is successful struggle against demonization (i.e. the elevation of the finite to ultimate significance) and against profanization (i.e. contentment with a world and its affairs dissociated from the holy). This struggle is conducted in the consciousness of the power of the Spirit and of the reality of the New Being in Jesus as the Christ. It leads to reformation movements within the churches themselves, and gives them 'the right to consider themselves vehicles of the Kingdom of God'.[46] But the Spirit's presence and activity is not restricted to the manifest Church. The power of the Kingdom of God is expressed also, in a preparatory way, in those individuals and groups in which, despite the fact that they are outside the churches, elements of faith and love are discernible. This consideration calls the churches to humility.

In words which are as close to a definition of the Church as anything we find in Tillich, he declares that 'where there are churches confessing their foundation in the Christ as the central manifestation of the Kingdom of God in history, there the church is'.[47] The history of the churches, however, though they are never without some manifestations of the Kingdom of God, is not to be identified with the history of the Kingdom of God. Church history falsifies any such claim. The churches—all churches—in their historical existence, being subject to ambiguity, both reveal and hide saving history. They reveal it when they are faithful to the criterion of the New Being. They hide it in that they are confined to particular sections of mankind,[48] in their many contradictory interpretations of the saving event on which their history is based,[49] and the recurring profanization of the holy of which church history records so many examples. No more can be said than that the churches are the representatives of the Kingdom of God in history, and that in them the Kingdom struggles for victory. Victories are achieved, even though they are fragmentary.

When these victories occur, answers begin to appear to the questions which arise out of the threefold function of life, self-integration, self-creativity, and self-transcendence.[50] Where the Kingdom of God is manifested, there is a power which controls but does not obliterate individuality. The ambiguities of self-integration are conquered.[51] Where the Kingdom of God is manifested, there it is recognized that 'revolution is being built into tradition in such a way that, in spite of the tensions in every concrete situation and in relation to every particular problem, a creative solution in the direction of the ultimate aim of history is found'.[52] The ambiguities of self-creativity (the conflict between the old and the new, between tradition and change) are conquered. Where the Kingdom of God is manifested, concern for social transformation is not allowed to obscure the truth that salvation lies beyond history. Utopianism is inevitably the seed-bed of cynicism.[53] The Kingdom of God requires emphasis both on the horizontal line of active social transformation and the vertical line of salvation. It is the task of the churches as representatives of the Kingdom of God 'to keep alive the tension between the consciousness of presence and expectation of the coming'.[54] Thereby the ambiguities of self-transcendence are conquered.

All these answers to the ambiguities of the functions of life represent but partial and fragmentary conquests, since they are given through finite institutions within history. The final answer to man's existential questions is given at the end of history, in eternal life. Tillich concludes his system[55] with a discussion of eternal life as the exclusion of all that is negative in history and in man's life, and the raising of the positive into unity with God who is being-itself.

SOME COMMENTS ON TILLICH'S ECCLESIOLOGY

It is obvious that Tillich's ecclesiology departs considerably from traditional lines. It might be said that it provides an example of that reconciling of tradition and revolution which he has noted as a sign of the overcoming of the ambiguities of self-creativity. I note here briefly first the traditional elements, and then those which, if not altogether revolutionary, are new in relating ecclesiology to the situation, questions, and needs of contemporary man.

TRADITIONAL ELEMENTS

He is emphatic that the Church is the creation of the Holy Spirit who builds up the Spiritual Community on the foundation of Jesus Christ. The Spiritual Community is no man-made association of persons. This is completely in accord with N.T. teaching.

Certain elements of ecclesiology which have been stressed in Catholic and Protestant theology are taken up by Tillich who frequently insists on adherence to the 'Protestant principle' and the preservation of 'Catholic substance'.[56] By the former he means essentially the principle that man's salvation and all that relates to it is from God, 'the principle of justification by grace through faith'.[57] By Catholic substance he means 'the concrete embodiment of the Spiritual Presence',[58] and in particular the concept of the sacraments as powerful symbols which mediate the New Being in Jesus as the Christ.[59] In the Introduction to *ST* 3 Tillich writes:

> Although my system is very outspoken in its emphasis on 'the Protestant principle', it has not ignored the demand that the 'Catholic substance' be united with it, as the section on the church . . . shows (ibid., p. 6).

Tillich has a wide-reaching doctrine of sacraments. He holds that the Spiritual Presence always manifests itself through word and sacrament: 'Reality is communicated either by the silent presence of the object as object or by the vocal self-expression of a subject to a subject.'[60] The sacraments of the Church are symbols grounded in the New Being which have inherent power to actualize and nourish the Spiritual Community. They are neither to be distorted into magical means of manipulating the divine (naive Catholicism) nor reduced to mere outward marks of faith (Zwinglianism). Moreover, there must be emphasis on the sacramental presence of the divine if a church is to represent the Kingdom of God in the struggle against profanization:

Strongly sacramental churches, such as the Greek Orthodox, have a profound understanding for the participation of life under all dimensions in the ultimate aim of history. The sacramental consecration of elements of all life shows the presence of the ultimately sublime in everything and points to the unity of everything in its creative ground and its final fulfilment. It is one of the shortcomings of the churches of the 'word', especially in their legalistic and exclusively personalistic form, that they exclude, along with the sacramental element, the universe outside man from consecration and fulfilment (ibid., p. 377).

While the details of Tillich's sacramental theology do not concern us here, it supports the contention that his ecclesiology is, despite some appearances to the contrary, 'built into tradition'.

NEW ELEMENTS

I turn to those elements which are, or have the appearance of being new. In accordance with his method of correlation, by which he seeks to show how revelation answers vital questions which are raised by man's existence, Tillich's ecclesiology is directly related to the contemporary situation of man in his world. He provides the groundwork for this by a searching analysis of man's situation in existence. His analysis of the functions of life reveals their inherent ambiguities, and raises the questions to which he believes the doctrines of the Spiritual Presence and the Spiritual Community provide the answers. He is not content with any academic definition of the Church, however theologically balanced. The Church is the gift of God in the world and for the world, and therefore must be seen by men to be relevant to the world's situation.

Tillich rejects triumphalism. 'The claim to have or to bring the ultimate towards which history runs'[61] by a church or by any group is demonic. Moreover, he insists constantly that the victories of the Spiritual Community over life's ambiguities, though real, are and must be fragmentary. Only at the end of history in eternal life are the ambiguities of life fully resolved, and the estrangement of man from his essential self, from others, and from God completely overcome.

The recognition of the tension between the imperfection of the Church and the holiness of its calling and purpose is, of course, not new. We have seen the problem faced, and attempts made to solve it by distinctions between the empirical Church and the heavenly, between the Church visible and invisible. But a triumphalism is often hidden beneath these distinctions: the claim that there does exist in history, in this or that group, the perfect Church of Christ, a Church of the impeccably orthodox, of the spiritual ones or the saints. What is fresh in Tillich's ecclesiology is his cogent presentation of the reasons why any such claim is, and must be false. The Spiritual Community manifests itself in the churches *under the conditions of finite existence*. That there is healing and victory over estrangement Tillich does not deny, but it is fragmentary and partial. He speaks of the churches as the representatives of the Kingdom of God,[62] but in history the Kingdom of God does not manifest itself as a static, structurally perfect entity, composed of perfect human beings. It is engaged in a struggle, and 'the struggle of the Kingdom of God in history is, above all, this struggle within the life of its own representatives, the churches'.[63] 'Struggle', 'conflict', 'fight' are words which Tillich frequently uses of the life of the Spiritual Community. Here on earth it is most truly the Church militant.

The distinction between the latent and manifest church also has the appearance of a new element in ecclesiology. It certainly breaks down the sharp distinction between Church and world which is characteristic of much traditional ecclesiology. Yet it is no more than an acknowledgement of what modern comparative study of religion has made plain to many students, namely that the non-Christian religions cannot be regarded as totally in error and lacking any sign of what Tillich calls the Spiritual Presence. This acknowledgement is implicit in the changed strategy of modern Christian mission. No longer does the Christian missionary hold that the religion and culture which he finds in his mission field must be demolished root and branch so that the Christian Church may be planted there (and all too often after a western model). He knows that the Spiritual Presence has been manifested there long before his arrival. He has the lengthier and more difficult task of helping a latent church respond anew to the Spiritual Presence and root itself in the New Being in Jesus as the Christ, in whom the Spiritual Presence is fully manifested.

Tillich included humanism among his examples of the latent church.[64] It is a striking witness to the increasing acceptance of something very close to his concept of the latent church that Bishop B. C. Butler, the Roman Catholic author of a somewhat conservative book entitled *The Idea of the Church*,[65] published in 1962, could nine years later publicly express the hope[66] for a wider scope not only for Christian ecumenism, but also for dialogue and co-operation between religious believers and non-believers, and in the European context could call upon Christians, Jews, and humanists to promote jointly the values which they share. It is a confession that the activity of the Holy Spirit is not restricted, despite St Augustine, to the confines of the Catholic Church.

It must not be supposed that Tillich advocates complacence in a state of things in which members of the manifest church are greatly outnumbered by those of the latent church. Receptive encounter with the New Being in Christ (repentance and faith) is the boundary point between the two. It is the work of the Spiritual Community to invite and help the latent community to engage in this encounter so that the Spiritual Presence may be the more widely experienced in love and unifying power.

24

The Ecclesiology of
Hans Küng

Hans Küng, of the Catholic Theological Faculty of the University of Tübingen, has written two major works on ecclesiology, *Structures of the Church*[1] and *The Church*.[2] In his Foreword to the latter Dr Küng says that *Structures* is to be understood as a *prolegomenon*. *Structures* was written after the announcement of Pope John XXIII convoking an ecumenical council (Vatican II).[3] The announcement was surprising because, both within and outside the Roman Catholic Church, it was widely assumed that the authority of the pope as defined in the First Vatican Council in 1870 rendered a council unnecessary. Küng sets out to suggest a theology of ecumenical councils, and to show how the Church's structures, the laity, ecclesiastical offices, and the Petrine office relate to councils.

The Church was published two years after the conclusion of Vatican II. In *Structures* Küng had outlined the theological re-examination and reforms which he hoped the Church would undertake. These, he recognized, were matters requiring time. But in the Preface to *The Church* he speaks of the Council as achieving 'a powerful breakthrough in terms of freedom, openness, and flexibility on behalf of the Catholic Church' and as 'evidence of a new lease of life breaking through after centuries of reserve and isolationism'.[4] He is convinced that the Church is on the right path. To be on the right path does not merely mean that it is adapting itself to the present, which would content some, nor that it is holding fast to the past, which would content others. Rather it means reform and renewal in accordance with its origins, 'the events which gave it life'. He now undertakes a systematic theology of the Church, based on biblical themes, 'so that the original Church may light the way once more for the Church of today'.[5] The two books together provide a thorough treatment of the doctrine of the Church which I shall here summarize under headings which Küng himself suggests: the Nature of the

Church; the Marks (or dimensions) of the Church; its Structures.

THE NATURE OF THE CHURCH

Throughout these two books Küng's preference for the N.T. concept of the Church as the people of God (though he by no means denies the theological value of the other biblical images), and his recognition that the idea of the Church as the *congregatio fidelium* (assembly of believers) is basic, constantly appear. 'In the history of theology', he writes, 'the Church as assembled community of the faithful has been too often neglected in favour of the Church as institution.'[6] This underlies the description of the Church (Küng would be chary of using the word 'definition') which he gives at the beginning of *Structures*. After an examination of the biblical use of the word *ekklesia*, during which he notes that the Latin *concilium* (council) has the same root meaning,[7] he declares that 'the Church is an ecumenical council by divine convocation'.[8]

> The Church presents and constantly renews herself as the council of believers convoked by God through Christ in the Spirit: in the proclamation of the Word as appointed by Christ through the apostolic office and in the celebration of the sacraments; in the profession of the common faith; in the exercise of an all-uniting love; in the hopeful expectation of the Second Coming of the Lord. The Church manifests herself most intensively during the act of worship, and in the common participation in the sacrament of the Eucharist (*Structures*, p. 15).

ESSENCE AND FORM

Küng believes that the old controversy about the visibility and invisibility of the Church is long out of date.[9] A real Church whose members are real people cannot possibly be invisible. There are, however, hidden and invisible aspects which it would be disastrous for the Church to neglect: the activity of the Spirit, the operation of grace, the inward response of faith. These are its vital elements. In truth, 'the one Church, in its essential nature and in its external forms alike, is always at once visible and invisible'.[10] The Church is 'first and foremost a happening, a fact, an historical event. The real essence of the real Church is expressed in historical form.'[11] That is to say, its essence *must* take historical form. Essence and form, though not to be separated, are nevertheless not identical. No form of the Church, even that of the N.T., embodies its essence perfectly and completely. The essence of the Church, permanent but not immutable, is given in its origins in the gospel of Christ. It is the gospel, and not the earliest form of the Church, which is the criterion by which any subsequent form of the Church is to be judged. It is mistaken, therefore, to advocate a return to the first century in an attempt to imitate the N.T. community:

> The New Testament Church is not a model which we can follow slavishly without any regard to the lapse of time and our constantly changing situation. .... On the other hand ... the New Testament Church ... beginning with its origins in Jesus Christ, is already the Church in the fullness of its nature, is therefore the original design; we cannot copy it today, but we can and must translate it into modern terms (*Church*, p. 24).

THE CHURCH AND THE KINGDOM (REIGN) OF GOD

Jesus' message was that 'the time is fulfilled, and the kingdom of God is at hand; repent, and believe in the gospel' (Mark 1.15). By the reign of God (Küng prefers to translate the Greek *basileia* by 'reign' rather than 'kingdom' because of the misleading associations of the latter word) Jesus 'means the eschatological, that is the fully realized, final, and absolute reign of God at the end of time'[12] which he says is now at hand. It is not to be brought about by man, but appears as a sovereign act of God. It is not an earthly, religio-political theocracy, but is purely religious: God's rule, God's salvation offered to all men under the one condition of repentance and belief in the gospel. Küng believes that Jesus announced the reign of God both as something to come and as something now present, Jesus himself and his work being the signs that it has already begun. He agrees with Bultmann that 'the decisive element of Jesus' message lies not in an imminent end, but in the challenge to decide here and now for the reign of God'.[13] But the futurist perspective of the biblical teaching about the kingdom is not to be pushed aside. The reign of God will be perfected. Christian existence, therefore, is in the interim period.

But what, Küng asks, has all this to do with a Church? Did Jesus intend a Church at all? 'To the very last, despite all his lack of success, Jesus addressed himself to *all* the ancient people of God.'[14] 'The Gospels do not report any public announcement by Jesus of his intention to found a Church or a new Covenant or any programmatic call to join a community of the elect.'[15] 'Not until Jesus is risen from the dead do the first Christians speak of a "Church". The Church (and in this sense the new people of God) is therefore a post-Easter phenomenon.'[16] But '*in the pre-Easter period*, Jesus, by his preaching and ministry, *laid the foundations* for the emergence of a post-resurrection Church'.[17] 'As soon as men gathered together in faith in the resurrection of the crucified Jesus of Nazareth and in expectation of the coming consummation of the reign of God and the return of the risen Christ in glory, the Church came into existence.'[18] The Church's origins, therefore, lie in the entire action of God in Christ, his birth, ministry, his calling of the disciples, his death, resurrection, and the sending of his Spirit to the witnesses of his resurrection.

The Church is neither to be identified with the Kingdom of God, nor dissociated from it. It is not the perfected Kingdom which is to come, but it is already under the reign of God which has begun; it 'lives and waits and makes its pilgrim journey under the reign of Christ, which is at the same time, in Christ, the beginning of the reign of God'.[19] It can be termed 'the fellowship of aspirants to the Kingdom of God'.[20] Its function is to *serve* the Kingdom of God. The same divine demands which Jesus preached under the heading 'the reign of God', the Church preaches under the heading 'Jesus the Lord'. The preaching of the reign of God as the decisive, future, and final act of God, as purely religious, as a saving event for sinners, and as demanding a radical decision now for God has become, Küng asserts, an ecclesiological imperative.

Throughout this section[21] Küng's abhorrence of ecclesiastical triumphalism, so often expressed in these two books, comes out clearly. The Church 'should not pretend to be an end in itself or appear to claim for itself the glory which rightly belongs to God. . . . It must not give the impression that the *Church* itself is the end and consummation of world history . . . that man exists for the Church, rather than the Church for mankind, and hence for the reign of God.'[22]

THE NEW TESTAMENT DOCTRINE OF THE CHURCH

1 THE PEOPLE OF GOD

We mentioned previously Küng's stress on the biblical concept of the people of God. This is, he says, 'the oldest and most fundamental concept underlying the self-interpretation of the *ekklesia*. Images such as those of the body of Christ, the temple and so on, are secondary.'[23] He supports this statement with a wealth of biblical evidence. Here another characteristic of Küng's ecclesiology appears—his opposition to clericalization in the Church.

The Church is always the whole people of God. Everyone belongs to the chosen race, the royal priesthood, the holy nation. 'This fundamental parity is much more important than the distinctions which exist in the people of God and which it would be foolish to deny.'[24] The word *laos* in the N.T. means the whole people of God, not 'the laity' in the sense of uneducated members incapable of holding office. Not before the third century did the distinction between 'clerics' and 'laymen' appear, a distinction which later led to the characterization and treatment of the 'laity' as second-class members.

2 THE CREATION OF THE SPIRIT

Küng examines thoroughly the biblical basis of this concept. The Spirit is the Spirit of God acting in Christ who 'opens up for the believer the way to the saving action of God in Christ'[25] and who creates the unity of the body of believers, imparting charisms (gifts) in great variety to all. 'The Church owes to the Spirit its origin, existence, and continued life, and in this sense the Church is a creation of the Spirit.'[26]

But the Church is not to be in any way identified with the Spirit. Those who would make such an identification fall into a triumphalism which ignores the fact that 'the real Church ... is not only a Church composed of people, but of sinful people'.[27] The Church is subordinate to the Spirit, and it must know that the Spirit works where and when he wills:

> The Spirit of God cannot be restricted in his operation by the Church; he is at work not only in the offices of the Church, but where he wills: in the whole people of God. He is at work not only in the 'holy city', but where he wills: in all the churches of the one Church. He is at work not only in the Catholic Church, but where he wills: in Christianity as a whole. And finally he is at work not only in Christianity, but where he wills: in the whole world (*Church*, p. 176).[28]

Küng sees that this poses certain questions for Catholic sacramental theology, which has been reluctant to recognize the validity of the sacraments of other churches. He suggests that, if the starting-point of Catholic judgements were the freedom of the Holy Spirit, this 'in nearly all cases would make a definite *negative* judgement impossible' (ibid., p. 178).

Citing 1 Corinthians 7.7, 12.7 and 1 Peter 4.10, he shows that the

N.T. speaks of the gifts of the Spirit as distributed to all believers, and not limited to the ordained: 'Each Christian has his *charism*. Each Christian is a charismatic.'[29] While the Pastoral Epistles speak of charisms given through the laying on of hands in ordination, the early and authentic letters of Paul, which have much to say about charisms, make no reference to ordination even though gifts of leadership, teaching, and preaching are included (1 Cor. 12.28). The charisms are not simply natural talents (though these may become charisms); they are calls to service. Any state of life or situation is for the Christian a potential charism. Küng regrets that Catholic ecclesiology has too often, until recently, been based on the Pastoral Epistles, and has neglected the charismatic structure of the whole Church which is so clearly stressed in the authentic Pauline epistles. As we shall see,[30] he holds that the development of ecclesiastical offices within the Church, to which the Pastoral Epistles and the Acts of the Apostles bear witness, was legitimate. But he is emphatic that there should be no neglect of 'the fundamental truth about the ordering of the Christian Church',

> namely that *all* members of the Church are inspired by the Spirit, *all* members of the Church have their charism, their special call and their personal ministry, and that pastoral ministries are not the only ones in the Church (ibid., p. 432).

In his view the emergence of a clerical class regarded as set over the 'laity' in a relationship of teacher to learner, director to passive recipient, has disastrously weakened and disrupted the Church.

3 THE BODY OF CHRIST

Küng provides a penetrating examination[31] of the biblical passages which relate to the 'body' concept, including those on baptism and the eucharist. He sees the concept 'body of Christ' as describing very fittingly the unique nature of the new people of God. The two concepts, people of God and body of Christ, are closely linked both in Paul's thinking and through their Jewish roots.[32] The meaning of the doctrine of the body of Christ is that Christ is present in the Church as the risen Lord. He is for the Church not only an event in the past—or in the future—but is present in its life and work. 'Christ is above all present and active in the *worship of the congregation* to which he called us in his Gospel, and into which we were taken up in baptism, in which we celebrate the Lord's Supper and from which we are sent again to our work of service in the world.'[33] Not that Christ is wholly contained in the Church. The N.T. references to the body and head, especially in Colossians and Ephesians 'are concerned not so much with the Church as the body, but with Christ as the head of the Church'[34] who gives it unity through his Spirit. Although he is continually present with his Church, Christ is its Lord.

It is misleading, therefore, to use language which implies the identity of the Church with Christ, such as to speak of the Church as 'a divine–human reality' or 'the extension of the incarnation'.[35] He adds a note which must disconcert not a few theologians, both Roman Catholic and others:

> To talk of the 'mystical body' of Christ is misleading, since the word is very often taken in the sense of what we nowadays understand by mysticism; this gives rise to a view of the Church as united with the divinity in a way that overlooks human creatureliness and sinfulness, and suggests a direct relationship with Christ, an identity with Christ, which is quite wrong.[36]

There is indeed a union between Christ and the Church, but it is one in which the personal differences between them are maintained. The Church remains the fellowship of believers *in Christ*. It is composed of sinful men: 'With good reason it says its *Confiteor* and repeats "Lord I am not worthy".'[37] Its growth is not an organic or automatic process. It takes place only in obedience to Christ, and when Christ through the activity of the Church in history penetrates the world, outwards through missions, or inwards through men of faith and love revealing the reign of God.

The claim that the Church as body of Christ is identified with Christ or possesses him wholly is triumphalism. It leads to the assumption that the Church is only responsible to itself: 'Its all too human directives are given out as the directives of Christ, human commandments are turned into divine commandments. Such a Church is a caricature of itself. Is there such a Church? ... Such a Church always exists, at least as a powerful temptation.'[38] Küng indeed recognizes that it is of this that the Catholic Church is often accused.[39] But as Christ is Head of the Church, so his word is over the Church: 'The teaching authority of the Church can never lie in its own first-hand teaching; it must always be derived from Christ and his word.'[40] Küng keeps this principle in clear view in his discussions of the Petrine office and papal infallibility.[41]

THE MARKS (DIMENSIONS) OF THE CHURCH

Both in *Structures* and *The Church* Küng devotes long sections to the credal 'marks' or 'notes' of the Church: one, holy, catholic, apostolic. These are not 'static labels'; he prefers to speak of them as dimensions which 'dynamically penetrate each other at every point'.[42] They are definitive, essential features of the Church, but all of them are only imperfectly realized on earth. They are divine gifts to the Church by virtue of its foundation in Christ, but they are also tasks to be carried out. The effectiveness of the Church's work in the world ('that the world may believe')

> depends entirely upon whether the Church presents her unity, catholicity, and apostolicity credibly. . . . Credible here does not mean without any shadows; this is impossible in the Church composed of human beings and indeed sinful human beings. Credible does mean, however, that the light must be so bright and strong that darkness appears as something secondary, inessential, not as the authentic nature but as the dark flecks on the luminous essence of the Church during the time of pilgrimage (*Structures*, p. 63).

This is a passage which invites comparison with Barth's reminder that the Church exists 'within Adamic humanity', and with Tillich's insistence that in the situation of existence there can only be fragmentary and partial victories over estrangement.[43]

In his treatment of the four 'dimensions' Küng naturally covers ground which many theologians before him had traversed. I shall therefore note here only his own emphases and new contributions under each head.

One The Church's unity does not imply 'a centralized egalitarian or totalitarian monolith'.[44] Unity is not a synonym for uniformity. It has room for churches coexisting with different rites and forms of devotion, even with different theologies and styles of thought, different laws, customs, and administrative systems. Unity is broken when churches coexist without co-operation but in hostile confrontation. Divisions can arise from honest convictions and cannot always be described in terms of 'Church' and 'heresy'; they seem more like the breaking-up of the one great Church. Küng sees two major schisms of this kind, that between the western and eastern Churches, and that between the western Church and the Church of the Reformation. This is, he says, a state of things 'so abnormal, so contradictory, and so hopeless that it is easy to understand how ways have been sought to justify the unjustifiable'.[45] One such way is to place all emphasis upon an invisible, ideal Church; another is to assert that the divisions are divinely intended, and to be reconciled in the eschatological fulfilment; another (popular with Anglicans) is to regard the different churches as branches of the one Church; another is the claim that only one empirical church is identical with the Church of Christ, and that the others are no part of it. Küng is aware that the Roman Catholic Church has been accused of such 'pharisaical self-conceit, self-righteousness, and impenitence' but believes that 'although there are still some ambiguities, Vatican II largely clarified the attitude of the Catholic Church to the other Christian churches'.[46]

All these are evasions. There can be no justification for Church divisions, for they are sinful. 'The first step in healing the breach must be an admission of guilt and a plea for forgiveness addressed both to God, the Lord of the Church, and to our brothers.'[47] Küng formulates five theological principles for the ecumenical journey of all the churches.[48]

1   The recognition of the *existing* common ecclesiastical reality: one Lord, one Spirit, one Father, one gospel, one baptism, one Supper of the Lord.
2   Prayer: for deliverance from the evil of divisions; of churches for one another. Action: churches listening to and learning from one another; working together to witness to Christ before the world.
3   Discovery of the true nature of one's own church; attention to what F. D. Maurice[49] had called 'the positive principles' of other churches.
4   The rediscovery of truth. Churches must make sacrifices, but not that of truth. There are irreformable constants of truth given by God's revelation. The dogmas and articles in which they have been formulated are not irreformable. The constants have to be 'prised out of their historical setting' so that they can be understood more fully.
5   Acceptance of the gospel of Jesus Christ, taken as a whole, as the standard for unity. Reunion will come in sight by the conversion of all the churches to Christ.

Holy   The Church is not holy because its members make it so by their own moral endeavours. On the contrary, the Church is a 'communion of sinners', totally in need of justification and sanctification.

The Church is holy because it is called by God to be the 'communion of saints', and 'by virtue of the sanctifying Spirit who continually establishes and animates the Church anew, and preserves, illuminates, guides, and sanctifies'.[50] The Church is both a communion of sinners and a communion of saints. Holiness is at once God's gift to it, and a challenge, a dimension into the depths of which it must grow. Many theologians have interpreted the holiness of the Church in a similar way, but Küng brings the subject down to earth by the reminder[51] that the Holy Spirit is not the captive of the Church, and that until the Church is 'open to the Holy Spirit which bloweth where it listeth, within or without any institution'[52] its own holiness will not be credible, and by the statement that the Church's holiness is not credibly represented by magnificence, pomp, or splendour, but rather in making clear its purpose to serve the world in humility.

Catholic   After a discussion of the different senses in which the phrase 'Catholic Church' has been used, Küng affirms that originally and basically it means the whole, universal Church.[53] A local church, however, is properly called catholic in that it represents the entire Church in a particular place.

But spatial extension alone does not make a church catholic; nor do numerical quantity, cultural variety, and temporal continuity. A church possessing all these characteristics may yet have become unfaithful to its nature.

> It is an all-embracing identity which at bottom makes a Church catholic, the fact that despite all the constant and necessary changes of the times and of varying forms, and despite its blemishes and weaknesses, the Church in every place and in every age remains unchanged in its essence (*Church*, p. 302).

'Identity' here indicates no kind of 'ecclesiastical narcissism'. The Church does not exist for itself, but for mankind as a whole, the world. By its very origin and nature the Church must be and act with reference to the whole inhabited earth (Greek, *oikumene*). 'Ecumenical' and 'catholic' are closely related words.

Küng maintains that a manifold variety is as necessary to the Church's true catholicity as it is to its unity: 'The Church must show herself as the Church which respects all languages, traditions and spiritual experiences in the forms peculiar to each of the different nations.'[54] He counsels a realism about the unlikelihood of Asiatic and African peoples accepting a 'centrally directed Western, Latin, unified

Church', and recognizes that it is 'untenable theologically' for the Roman Catholic Church to demand that Orthodox and Protestant Christians who have experienced a development of autonomous Christianity for centuries should surrender their own sound Christian values.[55]

During his discussion of catholicity in *The Church* Küng deals with two questions which have long bedevilled Church relations. The first is the claim to be the one Church by that church which is commonly referred to by its own members and by others as 'the Catholic Church'.[56] The churches of the East and of the Reformation, however they explain their relationship with the Church of the Apostles, were once, directly or indirectly, linked with this so-called Catholic Church. Might not their relationship to it, he cautiously asks, be thought of as that between mother and daughters who, for what they sincerely believe to be good reasons, 'could no longer live with mother'. The analogy is worked out in an illuminating way, and Küng concludes that neither the Catholic Church nor the other churches will achieve the necessary unity and catholicity of the Church without 'working out' their relationship with one another and mutually making peace.

The second question relates to the dictum, 'No salvation outside the Church'.[57] Küng rejects the 'theological sleight of hand' which attempts to include within the Church non-Christians of upright life. An explicit belief in Christ is fundamental to the concept of the Church. Those who make no such profession and might not even wish to do so cannot be silently claimed as members. He would probably doubt the usefulness of Tillich's idea of 'the latent Church'.

Küng believes that the negative and exclusive formula was dubious from the beginning, is open to misunderstanding, and damaging to the Church's mission. He would prefer the positive formulation 'salvation inside the Church', which does not imply that there is no salvation outside. The whole world is in God's hand, and the Church can lay no exclusive claim to certainty of salvation.

Apostolic   The apostolicity of the Church is its possession of and faithfulness to the apostolic commission. The apostolic office is 'unique and unrepeatable',[58] for the apostles were the original witnesses to Christ and their preaching is the original, fundamental testimony to him. But the apostolic *commission* and task remain. There is still an apostolic ministry, and it is the Church, 'the whole Church, not just a few individuals',[59] which succeeds to it. The Church's real link with the apostles, its apostolicity, resides in its preservation of agreement with the witness of the apostles and of a vital continuity with their ministry. Moreover, 'to be itself, the Church must follow the apostles in continually recognizing and demonstrating that it has been sent out into the world'.[60]

Like the other three marks of the Church, apostolicity is not a static attribute, but a dimension which has constantly to be fulfilled anew in history. Küng dares to express the opinion[61] that agreement by the Christian churches on these four fundamental dimensions of the Church is not an impossible hope: not an agreement which would exclude differences in theological interpretation, but one which would overcome the divisions in the one holy, catholic, and apostolic Church.

THE EXTERNAL STRUCTURE OF THE CHURCH

Küng is well aware that disagreement about external structure and about the place of ecclesiastical office is a most—perhaps the most—cogent cause of the Church's continuing disunity. To these subjects he allots a great deal of space both in *Structures* and *The Church*.

THE LAITY[62]

The basic structure of the Church is its standing as the people called by God. Küng maintains that the doctrine of the universal priesthood of all believers is a fundamental truth of Catholic ecclesiology, and he regrets that so often, until recently, Catholic theology has treated ecclesiology as a hierarchology, as though ecclesiastical offices constituted the basic structure of the Church.[63] He notes that the N.T. nowhere speaks of the ordained minister of the gospel as a priest. Christ is the High Priest, who has 'fulfilled definitively the truth of the priestly idea',[64] and is the representative of mankind before God, the Mediator. But the N.T. does speak of all believers as 'a royal priesthood'.[65] Through Christ's universal priesthood all who believe in him have a priestly function. They have direct access to God; they are to offer sacrifices, not of atonement since as sinners they can add nothing to Christ's sufficient sacrifice, but of praise, thanksgiving, and above all the humble and penitent offering of themselves wholly to God; they are 'called to preach the gospel in the sense of their personal Christian witness, without being all called to preach in the narrow sense of the word or to be theologians';[66] they have an essential role in the administering of baptism, the Lord's Supper and forgiveness of sins; they have a mediatory function between the world and God by devoting themselves to their fellow-men in service and by praying for them. Does then every member of the Church have the right and responsibility to do all things in the Church? Is there need for any kind of ecclesiastical office?

ECCLESIASTICAL OFFICE

Martin Luther had interpreted the priesthood of all believers as meaning that any baptized person 'may claim that he has already been consecrated as a priest, bishop, or pope, although it is not seemly for any one person to exercise this authority arbitrarily',[67] and that the Christian community has the right to call and appoint office-bearers, and to depose them. Küng concedes that Luther believed the situation in his day presented an emergency in which there was no alternative to reformation without the bishops, and that he believed this with some reason: 'The Reformation would have taken a different turn if the bishops (and the pope) had taken a different, an *apostolic* attitude ... if they had espoused a serious Church reform.'[68] But he considers that Luther failed to provide a theological foundation for ecclesiastical office. He tended to regard it as little more than a matter of convenience, and to neglect the scriptural doctrine (1 Tim. 4.14; 2 Tim. 1.6) that in ordination a grace is bestowed and not only ratified. On the other hand he notes with approval Luther's great emphasis on vocation, and his later willingness to distinguish between induction into a pastoral charge, and ordination which does not have to be repeated. Küng reveals his own conviction when he asks whether spiritual and ecclesiastical office in the Church is not

> something that emanates from the apostolic attestation of Scripture, namely succession in the apostolic *office*? Not, of course, in an ecclesiastical office for the exercise of power, or in an office for self-glorification, but in an office of service, of service in the apostolic spirit for the maintenance, defence, and expansion of the apostolic faith and the apostolic confession? And yet an office that is not merely an ecclesiastical officialdom delegated by men, but an authority established and legitimatized from above within the royal and priestly community, as a

special authority derived from a grace-dispensing apostolic vocation, blessing and commission? (*Structures*, p. 107).

Küng insists that ecclesiastical office is essentially diaconal.[69] The word chosen in the N.T. to describe the place and function of the Church officer 'carried no overtones of authority, officialdom, rule, dignity, or power: the word *diakonia*, service'.[70] Commenting on the frequency of the word 'serve' and its synonyms in the recorded teaching of Jesus, he says: 'In contrast to all the concepts of office in existence at the time, Jesus chose and emphasized this new conception of service.'[71] The Church is a fellowship of gifts of the Spirit (charisms). Charisms are calls to service. This is the very basis of Christian discipleship. The whole Church has, therefore, both a charismatic and a diaconal structure, and those who have received the gift of office stand within this structure.

Küng gives close attention to the evidence of the N.T. about the development of ecclesiastical office in the Church.[72] The ministries of which the New Testament speaks are many and varied. Some are exercised publicly and regularly, others are more private and occasional. Some have endured, others have disappeared. All are based on charisms, gifts of the Spirit, recognized and used in the service of the community.

Küng notes again that in the Christian communities founded by Paul there were no formal ministerial appointments. Those responsible for the various ministries derived their authority from their charisms and their call, 'not from the community and not from the apostle, not even from their own decision'.[73] There were no presbyters, no monarchical episcopate, no ordination by laying on of hands,[74] even though Paul's lists of charisms include administrators and overseers (*episkopoi*).

The office of presbyter, or elder, originated in Jewish–Christian communities, as did ordination by laying on of hands, following Jewish tradition. Küng suggests[75] that the two types of ministry, one charismatic and the other more institutional, influenced one another, and began to interlock at the end of the Pauline period. For example, the titles 'presbyter' and *episkopos* came to be used interchangeably. Within a generation or two the Palestinian form of constitution obscured the Pauline, and in the Pastoral Epistles we see the beginning of the monarchical episcopate. Yet the apostle Paul would have resisted the suggestion that the churches he founded were lacking in any essential because they had no monarchical *episkopoi* and the laying on of hands was not practised.

Küng believes that the rise of the threefold ministry was justifiable, but regrets that it led to 'a loss of the general *charismatic structure* of the Church and ... the forgetting of the particular diaconal structure of *all* ministries'.[76] The later forms of ministry and Church order, which took on a canonical force, were the realization of certain possibilities among many, and should not be mistaken for dogmatic necessities.[77] Following a discussion in *Structures* which covers much the same ground, he is prepared to say that in the new situation of ecumenical encounter between the Catholic Church and other Christian bodies questions such as that of the recognition of other means of reaching ecclesiastical office than by the imposition of episcopal hands deserve thorough theological examination.[78] Other questions ripe for renewed study are the relationship between the offices and functions of the *episkopos*, the *presbyteros* and the *diakonos*, and the spiritual and ecclesiastical acts which may be performed by any Christian as one who participates in the priesthood of all believers.[79]

However such questions may be decided in his own Church, Küng is insistent that those who are ordained to the pastoral ministry are not 'a separate caste of consecrated priests, as they often are in primitive religions. ... In the Church of Jesus Christ, who is the only high priest and mediator, all the faithful are priests and clergy.'[80] This priesthood of all believers, however, does not exclude a particular ministry of pastors whose authority is not simply by delegation from the community: 'It is the glorified Lord who creates them through his gifts, encouraging each to make a contribution to the community through his ministry (Eph. 4.12).'[81]

ECCLESIASTICAL OFFICE AND APOSTOLIC SUCCESSION

Küng notes and welcomes the increasing attention being given to the doctrines of ecclesiastical office and episcopacy by the Reformed Churches. Of the important 'Declaration concerning the Apostolic Succession', published by the United Evangelical Church of Germany in 1957, he says that 'many ambiguities in Luther's theology of office ... were cleared up ... and *several Catholic desiderata were fulfilled*'.[82] Points on which the Catholic can agree with the Declaration are:[83]

(a) All believers are called to the royal priesthood.

(b) The office of the apostles precedes all other ministries. It is unique, but standard-setting.

(c) Ecclesiastical office, while it is to be distinguished from that of the apostles, continues their function of leadership. Holders of pastoral office are subordinate to Christ and constantly in need of the grace of the Holy Spirit. They are subject also to the apostles, as being bound by the authority of the apostles' witness. Their office excludes neither other special ministries nor the priesthood of all believers.

(d) The basic apostolic succession is that of the whole Church. It is manifested in the continuous process of baptizing and being baptized, in the transmission and reception of the faith, in the Church's worship and work.

(e) Within the apostolic succession of the Church there is a succession of office, entry into which 'occurs with the co-operation . . . of the office-holders and the congregation'. The holder of pastoral office is not set in an exclusive position; he needs the co-operation of the priesthood of all believers which is itself an expression of the apostolic succession.

In the protest of the 'Declaration' against 'papalistic formalization of the succession' Küng sees misunderstanding of the Catholic doctrine. He defends the Catholic doctrine against the charge of mechanical formalism by the following points:[84] Apostolic succession is not an arbitrary human invention, but a work of the Spirit of Christ. The imposition of hands is its sacramental sign. Ordination is an *opus operatum* (a work worked) not of the ordaining minister, but of the Spirit:

> The power of ordination is not handed down on a horizontal level from the past, although in the temporal dimension the man who received his ordination from his predecessors in turn ordains his successor. Rather, the power of ordination is passed down in the vertical dimension, from the Spirit, transcending time and space (*Structures*, p. 166).

The consecration of a bishop is not the mechanical succession of an individual to a predecessor, but entrance into a community, the corporate body, or college of bishops which as a whole succeeds the college of the apostles. Apostolic succession does not contradict the Word of God, but serves it. The Word is not only to be read, but preached, and therefore needs a succession of preachers with a commission and continuity which goes back to the apostles. The doctrine of apostolic succession presupposes faith awakened by God's grace in the person to be ordained. Without this 'all that occurs is sacrilege'. The office bestowed imposes the obligation of faithfulness to the Lord, and service of the Church in an apostolic spirit. Such a doctrine, Küng maintains, is unjustly described as formalistic, mechanical, and dangerous.

At the close of a similar summary of the meaning of apostolic succession in *The Church*,[85] Küng writes:

> In the light of the Pauline or Gentile Christian view of the Church, other ways of entry into the pastorate and into the apostolic succession of the pastors must remain open. The other view of the Church, the presbyterial and episcopal view, which rightly became established in the Church in practice, must still be basically open to other and different possibilities, such as existed in the New Testament church (*Church*, p. 442).

In view of the theological and ecumenical implications of this question there is, he says, 'serious need for them to come under urgent discussion'.[86]

THE PAPACY

Both the books which we have considered include a discussion of the relationship of the papacy to the structure of the Church.[87] As we have seen, Küng has been able to note an increasingly positive attitude to episcopacy on the part of the Reformed churches. He is aware that there is no similar attitude towards the papacy. He attempts 'to present the Petrine office credibly',[88] and his treatment is explanatory and more patently apologetic. To summarize his main points:

a Christ founded the Church on the rock of the Petrine office. Küng adds in brackets 'and also the apostolic office'.[89]

b The Petrine office has the task of representing and guaranteeing unity, of strengthening faith, and of pastoral care.[90] It is a ministry, and only as such is it an authority in (not over) the Church.[91]

c Canon 218 gives to the pope 'supreme and juridical power over the universal Church', and Canon 1156 declares that 'the first See is under judgement of nobody'. The First Vatican Council in 1870 elaborated this papal status and authority in great detail. But Küng reminds us that this Council was interrupted by war before it could discuss the episcopate. There are, he maintains, limitations to papal authority both by natural and divine law.[92] Among these are the existence of the episcopate, and the orderly exercise of office by the bishops which the pope may not disturb; the *aim* of the pope's exercise of power, which must share the diaconal character of every ecclesiastical office; the *mode* of the papal exercise of power, which must be through the self-administration of individual churches with very rare interventions. Moreover, the Church has a legal defence against an unworthy pope through an ecumenical council.

d Canon 228 declares 'an ecumenical council holds supreme power over the universal Church'. This assertion can be supported from the Council of Constance, the binding character of whose decrees cannot be evaded.[93] That Council defines a distinct kind of superiority of ecumenical councils, namely their function as a 'control authority', not only for the emergency of the fifteenth century, but 'on the premise that a possible future pope might again lapse into heresy, schism, or the like'.[94] Küng suggests that the relationship of the supreme authority of the ecumenical council (Canon 228) to that of the pope (Canon 218) 'is not to be understood as a relationship of super-ordination and subordination, but as a reciprocal ministerial relationship in the service of the Church under the one and only Lord'.[95]

e Küng disagrees with Canon 222 which accords to the pope the exclusive right to convoke councils. He argues that this Canon does not base itself on a divine law. In times of crisis 'one could not dispute, *ex iure divino*, even the right of lay persons to convoke a council for the welfare of the Church',[96] granted that they have the support of the whole Church. Constantine and other emperors convoked councils, some of which are reckoned ecumenical, without consulting the popes, and even promulgated their decrees prior to papal confirmation.

f He welcomes certain ways in which Vatican II corrected and modified Vatican I's definition of the papacy.[97] The Petrine ministry is emphasized as a ministry, and not a dominion. The pope is referred to as 'the pastor of the whole Church' instead of 'the head of the Church'. Bishops are said to receive their full authority by episcopal consecration, and not by papal appointment, and pope and bishops together are to share a collegial responsibility for the government of the whole Church. The council also called for a reform of the centralized papal system by the setting-up of national and regional conferences, by representing the whole episcopate in Rome by a synod of bishops, and by making the Roman curia more international.

g Küng recognizes the stumbling-block which the doctrine of papal infallibility, defined by Vatican I, raises for the Reformed Churches. On the principle that no human formulation is ultimate, and that doctrine develops and should develop, provided that it is in keeping with revelation, and bearing in mind that 'dogmas are no more and no less than emergency measures which the Church was forced to adopt because of heresies',[98] he sees reason to suggest that the questions of the infallibility of the Church and of the pope merit further study in the light of criticism made since Vatican I, for example by Karl Barth.[99] He himself undertakes a contribution to such a study.[100] It is to be understood that a papal definition is not a new revelation, but an authoritative bearing of witness to the revelation which has occurred, 'not a divine word but only a human utterance about the Word of God'.[101] Vatican I defined limits to the pope's infallibility. It is operative only when he speaks as chief pastor and teacher (*ex cathedra*) and when he intends to define a matter of faith and morals; and his infallibility is that 'with which the divine Redeemer willed his Church to be endowed'. This phrase from the Vatican I definition must be given full weight. Papal infallibility is not separate from that of the Church. Vatican I's declaration that papal definitions do not depend on the *consensus* (agreement) of the Church does not mean that a pope can define a dogma *against* the *consensus* of the Church. This would incur the charge of schism, if not of heresy. He is under obligation to consult in order to obtain the *sensus* (mind) of the Church.[102] Küng puts these considerations forward to enable ecumenical discussion on the subject to proceed with fewer misunderstandings.

h Küng realizes, however, that many Christians call into question the very existence of the papacy. He frankly faces the theological and historical difficulties of this question. He expresses sorrow that the Petrine ministry has so often appeared to men to be a Petrine dominion. But he does not believe that the concept of the primacy is in opposition to Scripture. He sees in Pope John XXIII one who 'inaugurated a new epoch of hope for the whole of Christendom and for the Petrine ministry itself'.[103] He pleads for a voluntary renunciation of spiritual power on the part of the papacy, and 'a way back, or rather a way forward to the original idea of a primacy of service'[104] which serves the whole Church in evangelical humility, simplicity, and brotherliness, and which furthers evangelical freedom.[105]

In summary, for Hans Küng the Church is the people of God called into being by the Spirit of God through Christ, the community of those who believe in God through Christ, with whom Christ is present as their risen Lord. It is a worshipping and serving people; it is called to preserve and to perfect its essential marks of oneness, holiness, catholicity, and apostolicity. Its structures are: first and basically, the whole body of the faithful as a priestly community; second, the ecclesiastical offices in the succession of the apostles; and third, the Petrine office or papacy, succeeding to the Apostle Peter's position among the apostles. These three are not set apart from each other. They exist in a communion of reciprocal ministries, and have a common ministry to the world.

Postscript

Every book, if the author hopes for its publication, must come to an end. But every book which deals with a subject historically comes to an end which must be unsatisfying. In dealing with the past the writer has to omit much that is relevant in one way or another. He has to be selective, thus opening himself to the charge that his selection is prejudiced. Moreover, the end of an historical study has to be unsatisfactory, because, as the last sentence is written, history goes on, history which, as Tillich says, is characterized by 'the production of new and unique embodiments of meaning'.[1]

What is often described as the Church's first history book, the Acts of the Apostles of St Luke, ends in a way which many find abrupt. It concludes with the information that Paul spent two years in Rome, 'preaching the kingdom of God and teaching about the Lord Jesus Christ quite openly and unhindered'.

Readers down the centuries have regretted that Luke has told us nothing of the activities of the other apostles during the period in which the Acts concentrated on the story of Paul. So of this book it is possible to ask why no mention is made of the ecclesiology of such men as Karl Rahner, the most eminent of contemporary Roman Catholic theologians; of the studies of the biblical doctrine of the Church of the Anglican Lionel Thornton of the Community of the Resurrection; and of the missionary's viewpoint on ecclesiology of Lesslie Newbigin, formerly a bishop in the Church of South India.[2] The author is aware of many such gaps, and not only in his treatment of the twentieth century. He can only plead his inability to master all the relevant material, and the consideration of space.

Readers of the Acts have also regretted that Luke did not take his account a few years further. Writing, as most scholars assume, some twenty years after Paul's arrival in Rome, he must have been in a position to tell us more about the early history of the Church in Rome, of its growth and its struggles, of the persecution under the Emperor Nero in 64 when, according to tradition, the apostles Peter and Paul were martyred. It may be, as some suggest, that Luke's purpose was not so much to write a detailed history as to describe the passage of the gospel of Christ from Jerusalem to the capital of the ancient world, and that therefore he felt that his work had a satisfactory completeness.

I have attempted to bring my account of the ways in which Christians have understood the nature of the Church as close as possible to the date of publication. It has been seen how, in different ways, recent theologians have brought into prominence the image of the Church as servant—servant of the world, because servant of God and because this is God's world. This recovered insight must surely be retained. It needs to be deepened, for it is not yet fully recognized at what we now call 'the grass roots level', nor by many a Church leader, and still less by parish and congregational finance committees. Too often the unbiblical saying 'charity begins at home' is in mind, and it is forgotten that, according to the Scriptures, it is judgement which begins at the household of God (1 Pet. 4.17).

For the future, who can prophesy? There are signs that in many ways the future belongs to the Third World. Western industrialized nations have recently begun to realize that what they have been pleased to speak of as undeveloped nations can no longer be regarded as a source of cheap raw materials and labour in return for some paternalistic gestures. In many of these countries the Church has become indigenous, and in some of them is having to struggle for its very existence—the situation of the early Church. Perhaps we must now look to these Christians whose history, culturally, socially, economically, and politically, has differed greatly from that of those whose writings *de ecclesia* have been considered in this book, to help us to understand what God means his people, the body of Christ, and the communion of the Holy Spirit to be in the years which lie ahead of us.

Notes

CHAPTER 15

[1] G. R. Cragg, *The Church and the Age of Reason, 1648–1789* (Harmondsworth, 1970), p. 37.

[2] Ibid., p. 16.

[3] F. L. Cross, ed., *The Oxford Dictionary of the Christian Church* (London 1957), p. 789.

[4] I. T. Ramsey, ed., *John Locke, 'The Reasonableness of Christianity'* (California, Stanford University Press, 1958), pp. 60–62. This is an abridgement of the 1731 edn. Ramsey has numbered the *paragraphs* in this edn. Numbers here in brackets refer to these paragraphs.

[5] Ramsey, op. cit., pp. 45, 46, 50.

[6] Ibid., pp. 48–9.

[7] Quoted from Owen Chadwick, *The Reformation*, 'Pelican History of the Church', vol. 3 (Harmondsworth 1964), p. 402.

[8] Locke wrote three more letters on the subject, in answer to attacks on the first by Jonas Proast who argued that force was justified to promote true religion. Locke's fourth letter was only in draft form when he died.

[9] John Locke, *A Letter Concerning Toleration* (New York, The Liberal Arts Press, 1955), p. 16.

[10] Ibid., p. 29.

[11] Ibid., pp. 23–4, 27, 28, 35, 40.

[12] Ibid., p. 40.

[13] Ibid., p. 50.

[14] Ibid., pp. 50–51.

[15] Ibid., p. 51.

[16] Ibid., p. 52.

[17] 'Denomination' strictly means a designation by class; the naming of a particular category among entities which share the same characteristics. It is in this sense that we speak of banknotes as having denominations of one, five, ten, etc.

[18] Ibid., p. 20.

[19] More recently the word has been used to denote zealous partiality for *one* 'denomination' over others.

[20] See vol. 1, p. 139.

[21] Gallicanism took differing forms, some more radical than others. See Yves Congar, *L'Eglise de saint Augustin à l'epoque moderne* (Paris 1970), pp. 392–412 *passim*, and for a brief account, G. R. Cragg, op. cit., pp. 21–5.

[22] Cragg, op. cit., p. 99.

[23] Probabilism was thus defined by Bartolomeo Medina (1527–80): 'If an opinion is probable it is permissible to follow it, even though the opposite be more probable.' The

doctrine was vehemently attacked by Blaise Pascal in his *Provincial Letters* (1656).

[24] The Conference adopted a form of ordination with the laying on of hands, in 1836.

[25] The Augustinian doctrines of the early Jansenists are no longer emphasized.

[26] *The Deed of Union* (1932), drawn up when the separate Primitive Methodist, United Methodist, and Wesleyan Methodist Churches in England entered into union.

[27] See vol. 1, pp. 163 and 231 nn.

[28] 'The Methodists: Statement approved by the British Methodist Conference, Bradford, 1937' in R. Newton Flew, ed., *The Nature of the Church* (London 1952), pp. 207–8.

[29] See Warren W. Slabaugh, 'The Church of the Brethren', in Flew, op. cit., pp. 298–302.

[30] Cragg, op. cit., p. 283.

[31] Cragg, op. cit., p. 254.

[32] See above, p. 9.

[33] Congar, *L'Eglise*, p. 418.

[34] Ibid.

[35] Ibid., pp. 418–19.

[36] Ibid., p. 421.

[37] 'Symbolism' is used here in its theological sense of 'study of the creeds'. The Greek *symbolon* was the usual word for a creed in the early Church. The sub-title of Möhler's *Symbolik* is 'an account of the doctrinal differences of Catholics and Protestants according to their published confessions'.

[38] *Symbolik*, para. 36, quoted in Congar, op. cit., p. 422.

[39] R. H. Nientaltowski, 'Möhler', in *The New Catholic Encyclopedia* (New York, McGraw-Hill, 1967), vol. ix; see also Congar, op. cit., p. 423.

[40] These figures indicate that about a hundred bishops were not present for the voting.

[41] H. Denzinger, *Enchiridion Symbolorum, Definitionum et Declarationum de rebus fidei et morum* (Freiburg 1960), p. 1859, quoted in H. Küng, *Structures of the Church* (Notre Dame, U.S.A., 1968), p. 314.

[42] Congar, op. cit., p. 460.

[43] F. von Hügel, *Essays and Addresses on the Philosophy of Religion*, 2nd ser. (London 1930), p. 106.

[44] F. von Hügel, *Selected Letters, 1896–1924* (London 1927), p. 334.

[45] E.g. in *Eternal Life* (Edinburgh 1912), pp. 336 ff; *Essays and Addresses*, 1st ser. (London 1927), pp. 257–9, 267.

[46] In *Some Notes on the Petrine Claims* (London 1930), pp. 16–33. These notes were written in 1893.

[47] Maurice Nédoncelle, *Baron Friedrich von Hügel* (London 1937), p. 133.

[48] Von Hügel gives a striking example of what he means in *Essays and Addresses*, 1st ser., p. 285, citing the incident of the Jewish rabbi of Lyons, a chaplain in the First World War, 'holding up at a dying Catholic soldier's request, this soldier's crucifix before his eyes, and this amidst a hail of bullets and shrapnel'. For von Hügel's ecclesiology, *Essays and Addresses*, 1st ser., essays 8–11, pp. 227–98 are important.

CHAPTER 16

[1] In an introduction to a reprint in 1926 of the 1st edn; quoted here from Friedrich Schleiermacher, *On Religion: Speeches to its Cultured Despisers* (New York, Harper & Row, 1958), p. xi. This vol. gives the E. T. of John Oman of the 3rd edn of 1831, together with Schleiermacher's own 'Explanations' of certain passages. Quotations here from the *Speeches* are from this work.

[2] J. M. Creed, *The Divinity of Jesus Christ* (London 1964), p. 39.

[3] *Speeches*, p. 147.

⁴ Ibid., p. 149.
⁵ Ibid.
⁶ Ibid., p. 151.
⁷ Ibid., pp. 151–2.
⁸ Ibid., pp. 185–6.
⁹ Ibid., p. 155.
¹⁰ Ibid., p. 188.
¹¹ Ibid., p. 187.
¹² Ibid., p. 188.
¹³ Ibid., pp. 156–66.
¹⁴ Ibid., p. 157.
¹⁵ Ibid., pp. 158–9.
¹⁶ Ibid., p. 190.
¹⁷ Ibid., p. 157.
¹⁸ Ibid., p. 190.
¹⁹ Ibid., p. 163.
²⁰ Ibid., p. 166.
²¹ Ibid., p. 191.
²² Ibid., p. 166.
²³ Ibid., p. 191.
²⁴ Friedrich Schleiermacher, *The Christian Faith*, E. T. of the 2nd German edn, ed. H. R. Mackintosh and J. S. Stewart (Edinburgh 1960), p. v (Editors' Preface).
²⁵ Ibid., p. 3.
²⁶ Ibid.
²⁷ Ibid., pp. 5–6.
²⁸ Ibid., p. 31.
²⁹ Ibid., p. 34.
³⁰ Ibid., pp. 39–40.
³¹ Ibid., p. 53.
³² Ibid., p. 88.
³³ Many modern Catholic and Protestant theologians would disagree with the sharp distinction between Catholic and Protestant doctrine which Schleiermacher asserts here.
³⁴ Ibid., p. 107.
³⁵ Ibid.
³⁶ Ibid., pp. 355–70.
³⁷ Schleiermacher notes that the word 'mystical' is often used vaguely, but is prepared to admit its use in connection with his presentation of the redeeming activity of Christ (and therefore with his concept of the Church), provided that it is used in its original sense, which is decidedly less than 'magical', but decidedly more than 'empirical'. See ibid., pp. 428–31.
³⁸ Ibid., pp. 362–3.
³⁹ Ibid., p. 367.
⁴⁰ Ibid., pp. 525–722.
⁴¹ Ibid., p. 586.
⁴² Ibid., pp. 525–81.
⁴³ Ibid., pp. 676–95.
⁴⁴ Ibid., pp. 696–722.
⁴⁵ Ibid., p. 529.
⁴⁶ Ibid., p. 533.
⁴⁷ Ibid., p. 529.
⁴⁸ Ibid.
⁴⁹ Ibid., p. 533.
⁵⁰ Ibid., p. 538.

[51] Ibid., p. 544.
[52] Ibid., pp. 548–9.
[53] Ibid., p. 540.
[54] Ibid., p. 559.
[55] Ibid., p. 565.
[56] Ibid., p. 568.
[57] See also Schleiermacher's earlier treatment in the *Speeches*, above, pp. 25–6.
[58] Ibid., p. 676.
[59] See above, p. 32.
[60] Ibid., p. 678.
[61] Ibid., p. 681.
[62] Ibid., p. 683.
[63] Ibid., p. 697.
[64] Ibid., p. 696.
[65] An E.T. of vol. 3 was edited by H. R. Mackintosh and A. B. Macauley (*A. Ritschl: The Christian Doctrine of Justification and Sanctification*. Edinburgh 1900. References in this ch. are to this vol.
[66] Ritschl, op. cit., pp. 7, 202, 212, 238.
[67] Ibid., p. 388.
[68] Ibid., p. 8.
[69] Ritschl acknowledges many debts to Schleiermacher, although his references to the latter are often accompanied by a correction, and sometimes by the charge of inconsistency.
[70] Ibid., p. 2.
[71] Cf. also pp. 7, 546–7.
[72] See the discussion ibid., pp. 559–64.
[73] Ibid., p. 11.
[74] Ibid.
[75] Here Ritschl presents his view of the mutual relation of the two *foci*.
[76] E.g. ibid., pp. 130, 288, 590.
[77] Ibid., p. 109.
[78] Ibid., pp. 284–5.
[79] Ibid., p. 286.
[80] Ibid., p. 287.
[81] Ibid., p. 288.
[82] Ibid., p. 287.
[83] Ibid., p. 289.
[84] 'Not every one who says to me, "Lord, Lord," shall enter the kingdom of heaven, but he who does the will of my Father who is in heaven. ...'
[85] Ibid., p. 553. See also p. 603.
[86] These are p. 273 (in ch. 4, 'The Doctrine of God'); pp. 471–2 (in ch. 6, 'The Doctrine of the Person and Life-work of Christ'); pp. 532–4 (in ch. 7, 'The Necessity of the Forgiveness of Sins or Justification in General'); and pp. 603–8 (in ch. 8, 'The Necessity of Basing the Forgiveness of Sins on the Work and Passion of Christ').
[87] Ibid., p. 471.
[88] Ibid.
[89] Ibid.
[90] Ibid., p. 606.
[91] Ibid., p. 607.
[92] Ibid., p. 603.
[93] An E.T. by T. B. Saunders under the title *What is Christianity?* was published in London in 1901, and has been many times reprinted.
[94] 'The Preaching of Jesus on the Kingdom of God'.

[95] An E.T. by W. Montgomery under the title *The Quest of the Historical Jesus* was published in 1910.

CHAPTER 17

[1] Charles Smyth, *Simeon and Church Order* (Cambridge 1940), pp. 240–43.

[2] The Surrey Chapel belonged to the Countess of Huntingdon's Connexion. She was a wealthy and influential woman who devoted herself and her resources to promoting Methodism among the upper classes. She favoured the Calvinistic Methodism of Whitefield. Her 'connexion' included a number of Church of England clergymen whom she took on herself to appoint as her chaplains in the meeting-houses which she founded. The Bishop of London's consistory court declared this to be uncanonical in 1779, whereupon the Countess registered the meeting-houses as dissenting conventicles under the Toleration Act of 1689.

[3] Quoted in Charles Smyth, *The Church and the Nation* (London 1962), p. 143.

[4] William Carus, *Memoirs of the Life of the Rev. Charles Simeon, M.A.* (New York, Robert Carter, 1847), p. 23.

[5] See also H. C. G. Moule, *Charles Simeon* (London 1892); and Charles Smyth, *Simeon and Church Order*.

[6] Quoted in Moule, op. cit, pp. 102–3.

[7] Carus, op. cit., p. 171.

[8] Quoted in Smyth, *The Church and the Nation*, p. 143.

[9] Smyth, *Simeon and Church Order*, p. 299.

[10] Ibid.

[11] Carus, op. cit., p. 272.

[12] An advowson is the right to present a clergyman to a bishop for institution and induction as incumbent of a parish. The holder of an advowson, or patron, may be an individual or a corporation, such as a college. The right of advowson, which is not peculiar to the English Church, goes back to feudal times. English law regards advowsons as property which may be given away or sold.

[13] Quoted in Smyth, *Simeon and Church Order*, p. 292.

[14] References here are to Thomas Arnold, *Principles of Church Reform*, with an introductory essay by M. J. Jackson and J. Rogan. London 1962.

[15] See, e.g., J. R. H. Moorman, *A History of the Church in England* (London 1953), pp. 331–2.

[16] Arnold, op. cit., p. 97.

[17] Ibid., p. 99.

[18] Ibid., p. 101.

[19] Ibid., p. 103.

[20] Ibid., p. 104.

[21] Ibid.

[22] Ibid., p. 105.

[23] Ibid., p. 110.

[24] Ibid., p. 111.

[25] Ibid., p. 115.

[26] Ibid., p. 118.

[27] Ibid., p. 122.

[28] Ibid., p. 123.

[29] Ibid., p. 124.

[30] Ibid., p. 125.

[31] Ibid., pp. 125–7.

[32] Ibid., pp. 128–34.

33 Ibid., pp. 134–8.
34 Ibid., pp. 141–5.
35 Ibid., pp. 145–7.
36 Moorman, op. cit., p. 332.
37 See C. C. Richardson, *The Church through the Centuries* (New York, Scribner, 1938), pp. 217–18.
38 The Irish Church Act is referred to in Tract 2, written by Newman.
39 References here are to the American edn (2 vols.), *Tracts for the Times: by Members of the University of Oxford.* New York, Charles Henry, 1839–40.
40 Op. cit., vol. 1, pp. 9–10.
41 Ibid., p. 29.
42 Ibid., vol. 2, p. 3.
43 Ibid., p. 4.
44 Ibid., pp. 8–11.
45 Ibid., vol. 1, pp. 237–8.
46 Ibid., pp. 281–2.
47 Moorman, op. cit., pp. 344–5.
48 Newman explains his motives in writing Tract 90 at the end of part iv of his *Apologia pro vita sua* (1864).
49 J. H. Newman, *An Essay on the Development of Christian Doctrine.* New York, Longmans Green, 1927. References here are to this edn.
50 Newman, *Apologia pro vita sua* (London 1930), p. 185.
51 'It takes on strength as it proceeds.'
52 Typical, because he uses similar language in concluding arguments that the Roman Church is to be identified with the Church of the fifth and sixth centuries and with the Church of the first three centuries (op. cit., pp. 245–7, 321–2).

CHAPTER 18

1 A. J. Hartley, 'The Way to Unity: Maurice's Exegesis for Society', *Canadian Journal of Theology*, vol. xvi, nos. 1 and 2 (1970), p. 95.
2 Advertisement to the 1842 edn, F. D. Maurice, *The Kingdom of Christ*, ed. A. R. Vidler (London 1958), vol. 1, p. 25. References here are to this edn.
3 The 1842 edn was dedicated to the Revd Derwent Coleridge, son of Samuel T. Coleridge.
4 Vidler's edn gives only short extracts from the Introductory Dialogue. See the Everyman edn (London n.d.), p. 41.
5 Maurice's treatment of Luther is sympathetic. He is 'one of the few exceptions to the almost complete failure of Anglican theologians to understand Luther' (A. M. Ramsey, *F. D. Maurice and the Conflicts of Modern Theology* (Cambridge 1951), p. 28).
6 Maurice, *The Kingdom of Christ*, p. 163.
7 Ibid., p. 170.
8 Ibid., p. 175.
9 Ibid., p. 201.
10 Ibid., pp. 211–26.
11 Ibid., p. 220.
12 Ibid., pp. 220–21.
13 Ibid., p. 229.
14 Ibid., p. 235.
15 Ibid., p. 238.
16 Ibid., p. 251.

[17] Ibid., p. 253.
[18] Ibid., pp. 253–4.
[19] Ibid., p. 258.
[20] Ibid., p. 261.
[21] Ibid., p. 285.
[22] Ibid., vol. 2, p. 22.
[23] Ibid., p. 30.
[24] Ibid., p. 36.
[25] Ibid., p. 37.
[26] Ibid., p. 91.
[27] Ibid., p. 102.
[28] Ibid., p. 98.
[29] Ibid., p. 102.
[30] Ibid., pp. 106 ff.
[31] Ibid., pp. 139–40.
[32] Ibid., p. 146.
[33] Ibid., p. 151; cf. Augustine, *City of God* xiv, 28.
[34] Ibid., p. 164.
[35] Ramsey, op. cit., p. 30.
[36] Maurice, op. cit., vol. 2, p. 193.
[37] Ibid., pp. 197–204.
[38] Ibid., pp. 202–3.
[39] Ibid., p. 203.
[40] Ibid., pp. 203–4.
[41] Ibid., p. 259.
[42] Ibid., p. 263.
[43] Ibid.
[44] Ibid., p. 283.
[45] Ibid., p. 284.
[46] Ibid., pp. 293–300.
[47] Ibid., pp. 303–5.
[48] Ibid., p. 306.
[49] Ibid., p. 308.
[50] Ibid., p. 312.
[51] Ibid., pp. 313–19.
[52] Ibid., p. 315.
[53] Ibid., p. 319.
[54] See above, ch. 17.
[55] Ibid., p. 322.
[56] Ibid., p. 328.
[57] Ibid., pp. 328–9.
[58] Ibid., pp. 329–30.
[59] Ibid., p. 334.
[60] Ibid.
[61] Ibid.
[62] Ibid., p. 340.
[63] Maurice admits, however, that there have been periods, e.g. in the reign of Charles I, when 'the systematic tendency' became 'very prevalent' among English churchmen; see ibid., p. 316.
[64] See vol. 1, p. 158.
[65] See R. Rouse and S. C. Neill, eds., *A History of the Ecumenical Movement* (London 1954), pp. 264–5.
[66] Ibid., p. 265.
[67] Ibid., pp. 282–3.

[68] The text of this Appeal is given in G. K. A. Bell, ed., *Documents on Christian Unity, 1920–30: a Selection.* London 1955.

[69] *Report of the Anglican–Methodist Unity Commission: Part 2, The Scheme* (London 1968), p. 37.

[70] See Gregory Dix, 'The Ministry in the Early Church' in K. E. Kirk, ed., *The Apostolic Ministry* (London 1957), pp. 187–8, 297–8.

CHAPTER 19

[1] The Greek word *oikoumene* from which 'ecumenical' is derived means 'the inhabited world'. The New York gathering of 1900 was called the Ecumenical Missionary Conference 'because the plan of campaign which it proposes covers the whole area of the inhabited world' (quoted from Rouse and Neill, op. cit., p. 354).

[2] Rouse and Neill, op. cit., p. 362.

[3] Revisers' Preface to the N.T.

[4] This encouragement was welcomed and acted on by the Pontifical Biblical Institute under the rectorship of Cardinal Augustin Bea, and sustained by the Constitution 'On Divine Revelation' of Vatican II.

[5] The N.T. was published in 1961, the O.T. and Apocrypha in 1970.

[6] Vol. 1, ed. R. Rouse and S. C. Neill, takes the history to 1948. Vol. 2, *The Ecumenical Advance: A History of the Ecumenical Movement, 1948–1968*, ed. Harold E. Fey. London 1970.

[7] See Rouse and Neill, op. cit., p. 411.

[8] Quoted ibid., p. 416.

[9] Ibid., p. 422.

[10] Ibid., p. 423.

[11] Ibid., p. 433.

[12] Ibid.

[13] Although, as at Lausanne, Orthodox representatives participated fully in the discussions, Archbishop Germanos of Thyateira had earlier explained that the Conference's statements were often worded in a way in which the Orthodox could not conscientiously vote for them.

[14] Ibid., pp. 434–5.

[15] *The Churches Survey Their Task*, The Report of the Oxford Conference on Church, Community, and State (London 1937), p. 82.

[16] For brevity's sake I shall use the acronym W.C.C.; and for Faith and Order, F. and O.

[17] In 1961 this basis was enlarged to 'a fellowship of churches which confess the Lord Jesus Christ as God and Saviour according to the Scriptures and therefore seek to fulfil together their common calling to the glory of the one God, Father, Son, and Holy Spirit'.

[18] In 'The Toronto Statement', a document of the Central Committee issued in 1950.

[19] London 1952.

[20] *The Third World Conference on Faith and Order*, Oliver S. Tomkins (London 1953), p. 15.

[21] Ibid., p. 33.

[22] *The New Delhi Report: The Third Assembly of the World Council of Churches, 1961*, ed. W. A. Visser 't Hooft (New York, Association Press, 1962), p. 116.

[23] Oliver S. Tomkins, later Bishop of Bristol, had already written *The Church in the Purpose of God*, London 1950, in preparation for Lund.

[24] *The Fourth World Conference on Faith and Order, Montreal, 1963*, ed. P. C. Rodger and L. Vischer. London 1964.

[25] See *New Directions in Faith and Order, Bristol, 1967* (F. and O. Papers, 50). Geneva 1968.

[26] *The Old and the New in the Church* (F. and O. Papers, 34). London 1961.

[27] Ibid., p. 78.

[28] E. Troeltsch, *Die Soziallehren der Christlichen Kirchen und Gruppen* (1911); E. T., *The Social Teaching of the Christian Churches* (see p. 206, n. 1.).

[29] Fey, op. cit., pp. 419–20.

[30] *Drafts for Sections prepared for the Fourth Assembly of the World Council of Churches, Uppsala, 1968.* Geneva 1968.

[31] *The Uppsala Report 1968: Official Report of the Fourth Assembly of the World Council of Churches* (Geneva 1968), p. 16.

[32] Ibid., p. 12.

[33] Ibid., p. 13.

[34] Pp. 496–500.

[35] See Fey, op. cit., ch. 5, 'Confessional Families and the Ecumenical Movement'.

[36] See Rouse and Neill, op. cit., pp. 473–6. Also *The Constitution of the Church of South India* (Madras, Christian Literature Society for India 1952).

[37] Cf. the words of those who signed the report of the conversations between the Church of England and the Methodist Church: 'If it be said that the Scheme proposed is not free from anomalies, we reply that the present division of our Churches from each other, frustrating their work and running counter to the declared will of God, is an anomaly so great that all other anomalies taken together are insignificant beside it.' *Anglican–Methodist Unity: Part 2, The Scheme* (London 1968), p. 181.

[38] The words are from *The Principles of Union* (1965), a document accepted by the Anglican Church of Canada and the United Church of Canada, and later by the Christian Church (Disciples of Christ) in Canada as providing guidelines by which to prepare a plan of union. The whole context is instructive: 'The United Church of Canada has . . . declared that, in view of the fact that episcopacy was accepted from early times and for many centuries and is still accepted by the greater part of Christendom, it should be continued and effectively maintained in some constitutional form both at the inauguration of a union with the Anglican Church and thereafter. We are therefore agreed in accepting the threefold ministry of Bishops, Presbyters, and Deacons in some constitutional form and with the same freedom of interpretation that is now permitted within the Anglican Church. By the term "constitutional" we intend to point to the concept of the episcopacy as one element in the life of the Church in which councils and congregations also have their place, the episcopate not being separated from the life of the whole Church but integrated with it and exercised in it. By the phrase "freedom of interpretation" we mean to indicate a safeguard against any interpretation which would require either Church to repudiate or condemn the work of God in its own history, but we do not mean to imply that no agreement on the meaning of ministry in general or episcopacy in particular is necessary for unity in the faith.'

A *Plan of Union* for the three churches named was published by the General Commission on Church Union, Toronto 1973, and was remitted to the churches for study. The Anglican Church of Canada withdrew from the negotiations in 1975.

CHAPTER 20

[1] See above, p. 83.

[2] The Latin is *ordinentur*, the precise meaning of which is difficult to grasp in the context. Y. Congar (*L'Eglise*, p. 471) describes the word as *mystérieux*.

[3] *Sempiternus Rex*, 4; quoted in Fey, op. cit., p. 318.

[4] 'Ecumenical Council' here means an assembly of all bishops of the Roman Catholic Church. In some circles it was mistakenly thought that John XXIII's intention was to summon a council representative of all churches throughout the world.

[5] Quotations here are from Walter M. Abbott, S. J., ed., *The Documents of Vatican II* (New York, Guild Press, 1966).

[6] Ch. i, 1, Abbott, op. cit., p. 15.

[7] i, 4–7, pp. 16–22.

[8] Ibid., p. 24, n. 27.

[9] ii, 10, p. 27.

[10] See above, pp. 59, 62, 66 ff.

[11] ii, 13, p. 32.

[12] ii, 15, pp. 33–4.

[13] See vol. 1, pp. 86–91.

[14] As recently as 1949 it was necessary for the Holy Office to write to Archbishop Cushing of Boston to explain that Catholic doctrine does not deny that non-Roman Catholics may receive grace to salvation.

[15] ii, 15, p. 34.

[16] iii, 19, p. 38.

[17] iii, 20, p. 39.

[18] Ibid.

[19] iii, 22, pp. 42–3.

[20] See 'Prefatory Note of Explanation', sent to the Council 'from a higher authority' before the vote was taken on the Constitution: ibid., pp. 98–9.

[21] See vol. 1, pp. 69–70.

[22] Hans Küng, *The Church*, p. 418.

[23] iii, 28, p. 53.

[24] vii, 48, pp. 79–80.

[25] Ibid., pp. 199–308.

[26] Preface, para. 1, p. 200.

[27] Ibid., p. 184.

[28] Ibid., pp. 185–6.

[29] In 'A Response', ibid., pp. 309–16.

[30] Ibid., pp. 310–11.

[31] Ibid., pp. 311–14.

[32] Ibid., pp. 341–66.

[33] Ibid., p. 343.

[34] See above, pp. 98–9.

[35] i, 3, p. 346.

[36] i, 4, p. 347.

[37] ii, 8, p. 352.

[38] Fey, op. cit., pp. 343 ff.

[39] *The Evangelization of the Modern World*, Vatican City 1973.

[40] Ibid., p. 5.

[41] Ibid., pp. 7–8.

[42] Ibid., pp. 9–10.

[43] But perhaps it has never been so monolithic a structure as Protestants generally, and even some Catholics, have managed to persuade themselves.

[44] The latter question is discussed by Harry J. McSorley, C.S.P. in an article 'The Right of Catholics to Dissent from *Humanae Vitae*' in *The Ecumenist* (New York, Paulist Press), vol. 8, no. 1 (November/December 1969), pp. 5–9.

[45] For an account of some of the more influential of these see Robert S. Paul, *The Church in Search of Itself* (Grand Rapids, Michigan, Eerdmans, 1972), ch. vii, 'Catholic Reform or Roman Rebellion', pp. 226–71.

[46] 'The Church as *Sacramentum Mundi*', in *Structures of the Church* (*Concilium*, vol. 58), ed. Jiménez Urresti. New York, Herder, 1970.

[47] Op. cit., pp. 39–40.

[48] Richard McBrien has also written *Do we need the Church?* (New York, Harper & Row, 1969) and *Church, the Continuing Quest* (New York, Newman Press, 1970).

[49] E.g. in *God the Future of Man* (London 1969), ch. iv, 'The Church as the Sacrament of Dialogue'.

[50] v, 92, Abbott, op. cit., p. 120.

[51] Schillebeeckx, op. cit., p. 120.

[52] The reference is to *Gaudium et Spes*, ch. v, 92.

[53] Gibson Winter, *The New Creation as Metropolis* (New York, Macmillan, 1963), p. 130.

[54] Ibid., p. 121.

[55] Schillebeeckx, op. cit., p. 127.

[56] Ibid., p. 138.

[57] Gregory Baum, *The Credibility of the Church Today* (New York, Herder, 1968), pp. 88 ff.

[58] Ibid., pp. 106–13.

[59] Baum, *Faith and Doctrine* (New York, Newman Press, 1969), p. 93. See also *The Credibility of the Church Today*, pp. 113–20.

[60] Baum, *The Credibility of the Church Today*, p. 134.

[61] Ibid., p. 136.

[62] Ibid., p. 141.

[63] Ibid., p. 145.

[64] Ibid., p. 152.

[65] Ibid., pp. 152 ff.

[66] Ibid., p. 176.

[67] Rosemary Radford Ruether, *The Church Against Itself* (London 1967), p. 6.

[68] Ruether, 'Letter to the Editor', in *The Ecumenist*, vol. 6, no. 4 (May/June 1968), p. 160. The review was by Joanne Dewart in the same journal, vol. 6, no. 3 (March/April 1968), pp. 140–42.

[69] Ruether, *The Church Against Itself*, p. 138.

[70] Ibid.

[71] Ibid., p. 61.

[72] Ibid., pp. 159–60.

[73] Ibid., p. 163.

[74] Ibid., p. 173.

[75] Ibid.

[76] Schillebeeckx, op. cit., p. 134.

[77] Ibid., p. 136.

[78] Ibid., pp. 137–8.

[79] Baum, *The Credibility of the Church Today*, p. 196.

[80] Ibid., p. 197.

[81] Ibid., pp. 207–8.

CHAPTER 21

[1] Ernst Troeltsch, *The Social Teaching of the Christian Churches*, E.T. by Olive Wyon, 2 vols., London; New York, Macmillan, 1931. First published in 1911 under the title *Die Soziallehren der Christlichen Kirchen und Gruppen*.

[2] See J. C. McLelland, *Toward a Radical Church* (Toronto, Ryerson Press, 1967), pp. 62–3.

[3] J. C. McLelland, op. cit., p. 62.

[4] Troeltsch, op. cit., vol. ii, pp. 729 ff.

[5] Ibid., p. 730.

[6] Ibid.

[7] Ibid.

[8] For further elucidation of Troeltsch's conception of the third type, see ibid., pp. 816–17.

[9] Dietrich Bonhoeffer, *Letters and Papers from Prison*, ed. Eberhard Bethge (New York, Macmillan, 1972), letter of 30 April 1944, pp. 279–81.

[10] E.g. 'religionless Christianity', the idea of the world come of age, the concept that God has been edged out of the world, the error of treating God as a *deus ex machina*, or stop-gap, and the suggestion that Christians must live 'as though God were not given'.

[11] Ibid., 30 June 1944, p. 341.

[12] Ibid., 8 June 1944, p. 326.

[13] Ibid., p. 327.

[14] Ibid., 8 July 1944, p. 345.

[15] Ibid., 8 June 1944, p. 326.

[16] Ibid., 30 June 1944, p. 341.

[17] Ibid., 8 July 1944, p. 345.

[18] Ibid.

[19] Ibid., 30 June 1944, p. 342.

[20] Ibid., 30 April 1944, p. 282.

[21] Ibid., 3 August 1944, p. 378.

[22] Ibid., 30 April 1944, p. 281.

[23] Ibid., pp. 281, 286.

[24] Ibid., p. 382.

[25] *The Documents of Vatican II: Gaudium et Spes*, ch. i, 19, p. 217.

[26] Ibid., ii, 30, p. 228.

[27] Ibid., ii, 30–32, pp. 228–31.

[28] Ibid., iv, 43, p. 245.

[29] See R. S. Paul, op. cit., pp. 184 ff.

[30] Gibson Winter, *The Suburban Captivity of the Churches* (New York, Macmillan, 1962).

[31] Harvey Cox, *The Secular City* (New York, Macmillan, 1965).

[32] Winter, op. cit., p. 34.

[33] The adequacy of the resources and the responsiveness have both diminished since Professor Winter wrote.

[34] Ibid., pp. 42, 55.

[35] Ibid., p. 63.

[36] Ibid., p. 67.

[37] Ibid., p. 76.

[38] Ibid., p. 82.

[39] Ibid., p. 90.

[40] Ibid., p. 120.

[41] Ibid., p. 159.

[42] Ibid., pp. 164–5.

[43] Ibid., p. 166.

[44] Ibid., pp. 166–78.

[45] Ibid., p. 171.

[46] Ibid., p. 207.

[47] Ibid., pp. 208–9.

[48] See R. S. Paul, op. cit., p. 215.

[49] Cox, op. cit., p. 110.

[50] Ibid., p. 112.
[51] Ibid., ch. 2.
[52] Cox provides an excellent discussion (pp. 18–21) on the important distinction between secularization and secularism. The latter is 'an ideology, a new closed worldview which functions very much like a new religion'.
[53] Ibid., p. 20.
[54] Ibid., p. 25.
[55] Ibid., p. 32.
[56] Ibid., p. 105.
[57] Ibid., p. 125.
[58] Ibid., p. 127.
[59] Ibid.
[60] Ibid., p. 128.
[61] Ibid., pp. 143–4.
[62] Ibid., p. 145.
[63] Ibid., p. 154.
[64] Ibid., p. 156.
[65] Ibid., p. 160.
[66] Ibid., p. 226. See R. S. Paul, op. cit., pp. 215–25, for a critique of *The Secular City*. The question whether Cox identifies the Church too closely with the secularized technopolis is discussed on pp. 224–5.

CHAPTER 22

[1] For a succinct account of Barth's theology see W. Nicholls, *Systematic and Philosophical Theology* (Harmondsworth 1969), pp. 75–149. References to the *Church Dogmatics* are to the E.T., ed. G. W. Bromiley and T. F. Torrance, *Karl Barth: Church Dogmatics*, Edinburgh. It is to be remembered that the date of each volume is about three years later than the Swiss edn.
[2] E.T. by E. C. Hoskyns, *Karl Barth: The Epistle to the Romans*, Oxford 1933.
[3] Karl Barth, *The Humanity of God* (Richmond, Virginia, John Knox Press, 1968), p. 62. The volume includes another lecture, delivered in 1957, on 'Evangelical Theology in the Nineteenth Century', in which he is much more generous in his estimate of its accomplishments than he had been thirty years earlier.
[4] Ibid., p. 42.
[5] Ibid., p. 37.
[6] Ibid., p. 46.
[7] E. Lamirande, o.m.i., 'Roman Catholic Reactions to Karl Barth's Ecclesiology', in *Canadian Journal of Theology*, vol. xiv, no. 1 (January 1968), pp. 28–42.
[8] Ibid., p. 33.
[9] H. R. Mackintosh, *Types of Modern Theology* (London 1937), pp. 309–13.
[10] Hoskyns, op. cit., pp. 353, 371, 418.
[11] Ibid., p. 418.
[12] This underlies the whole section 'Justification by Faith Alone' in *Church Dogmatics*, vol. iv, 1. See especially pp. 629–34. Cf. also in the *Römerbrief*, 'Faith cannot be a concrete thing that once began and then continued its course. Faith is the Beginning, the Miracle, the Creation in every moment of time' (Hoskyns, op. cit., p. 499).
[13] *CD* (*Church Dogmatics*), vol. iv, 1, pp. 650 ff.
[14] Lamirande, op. cit., p. 34.
[15] E.g., H. R. Mackintosh, op. cit., pp. 314–16.

[16] H. Hartwell, *The Theology of Karl Barth: an Introduction* (London 1964), pp. 36–7.

[17] See above, p. 137.

[18] The closeness to the idea of the Church as *Sacramentum mundi* (see above, pp. 109 ff) should be noted.

[19] *CD* iv, 1, p. 653.

[20] Ibid.

[21] Ibid., p. 654.

[22] Ibid., p. 661. It is possible to suggest that this phrase gives the essential meaning of the doctrine that the Church is the extension of the incarnation, favoured by some Anglican theologians, but usually rejected by Protestants on the ground that it identifies the Church with the risen Christ and that it is triumphalistic in assuming the Church to be a perfect society. Yet Barth himself sharply rejects this Anglican doctrine as 'not only out of place but even blasphemous' (*CD* iv, 3, 2nd half, p. 729).

[23] *CD* iv, 1, pp. 661–8.

[24] Ibid., p. 669.

[25] Ibid., pp. 669–70.

[26] Ibid., p. 671.

[27] Ibid., pp. 681–2.

[28] Ibid., p. 688. Cf. the Orthodox theologian, J. Meyendorff, quoted, in vol. 1, p. 154.

[29] Ibid., pp. 688–9.

[30] Ibid., p. 690.

[31] Ibid., pp. 698–9. Cf. the treatment of this credal clause in the Catechism of the Council of Trent; see vol. 1, pp. 200–1.

[32] Ibid., p. 701.

[33] Ibid., p. 702.

[34] Ibid., p. 703.

[35] Ibid., p. 704.

[36] Ibid.

[37] Ibid., p. 705.

[38] Ibid., pp. 706–7.

[39] Ibid., p. 708.

[40] Ibid.

[41] Ibid., pp. 710–12.

[42] Ibid., pp. 712–13.

[43] Ibid., p. 715.

[44] *CD* iv, 1, pp. 715–18 deserve the careful study of those who claim that apostolicity depends upon a traceable line of bishops from the present day to the apostles.

[45] Ibid., pp. 718–19.

[46] Ibid., p. 721.

[47] *CD* iv, 3, 2nd half, pp. 681–901.

[48] Ibid., p. 687.

[49] Ibid., p. 693.

[50] Ibid., p. 695.

[51] Ibid., p. 710.

[52] Ibid., p. 711.

[53] Ibid., p. 720.

[54] See also *CD* iv, 1, pp. 725–39, 'The Time of the Community'.

[55] Karl Barth, *Dogmatics in Outline* (London 1949), pp. 122–3.

[56] See vol. 1, p. 203.

[57] *CD* iv, 3, p. 724.

[58] Ibid., p. 726.

[59] Ibid., p. 727.

[60] Ibid., p. 728.

[61] Ibid., p. 766.
[62] Ibid., p. 767. Barth here cites also John 3.16, Colossians 1.16, and Hebrews 1.3.
[63] Ibid., pp. 769–77.
[64] Ibid., p. 796.
[65] Ibid., p. 797.
[66] Ibid., p. 798.
[67] Ibid., p. 800.
[68] Ibid., p. 803.
[69] Ibid., p. 811.
[70] Ibid., pp. 812–30.
[71] Ibid., p. 831.
[72] Ibid., pp. 838–43.
[73] Ibid., pp. 843–54.
[74] Ibid., p. 855.
[75] Ibid., p. 863.
[76] Ibid., pp. 865–82.
[77] Ibid., pp. 882–901.
[78] Ibid., p. 858.
[79] *CD* iii, 4, pp. 488–90.
[80] See above, p. 136.
[81] Karl Barth, *The Humanity of God*, p. 62.
[82] Ibid., p. 63.
[83] Ibid.
[84] Ibid., p. 64.
[85] Ibid.
[86] Ibid., p. 65.

CHAPTER 23

[1] R. T. Handy, 'Paul Tillich', in Alan Richardson, ed., *A Dictionary of Christian Theology* (London 1969), p. 340.
[2] Paul Tillich, *Systematic Theology* (London; Chicago, Chicago University Press, vol. 1, 1951; vol. 2, 1957; vol. 3, 1963). Hereafter designated as *ST*. Page references are to the Chicago edn.
[3] *ST* 1, p. 60.
[4] *ST* 2, p. 25.
[5] Ibid., p. 45.
[6] Many students of Tillich are baffled by his apparent equation of the fall with creation.
[7] *ST* 1, p. 261.
[8] Ibid., ch. 7.
[9] *ST* 2, pp. 46 ff.
[10] Ibid., p. 138.
[11] *ST* 3, pp. 30–110.
[12] Ibid., p. 107.
[13] Passages like this have incurred the charge that Tillich's Christology is adoptionist: see A. J. McKelway, *The Systematic Theology of Paul Tillich* (New York, Dell Publishing Co., 1964), pp. 166–8. It is my belief, however, that he can be strongly defended against the charge.
[14] *ST* 3, p. 147.
[15] Tillich uses the words 'ecstatic' and 'ecstasy' in the sense of the human spirit being

lifted beyond itself but without loss of its rational character. It is not to be confused with 'enthusiasm'.

16 Ibid., pp. 150–52.

17 The Greek word *kairos* means 'time' in the sense of an opportune or particularly significant moment.

18 Ibid., p. 155.

19 Ibid., p. 154.

20 Ibid., pp. 155–6.

21 Ibid., p. 158.

22 Ibid.

23 Ibid., p. 159.

24 Ibid., pp. 231–7.

25 E.g., ibid., p. 157.

26 Ibid., p. 165.

27 Ibid., p. 167.

28 Ibid., p. 173.

29 Ibid., pp. 188–93.

30 Ibid., pp. 193–6.

31 Ibid., pp. 196–212.

32 Ibid., p. 197.

33 Ibid., pp. 212–16.

34 Ibid., pp. 212–13.

35 Ibid., p. 214.

36 Ibid.

37 Ibid., p. 216.

38 Ibid., p. 246.

39 See especially *ST* 3, pp. 374–82.

40 Ibid., p. 107.

41 Ibid., pp. 359–60.

42 Ibid., p. 361.

43 Ibid., p. 344.

44 Ibid.

45 Ibid., p. 376.

46 Ibid., p. 377.

47 Ibid., p. 378.

48 Ibid.

49 Ibid., p. 379.

50 See above, pp. 159, 162.

51 *ST* 3, pp. 385 ff.

52 Ibid., p. 389.

53 Ibid., p. 390.

54 Ibid., p. 391.

55 Ibid., pp. 394–423.

56 E.g., *ST* 3, pp. 6, 245.

57 Ibid., p. 223.

58 Ibid., p. 245. Tillich does not deny that the Protestant principle is recognized by sound Catholic theology; nor that Catholic substance is present in many Protestant churches.

59 Ibid., p. 122.

60 Ibid., p. 120.

61 Ibid., p. 344.

62 Ibid., p. 375.

63 Ibid., p. 381.

64 Ibid., p. 155.

[65] Baltimore, Helicon Press; and London.

[66] Bishop Butler, in a letter to *The Times* of London, dated 21 August 1971, writing in his capacity as president of the Social Morality Council.

CHAPTER 24

[1] Original title, *Structuren der Kirche* (Freiburg, Herder, 1962), E.T., London 1964; and in paperback, Notre Dame, U.S.A., University of Notre Dame Press, 1968, from which citations here are made (referred to as *Structures*).

[2] Original title *Die Kirche* (Freiburg, Herder, 1967). E.T., London 1967; and New York, Sheed & Ward, 1968, from which citations here are made (referred to as *Church*).

[3] See above, pp. 96 ff.

[4] *Church*, p. ix.

[5] Ibid., p. xiii.

[6] *Structures*, p. 12, n. 8.

[7] Ibid., p. 9: '*Con-cilium* is derived from *con-kal-ium*, or from *con-calare*. *Calare* is employed as a religious technical term for "to announce", "to summon".'

[8] Ibid., p. 14.

[9] *Church*, p. 34.

[10] Ibid., p. 38. Cf. Richard Field, in vol. 1, pp. 183–4; and Karl Barth, above, p. 140.

[11] Ibid., p. 5. Cf. Barth on the Church as 'event', above, pp. 137–8.

[12] Ibid., p. 48.

[13] Ibid., p. 62.

[14] Ibid., p. 72.

[15] Ibid., p. 73.

[16] Ibid.

[17] Ibid., p. 74.

[18] Ibid., p. 75.

[19] Ibid., p. 95.

[20] Ibid., pp. 95–6.

[21] Ibid., pp. 88–104.

[22] Ibid., p. 97.

[23] Ibid., pp. 119–20.

[24] Ibid., p. 125.

[25] Ibid., p. 167.

[26] Ibid., p. 172.

[27] Ibid., p. 174.

[28] Cf. Tillich: see above, pp. 160–61.

[29] *Church*, p. 187.

[30] See below, p. 188.

[31] *Church*, pp. 203–41.

[32] Ibid., pp. 224–5.

[33] Ibid., p. 235.

[34] Ibid., p. 236.

[35] Ibid., pp. 237, 239. Cf. Barth's rejection of this phrase, p. 209, n. 22.

[36] Küng's assertion in the same note (p. 237) that 'mystical' in this usage simply means 'mysterious' must be challenged. The word is connected with the Greek *mueomai*, 'to become an initiate', and the 'mystical body' basically means no more and no less than the company of those who have been baptized. See vol. 1, p. 77.

[37] Ibid., p. 237.

[38] Ibid., p. 239.

[39] Ibid., pp. 239–40.
[40] Ibid., p. 241.
[41] *Structures*, ch. viii; *Church*, pp. 444–80.
[42] *Structures*, p. 63.
[43] See above, pp. 142, 162–4.
[44] *Church*, p. 275.
[45] Ibid., p. 281.
[46] Ibid., p. 283.
[47] Ibid., p. 284.
[48] Ibid., pp. 285–96.
[49] See above, pp. 58–61.
[50] *Structures*, p. 48.
[51] Cf. above, p. 178.
[52] *Structures*, p. 48.
[53] *Church*, pp. 296–300.
[54] *Structures*, p. 40.
[55] Ibid., p. 39.
[56] *Church*, pp. 305–13.
[57] Ibid., 313–19.
[58] Ibid., p. 354.
[59] Ibid., p. 355.
[60] Ibid., p. 358.
[61] Ibid., p. 359.
[62] See also above, pp. 177–8, under 'The People of God'.
[63] As proof of the reversal of this trend in Catholic theology, he cites (*Structures*, pp. 86–7) numerous recent books and papal pronouncements on the laity.
[64] *Church*, p. 367.
[65] 1 Peter 2.4, 11; Revelation 1.5.
[66] *Church*, p. 377.
[67] *Structures*, p. 108. Quoted from M. Luther, *Werke* 6, 408 (Weimar, 1883 ff).
[68] Ibid., p. 120.
[69] *Church*, pp. 388 ff.
[70] Ibid., p. 389.
[71] Ibid., p. 391.
[72] Ibid., pp. 393–444. See also *Structures*, pp. 136–54.
[73] *Church*, p. 401.
[74] Acts 14.23 is anachronistic, Küng argues, in saying that Paul and Barnabas appointed elders.
[75] *Church*, p. 407.
[76] Ibid., p. 432.
[77] Ibid., p. 429.
[78] *Structures*, p. 184.
[79] Ibid., pp. 185–90.
[80] *Church*, p. 438.
[81] Ibid., pp. 438–9.
[82] *Structures*, p. 154. The italics are Küng's.
[83] Ibid., pp. 157–64.
[84] Ibid., pp. 165–8.
[85] *Church*, pp. 441–2.
[86] Ibid., p. 444.
[87] *Structures*, pp. 201–304; *Church*, pp. 444–80.
[88] *Structures*, p. 203.
[89] Ibid., p. 205.
[90] Ibid. This is based on the commission to Peter in Matthew 16.18–19; Luke 22.32;

John 21.15–19.

[91] At this point the non-Catholic reader looks in vain for an attempt to provide an historical and theological link between the office of Peter and the holder of the see of Rome.

[92] Ibid., pp. 209–23.

[93] See vol. 1, p. 138. Küng writes: 'The legitimacy of the new pope (Martin V) depended on these decrees [i.e. of Constance] ... according to the usual view, it is in turn the premise of the legitimacy of the popes in the last five hundred years' (*Structures*, p. 254).

[94] Ibid., p. 255.

[95] Ibid., p. 258.

[96] Ibid., p. 295.

[97] *Church*, p. 451.

[98] *Structures*, p. 349.

[99] Karl Barth, *Church Dogmatics* i, 2, pp. 544–72. Küng discusses this long note of Barth's in *Structures*, pp. 314–26.

[100] *Structures*, ch. 8; *Church*, pp. 449–50. In his more recent book, *Infallible? An Inquiry* (New York, Doubleday, 1971), he subjects the concept to even more searching examination.

[101] *Structures*, p. 322.

[102] Ibid., p. 334.

[103] *Church*, p. 471.

[104] Ibid., p. 472.

[105] Ibid., pp. 477–8.

POSTSCRIPT

[1] Tillich, *Systematic Theology*, vol. 3, p. 304.

[2] Significant are: Karl Rahner (among his many works), 'Questions on the Theology of History', part ii in *Theological Investigations*, vol. v [Later Writings] London, and Baltimore, Helicon Press, 1966; *The Shape of the Church to Come*, London, and New York, Seabury, 1974; L. S. Thornton, *The Common Life in the Body of Christ*, London 1942; Christ and the Church, part iii of a treatise on 'The Form of a Servant', London 1956; Lesslie Newbigin, *The Household of God*, London 1953.

Bibliography

Dates given are those of the editions used or referred to in this book, and do not always indicate the date of the first publication.

Barth, Karl, *Church Dogmatics* (E.T. ed. G. W. Bromiley and T. F. Torrance), 4 vols. each in several parts. Edinburgh, T. & T. Clark, 1936–62.

Barth, Karl, *Dogmatics in Outline*, SCM Press 1949.

Barth, Karl, *The Epistle to the Romans* (E.T. by E. C. Hoskyns). Oxford University Press 1933.

Barth, Karl, *The Humanity of God*. Richmond, Virginia, John Knox Press, 1968.

Baum, Gregory, *The Credibility of the Church Today*. New York, Herder & Herder, 1968.

Baum, Gregory, *Faith and Doctrine*. New York, Newman Press, 1969.

Bell, G. K. A., ed., *Documents on Christian Unity: a Selection, 1920–30*. Oxford University Press 1955.

Bonhoeffer, Dietrich, *Letters and Papers from Prison*, ed. Eberhard Bethge. New York, Macmillan, 1972.

Butler, B. C., *The Idea of the Church*. Darton, Longman & Todd; Baltimore, Helicon Press, 1962.

Carus, William, *Memoirs of the Life of the Rev. Charles Simeon, M.A.* New York, Robert Carter, 1847.

Chadwick, Owen, *The Reformation*, 'Pelican History of the Church', vol. 3. Penguin Books 1964.

Congar, Yves, *L'Eglise de saint Augustin à l'époque moderne*. Paris, Les Editions du Cerf, 1970.

Cox, Harvey, *The Secular City*. New York, Macmillan, 1965.

Cragg, G. R., *The Church and the Age of Reason, 1648–1789*, 'Pelican History of the Church', vol. 4. Penguin Books 1970.

Creed, J. M. *The Divinity of Jesus Christ*. Collins 1964.

Cross, F. L., ed., *The Oxford Dictionary of the Christian Church*. Oxford University Press 1957.

Denzinger, H., *Enchiridion Symbolorum, Definitionum et Declarationum de rebus fidei et morum*. Freiburg 1960.

Fey, Harold E., *The Ecumenical Advance: A History of the Ecumenical Movement, 1948–1968*. SPCK 1970.

Flew, R. Newton, ed., *The Nature of the Church*. SCM Press 1952.

Harnack, Adolf, *Das Wesen des Christentums*, 1900; E.T. by T. B. Saunders, *What is Christianity?* Williams & Norgate 1901.

Hartwell, H., *The Theology of Karl Barth: an Introduction*. Duckworth 1964.

Jackson, M. J. and Rogan, J., eds., *Thomas Arnold, Principles of Church Reform*. SPCK 1962.

Küng, Hans, *The Church*. Burns & Oates; New York, Sheed & Ward, 1967.

Küng, Hans, *Infallible? An Inquiry*. New York, Doubleday, 1971.

Küng, Hans, *Structures of the Church*. Nelson 1964; Notre Dame, University of Notre Dame Press, 1968.

Locke, John, *A Letter Concerning Toleration*. New York, The Liberal Arts Press, 1955.

Locke, John, *The Reasonableness of Christianity* (see under Ramsey, I. T., below).

Loisy, Alfred, *L'Evangile et l'Eglise*. Paris 1902; E.T. Christopher Howe, *The Gospel and the Church*. New York, Scribner, 1912.

McBrien, Richard, *Church, the Continuing Quest*. New York, Newman Press, 1970.

McBrien, Richard, *Do we need the Church?* New York, Harper & Row, 1969.

McKelway, A. J., *The Systematic Theology of Paul Tillich*. New York, Dell Publishing Co., 1964.

Mackintosh, H. R., *Types of Modern Theology*. Nisbet 1937.

McLelland, J. C., *Toward a Radical Church*. Toronto, Ryerson Press, 1967.

Maurice, F. D., *The Gospel of the Kingdom of Heaven*. Macmillan 1888.

Maurice, F. D., *The Lord's Prayer*. Macmillan 1861.

Maurice, F. D., *The Kingdom of Christ*, 2 vols., ed. A. R. Vidler. SCM Press 1958.

Möhler, Johann A., *Die Einheit in der Kirche* ('Unity in the Church'). Mainz 1825; ed. with commentary by J. R. Geiselmann.

Köln–Olten 1957; French tr., Collection Unam Sanctam 2. Paris, Les Editions du Cerf, 1938.

Möhler, Johann A., *Symbolik* ('Symbolism'). Mainz 1832; ed. J. R. Geiselmann. Köln–Olten 1958; French tr. F. Lachat. Besançon 1836.

Moorman, J. R. H., *A History of the Church in England.* A. & C. Black 1953.

Moule, H. C. G., *Charles Simeon.* Methuen 1892.

Nédoncelle, Maurice, *Baron Friedrich von Hügel.* Longmans Green 1937.

Newbigin, Lesslie, *The Household of God.* SCM Press 1953.

Newman, John Henry, *Apologia pro vita sua.* Dent 1930.

Newman, John Henry, *An Essay on the Development of Christian Doctrine.* New York, Longmans Green, 1927.

Nicholls, William, *Systematic and Philosophical Theology.* Penguin Books 1969.

Palmer, William, *Treatise on the Church of Christ,* 2 vols. Rivington 1839.

Paul, Robert S., *The Church in Search of Itself.* Grand Rapids, Michigan, Eerdmans, 1972.

Rahner, Karl, *The Shape of the Church to Come.* SPCK; New York, Seabury, 1974.

Rahner, Karl, *Theological Investigations,* vol. 5 (Later Writings). Darton, Longman & Todd; Baltimore, Helicon Press, 1966.

Ramsey, A. M., *F. D. Maurice and the Conflicts of Modern Theology.* Cambridge University Press 1951.

Ramsey, I. T., ed., *John Locke, 'The Reasonableness of Christianity'.* Stanford University Press, California, 1958.

Richardson, Cyril, *The Church through the Centuries.* New York, Scribner, 1938.

Ritschl, Albrecht, *The Christian Doctrine of Justification and Sanctification* (E.T. by H. R. Mackintosh and A. B. Macauley). Edinburgh, T. & T. Clark, 1900.

Rouse, R. and Neill, S. C., eds., *A History of the Ecumenical Movement, 1517–1948.* SPCK 1954.

Ruether, Rosemary Radford, *The Church Against Itself.* Sheed & Ward 1967.

Schillebeeckx, Edward, O.P., *God the Future of Man.* Sheed & Ward 1969.

Schleiermacher, Friedrich, *The Christian Faith* (E.T. by H. R.

Mackintosh and J. S. Stewart). Edinburgh, T. & T. Clark, 1960.

Schleiermacher, Friedrich, *On Religion: Speeches to its Cultured Despisers* (E.T. by John Oman). New York, Harper, 1958.

Schweitzer, Albert, *The Quest of the Historical Jesus* (E.T. by W. Montgomery). A. & C. Black 1956.

Smyth, Charles, *The Church and the Nation*. Hodder & Stoughton 1962.

Smyth, Charles, *Simeon and Church Order*. Cambridge University Press 1940.

Thornton, Lionel, C.R., *Christ and the Church*. Dacre Press 1956.

Thornton, Lionel, C.R., *The Common Life in the Body of Christ*. Dacre Press 1942.

Tillich, Paul, *Systematic Theology*, 3 vols. Nisbet; Chicago University Press, 1951–63.

Tomkins, Oliver S., *The Church in the Purpose of God*. SCM Press 1950.

Tracts for the Times: by Members of the University of Oxford, 2 vols. New York, Charles Henry, 1839–40.

Troeltsch, Ernst, *The Social Teaching of the Christian Churches* (E.T. by Olive Wyon of *Die Soziallehren des Christlichen Kirchen und Gruppen*, 1911), 2 vols. Allen & Unwin; New York, Macmillan, 1931.

Tyrrell, George, *Christianity at the Crossroads*. London and New York, Longmans Green, 1909.

von Hügel, Friedrich, *Essays and Addresses on the Philosophy of Religion*, 1st and 2nd ser. Dent 1927, 1930.

von Hügel, Friedrich, *Eternal Life*. Edinburgh, T. & T. Clark, 1912.

von Hügel, Friedrich, *Selected Letters, 1896–1924*. Dent 1927.

von Hügel, Friedrich, *Some Notes on the Petrine Claims*. Sheed & Ward 1930.

Winter, Gibson, *The New Creation as Metropolis*. New York, Macmillan, 1963.

Winter, Gibson, *The Suburban Captivity of the Churches*. New York, Macmillan, 1962.

ARTICLES IN JOURNALS; CHAPTERS IN BOOKS

Dix, Gregory, 'The Ministry in the Early Church', chapter in K. E. Kirk, ed., *The Apostolic Ministry*. Hodder & Stoughton 1957.

Handy, R. T., 'Paul Tillich', article in Alan Richardson, ed., *A Dictionary of Christian Theology*. SCM Press 1969.

Hartley, A. J., 'The Way to Unity: Maurice's Exegesis for Society', article in *Canadian Journal of Theology*, vol. xvi, nos. 1 and 2, 1970.

Lamirande, E., 'Roman Catholic Reactions to Karl Barth's Ecclesiology', article in *Canadian Journal of Theology*, vol. xiv, no. 1, 1968.

McBrien, Richard, 'The Church: Sign and Instrument of Unity', article in Jiménez Urresti, ed., *Structures of the Church* (*Concilium*, vol. 58). New York, Herder & Herder, 1970.

McSorley, Harry J., C.S.P., 'The Right of Catholics to dissent from *Humanae Vitae*', article in *The Ecumenist*, vol. viii, no. 1. New York, Paulist Press, 1969.

Nienaltowski, R. H., 'Möhler', article in *The New Catholic Encyclopedia*, vol. ix. New York, McGraw-Hill, 1967.

O'Dea, Thomas, 'The Church as *Sacramentum Mundi*', article in Jiménez Urresti, ed., *Structures of the Church* (*Concilium*, vol. 58). New York, Herder & Herder, 1970.

Rodes, Robert, 'Structures of the Church's Presence in the World of Today—through the Church's own Institutions', article in Jiménez Urresti, ed., *Structures of the Church* (*Concilium*, vol. 58). New York, Herder & Herder, 1970.

Ruether, Rosemary Radford, 'Letter to the Editor' in *The Ecumenist*, vol. vi, no. 4. New York, Paulist Press, 1968.

Slabaugh, Warren W., 'The Church of the Brethren', statement in R. Newton Flew, ed., *The Nature of the Church*. SCM Press 1952.

REPORTS OF COMMISSIONS, CONFERENCES, AND COUNCILS; AND OTHER DOCUMENTS

The Churches Survey Their Task, Report of the Oxford Conference on Church, Community, and State. George Allen & Unwin 1937.

The Third World Conference on Faith and Order, ed. Oliver S. Tomkins. SCM Press 1953.

The Fourth World Conference on Faith and Order, eds. P. C. Rodger and L. Vischer. SCM Press 1964.

The Old and the New in the Church, Faith and Order Papers, no. 34. SCM Press 1961.

New Directions in Faith and Order, Faith and Order Papers, no. 50.

Geneva, W.C.C., 1968.

The New Delhi Report: The Third Assembly of the World Council of Churches, 1961, ed. W. A. Visser 't Hooft. New York, Association Press, 1962.

The Uppsala Report, 1968: Official Report of the Fourth Assembly of the World Council of Churches. Geneva, W.C.C., 1968.

Drafts for Sections prepared for the Fourth Assembly of the World Council of Churches, Uppsala, 1968. Geneva, W.C.C., 1968.

The Documents of Vatican II, ed. Walter M. Abbott, s.J. New York, Guild Press, 1966.

The Evangelization of the Modern World (for the Use of the Episcopal Conferences). Vatican City 1973.

The Constitution of the Church of South India. Madras, Christian Literature Society for India, 1952.

Report of the Anglican–Methodist Unity Commission, Part 2, The Scheme. SPCK 1968.

The Principles of Union. Toronto, Anglican Church of Canada and The United Church of Canada, 1965.

Plan of Union. Toronto, General Commission on Church Union, 1973.

Index

NAMES

Abbott, W. M. 104, 205n
Abraham 62
Andrewes, Lancelot, Bp of Winchester 51
Aristotle 63
Arnold, Thomas 47–51
Athanasius, Bp of Alexandria 16
Augustine, Bp of Hippo 10, 39, 59, 99, 173, 202n

Bagot, Richard, Bp of Oxford 55
Baillie, Donald M. 84–5
Barth, Karl 42, 134, ch.22, 156, 181, 192, 212nn, 214n
Baum, Gregory 111–13, 115
Bea, Augustin, Cardinal 96–7, 203n
Bell, G. K. A., Bp of Chichester 203n
Bellarmine, Robert 106, 149
Benedict XV, pope 83, 95
Bentham, Jeremy 59, 61
Bergson, Henri 19
Berkeley, George, Bp of Cloyne 4
Berridge, John 44, 46
Bethge, Eberhard 120, 207n
Blondel, Maurice 19
Böhme, Jacob 118
Bonhoeffer, Dietrich 120–4, 130
Bousset, Jacques Bénigne, Bp of Meaux 9
Boyle, Robert 4
Bramhall, John, Abp of Armagh 51
Brent, Charles, Bp of Western New York 80, 82, 84
Brown, Robert McAfee 102–3
Brunner, Emil 42
Bultmann, Rudolf 134
Butler, B. C. 172
Butler, Joseph, Bp of Durham 6

Calvin, John 6, 28, 37, 39

Campion, D. R. 102–3
Carus, William 45
Castellio, Sebastian 6
Celsus 9
Chadwick, Owen 196n
Clarke, Samuel 4
Clement of Rome 52
Coleridge, Samuel Taylor 14, 201n
Congar, Yves 15, 19, 196n, 197nn
Constantine, emperor 67, 191
Cooper, Anthony Ashley, Earl of Shaftesbury 47
Cosin, John, Bp of Durham 51, 54
Cox, Harvey 129–34, 207nn, 208nn
Cragg, G. R. 10, 14, 196n, 197nn
Creed, J. M. 22
Cushing, R., Abp of Boston 205n
Cyprian, Bp of Carthage 15, 100

Descartes, René 4
Dewart, Joanne 206n
Dix, Gregory 203n
Döllinger, J. J. I. 18–19
Drey, J. S. 16
Dulles, Avery 98

Ebeling, Gerhard 134
Edwards, Jonathan 10

Faber, F. W. 55
Febronius see Hontheim, Johann von
Fey, Harold E. 203n, 204nn, 205n
Field, Richard 212n
Flew, R. Newton 87, 197nn
Franck, Sebastian 118
Francke, August 10
Froude, R. H. 52, 55

Germanos, Abp of Thyateira 203n
Goethe, J. W. 14

221

SUBJECTS

C. indicates Church